SHOUTS AND WHISPERS

SHOUTS AND WHISPERS

*Twenty-One Writers Speak about
Their Writing and Their Faith*

Edited by

Jennifer L. Holberg

WILLIAM B. EERDMANS PUBLISHING COMPANY
GRAND RAPIDS, MICHIGAN / CAMBRIDGE, U.K.

© 2006 Wm. B. Eerdmans Publishing Co.

Wm. B. Eerdmans Publishing Co.

2140 Oak Industrial Drive N.E., Grand Rapids, Michigan 49505 /
P.O. Box 163, Cambridge CB3 9PU U.K.

Library of Congress Cataloging-in-Publication Data

Shouts and whispers: twenty-one writers speak about their writing
and their faith / edited by Jennifer L. Holberg.

p.   cm.

Includes bibliographical references.

ISBN: 978-0-8028-3229-0 (pbk.: alk. paper)

1. Authors, American — 20th century — Interviews. 2. Authors, American —
21st century — Interviews. 3. Authorship — Religious aspects — Christianity.
4. Christianity and literature.   I. Holberg, Jennifer L.

PS129S56   2006

810.9′382 — dc22

2006003737

www.eerdmans.com

For Gayle

Contents

———

CONTENTS

Contents

Introduction

───────

What does it mean to be a writer working in a context of faith within the world of contemporary letters? What features characterize such a writer's work? Are these features different from those written from a secular perspective? Do they need to be? How should a religious perspective be expressed in literature — explicitly or implicitly? And what is faith anyway — what "counts" as belief?

The responses to these questions — and many others — are as different as the writers gathered in this volume. The powerful diversity of these writers' own literary approaches is reflected in their similarly complicated approaches to faith. In their richly nuanced explorations, these writers provocatively examine the fundamental nature of both literature and belief, articulating an aesthetics of what faithful, or perhaps "faithfull," writing might look like in the current literary scene. Some of their answers may even surprise.

What these reflections *do* share is a common beginning at Calvin College's Festival of Faith and Writing. Launched in 1990 as Contemporary Christian Writers in Community, a small conference of fewer than two hundred, the biennial Festival has grown in attendance tenfold over the last decade and a half. Begun under the aegis of Henry Baron, its first director, and Ed Ericson and directed for much of its history by Dale Brown, this massive undertaking involves the work of many hands across the English department, the campus, and the larger community in order to make it a success. Notably, many of these hands belong not just to faculty, staff, and community members but also to hundreds of student volunteers. Seeking to explore literature from writers — both within the broad Christian community and from other faith traditions — who are interested in questions of spiritual understanding and transcendence, the Festival continues to draw an exciting mix of readers, writers from almost every imaginable genre, publishers, and critics to participate in its three-day conversation.

Anyone who has ever attended the Festival, however, knows that no volume could ever come close to capturing the vitality and diversity of these many conversations. And "conversation" is the key word here: over the years, only 25 percent of the sessions at the Festival have been speeches. The rest have been sessions such as panels, readings, performances, roundtables, and academic discussions. As a small percentage of even the small category of Festival speeches, then, the selections in this book do not pretend to represent the full Festival experience. Nor is this volume intended as a characterization or commemoration of the Festival of Faith and Writing *as* an event; instead, it seeks to celebrate what is important *about* that event: the significant discussions around the intersections of literature and faith that occur there. And because these are discussions, I have edited these pieces to retain their oral quality; they should be read as lectures written for the ear, perhaps more than as texts written for the eye.

I think the metaphor of "intersections" is a particularly apt one. Thinking geometrically helps one realize the many points of convergence, not only between faith and writing but between these authors as well. I like the image of writers traveling on many roads — and then meeting up at critical junctures. Of course, none of these encounters is without risk. This is fraught territory indeed — and with the heavy freight that both literature and belief carry, the crossroads can be dangerous. Indeed, David James Duncan warns us in his essay that these convergences are often more like collisions than anything else.

Perhaps. Still, no matter how they may answer any other question or define any other term, all these writers are agreed on at least one fundamental assumption: that literature can help us be more faithful. How?

Barbara Brown Taylor begins the volume by noting the tension between what she terms the "languages of belief and beholding," yet simultaneously insisting that the two must exist together. In fact, she claims, the two enrich each other and ultimately lead us to experience God and one another in all the fullness God intended.

If this is true, then how do people of belief approach literature? Katherine Paterson and Frederick Buechner provide useful models of what that approach might look like for writers and readers alike. Paterson examines images of God taken from Genesis in order to make clear our own role as creators, as story-makers, while Buechner encourages us to begin to see ourselves within stories — in this case, the biblical story — as story-subjects. For both Paterson and Buechner, the way we imagine ourselves profoundly affects the way we are able to come to faithfulness.

Another question arises, of course. If we accept the importance of story, we still need to decide how best to tell it. Two quite different options emerge: shouts or whispers? Doris Betts sets up the dilemma quite nicely when she quotes Flannery O'Connor's view that "to the hard of hearing you shout, and for the almost-blind you draw large and startling figures." Bret Lott, whose essay follows Betts's, would seem to be a shouting man. But Betts posits a quite different model — and instead advocates "whispering hope." At heart, the question they both address seems to be what qualifies as a "Christian" novel, a label that Betts also finds problematic.

But it's not just what the end product — the novel or short story or poem — looks like; these writers interrogate what the very act of writing might resemble for the Christian. If Walter Pater argued that all art aspires to the condition of music, the authors in the book's middle section —Kathleen Norris, Walter Wangerin, Will Campbell, Elizabeth Dewberry, Ron Hansen, Paul Schrader, Jan Karon, James Calvin Schaap, and Silas House — suggest a thought-provoking range of metaphors for the *experience* of doing faith-filled writing, including subversion, worship, testimony, prayer, knowing, light, and praise. In so doing, they also increase our understanding of the richness of this creative gift and enhance the ways we think about using it to serve God.

That's the positive side. But Joy Kogawa, Betty Smartt Carter, David James Duncan, and Anne Lamott call our attention to the darker side as well — the tendency toward triumphalism or cynicism, the pain from a wounding background — and describe ways of finding hope while still acknowledging brokenness. Kogawa, for example, remarks:

> We cannot see the atom, and yet it unleashes that kind of immense power.
>
> I've wondered if there isn't a corollary: an unseen good that would be even more powerful than all of that evil. It seems to me that there is. It resides within the infinitesimal moral choices that we each make from moment to moment. Things that seem so tiny, so insignificant, so fleeting that they're hardly worth noting.

The book's final essays — by Luci Shaw, Madeleine L'Engle, Thomas Lynch, and a second from Katherine Paterson — ask us to consider how this attentiveness allows faithful readers to live incarnationally. These writers make the vital connection between language and embodiment and urge us to translate words into actions. Paterson's closing words perhaps say it best: "It is up to each of us not simply to write the words, but to *be* the word of hope, of faith, of love. To be the word made flesh."

My deepest thanks to each of the writers included here for their generosity and their graciousness, especially given the time constraints under which we were working: to Melissa Van Til for her valiant efforts with the transcriptions of so many of these selections and for her very able secretarial work; to Meagan Luhrs and Jon Pott of Eerdmans for their encouragement and assistance; to Jim VandenBosch, Roy Anker, and Shelly LeMahieu Dunn for their editorial feedback; and to Dale Brown for advice on this project as well as for the vision of bringing together faith and writing that inspired me. All royalties from the sale of this book will be donated to the children's literacy charity, Reading Is Fundamental.

I could not be more blessed than with the wonderful family and tremendous group of friends that surround me. They supported not only this project but enable everything I do. They have my sincere love and gratitude, as ever.

One friend, in particular, has been especially important. This book is for her.

JENNIFER L. HOLBERG
Grand Rapids, Michigan

BARBARA BROWN TAYLOR

··

Way Beyond Belief:
The Call to Behold

───────

I am both happy and surprised to be with you at Calvin College this weekend, especially since my literary genre is not what you would call mainstream. I write small religious essays and sermons, both of which have fairly limited, though I must say loyal, audiences.

In my case, of course, most of the writing has been for the purpose of speech. For the past twenty years, my primary vocations have been preaching and teaching, both of which depend heavily on oral presentation. While the words appear first on the page, they are not meant to stay there. They are meant for the ear, not the eye, which turns the page into the stage where the words audition and rehearse. They file in to show me what they can do. I weed them out. They explain themselves to me. I ask for more feeling. They arrange themselves one way. I suggest another. They focus on meaning. I make them give me rhythm. Finally it is my turn to say them out loud, which is when I usually have to let a few more of them go — because what is lovely on the page is often too heavy for the air.

That is only logical if you think about it, since a page is so much more substantial than the air. A page can hold hundreds of words still tethered to one another by commas and semicolons, so that a reader can go back and make sure that none has gotten away. As long as you have a page, you don't need a memory. If you don't get something the first time, then you may go back as many times as you like. The words will be right there waiting for you, as patient as rabbits in a pen.

But none of that works in the air. In order to survive that medium, words have to be fast and light. Pack too many syllables in them and they will sink before they have gone three feet out of your mouth. Link a long string of them together with a semicolon, and watch half of them take a wrong turn because those in the back lost sight of those up front. Or try keeping the words abstract, with no body odor to them at all, and you may also discover that words can be too light for air. Without any smell to them, without any color or heat in them to keep them down to earth, words can float clean out of human reach. Even in the air, words need enough ballast to anchor them in memory.

Since you are veteran listeners to airborne words yourselves, you know that sometimes the only memory they create is the memory of having felt deeply alive for a moment — or profoundly sad — or so close to the pulsing truth of things that all the hair on your arms stood up. While the words that carried you to that place are now entirely lost to you, you will never forget what the person sitting in front of you was wearing, or how the beam of sunlight that cut across your vision showed you everything that dances invisibly in front of your face all the time. Some of you even stood in line afterwards to say something to the speaker who held the door to that moment open for you, risking the awkward moment when you thanked him for something he never said, or complimented her on her hair when that was the absolute *last thing* that you meant to say to her.

All of these are significant liabilities for those of us in the oral presentation business, but the worst thing of all is that I have to be there — I have to be *here* — in order to put my words in the air. I guess that I could turn off all the lights and do a PowerPoint presentation, but I would still be able to hear you shifting in your seats. I would still be able to see one of you get up and head toward the back of this auditorium, without knowing whether it was what I was saying or what you ate for dinner last night that made you leave the room.

At the last church I served, I watched one man struggling to stay awake while I preached. The church only seated 82 people, so it was pretty easy to keep an eye on everyone. He was in the back pew on my right, with his eyes closed and his head leaned back against the wall. Every now and then his mouth would drop open, which would wake him up. Then he would go through the whole cycle all over again. I knew he had small children who were not in church with him that day, so when he shook my hand at the door, I said, "Are the kids okay? I couldn't help noticing that you looked really beat in there." He looked at me as if I had just recited his social security number.

"You can *see* us?" he asked.

Yes, I can see you. Most of the time I can even see how my words affect you, which was never the plan. The plan was to be a short story writer, not a preacher, so that you could read my stories or not — suit yourself — and unless you wrote me a letter that I could read in the privacy of my own home about a story of mine that you read in the privacy of your own home, then I would never have to know what you thought of it — or of me either, for that matter. I meant to wear bohemian clothes, sleep in garrets, live large and push language to its limits describing things few people saw. Instead I ended up with a closet full of black suits and clergy shirts, learning how to write twelve-minute Sunday sermons that might mean something to the children who heard them as well as their parents.

While I am not ungrateful for this turn of events, I have always harbored a kind of wistfulness about it — or, closer to the truth — a kind of envy for those poets and writers who are able to say things that I don't think I can say in church and keep my job. In some cases they are extreme things, both personal and political. In other cases they are erotic things or just plain sensual ones, but rightly or wrongly, it seems to me that there are large swaths of human experience — and of the English language as well — that are off limits for me because of the arena in which I have chosen to love the words.

My present shorthand for the tension I feel is the tension between what I call the language of beholding and the language of belief — the first being language devoted to *what is,* and the second being language devoted to *what is right.* In my lexicon, at least, the language of beholding calls me to full attention to real life on earth — not just mine, but the real lives of other people as well, along with the lives of nations, oceans, creatures, trees — and to describe their reality as faithfully as I can, even

3

when that is strange or frightening to me or causes me all kinds of ideological problems. When I am in service to the language of beholding, my primary responsibility is to *what is.*

When I serve the language of belief, I have many more responsibilities. I am accountable to a community of faith, for one thing, with whom I share certain scriptures, sacraments, and conceptual truths about God, all of which we believe call us to live in certain ways. While we sometimes confuse right thinking with right living, rightness remains important to us and we spend a fair amount of time calling one another to account for what we say we believe. When I exercise the language of belief, my primary responsibility is to *what is right.*

To add an extra twist to this tension, there exists in some churches a conviction that what *is* cannot, on principle, be *right* — because creation is fallen, because human beings are born in sin, because flesh is at war with spirit and Satan rules the earth. Since I did not encounter such beliefs until I was an adult, I remain fairly immune to them. But where they are present, I find they cut an even deeper chasm between the languages of beholding and belief.

I fell in love with words early, at least partly because my family moved so much. My dad was not a military man, but close. He was a psychologist with the Veterans' Administration for the first few years of my life, then a college professor, so we did not stay anywhere long before he was promoted and we were on the road again. Best friends did not last any longer for me than beloved backyards did. I became an experienced dish packer. The only true constants in my life were my family and the public library, where my mother took my two sisters and me every week to check out an armload of books no matter what town we were living in. My only constants were love and words, in other words, and I grew up as dependent on one as on the other.

I had the kind of parents who believed that religion should be chosen, not imposed. The way they told it, my baptism in the pre-Vatican II Catholic Church had pretty much put the lid on the church thing for both of them. When my southern Methodist mother from Georgia married my lapsed Catholic father from South Dakota, my Catholic grandmother was not pleased. When I was born two years later they tried to appease her with my baptism, but the whole thing backfired when the

Roman priest took me in his arms and said what sounded to my parents like some rude things about my character. Lacking an adequate doctrine of original sin, they were both deeply offended. As soon as the priest had handed me off and was safely out of earshot, my mother reportedly turned to my father and said, "We are getting out of here, and we are never coming back." And they never did.

They taught me reverence for the world instead, or did I simply catch it from them? My first cathedral was the field of broom grass behind my house in Kansas, my first Eucharist the saltine crackers I toasted over a stick fire with my friends. I will never forget my first look at the meteor shower called the Tears of Saint Lawrence from my backyard in Ohio, or the oily smell of the Black Warrior River in Alabama as I waded deeper and deeper with the clay bottom sucking at my feet. My immersion in these mysteries gave me sanctuary. Beholding them set me right when everything else was going wrong. If anyone had tried to tell me that creation was fallen, or that I should care more for heaven than earth, then I would have gone off to lie in the sweet grass by myself.

The books I liked best early on were biographies and fantasies — biographies because I was impatient with being a child and needed some larger lives I might grow into, and fantasies because the real world of the Deep South during the Civil Rights era was often a frightening place to be. Amelia Earhart and Florence Nightingale saved me in those days. So did Narnia and Camelot. They lent me their lives when my own fit as tightly as last year's shoes. They offered me alternative realities when my own neighborhood seemed dangerous to me, with tribes of mean kids who had soaked up their parents' politics, lying in wait for my sisters and me. I am pretty sure that we gave as good as we got, but I am equally sure that we did not understand what we were fighting about any better than our tormentors did. Like most young warriors, we took on the battles that our elders chose for us with all the idealism that they had lost.

The books did not provide an escape for me as much as they provided meaning. In their pages, the forces of evil were given shapes and names. Mordred. The Witch of Endor. As frightening as they were, I learned that their power was limited. I also learned that I was free to resist them, although no one could oppose them by using their own hateful tactics. The minute someone decided to fight evil by employing evil's own weapons, the battle was lost. There was a better way, a way that often involved suffering hurt instead of hurting others, which Aslan, the original Lion King, showed me before I ever read a Gospel.

Eventually I did read a Gospel — read the whole Bible in fact — where I was happy to discover the larger lives and alternate realities that I had come to expect in books. I could not help noticing the difference between the first and second sections of the book, however. While the first section of the Bible was full of lusty, often scheming and bloody human life, the second section seemed very cleaned up to me. The distinction between good people and bad people was much clearer in the second section, for instance, and while there was still a little violence, there was no sex at all. In fact, the second section made sex sound like something that only bad people did, or at least weak people. Most of the real heroes in that section were very serious single people who — like the kids I had grown up with — were involved in fights with their own neighbors that I did not fully understand.

So I continued to read fiction alongside the Bible as I grew into sexual adulthood myself, balancing Matthew and Luke with D. H. Lawrence and John Updike. While I looked to the first to tell me what was right, I looked to the second to show me what *was.* I even found a few writers, like Nikos Kazantzakis and Graham Greene, who seemed able to do both at the same time. I experimented with church membership in high school and found it a poor fit, but I was hooked on transcendence by then — if not on God — so that when I arrived at college, where I could finally choose my own courses, I gorged on English literature and religion.

While their interests were different, both disciplines confirmed my instincts about the power of the word. Both taught the art of exalted language, and while I spent four years leaping from Abraham Heschel and Paul Tillich to Wallace Stevens and Archibald MacLeish, I knew that eventually I was going to have to make a choice.

In the end, I chose the language of belief and packed my bags for Yale Divinity School, where I was finally indoctrinated into the faith I had been flirting with for so long. I became an Episcopalian. I learned to use "Christology" and "soteriology" in the same sentence. I worked as a cocktail waitress in the summertime, still drawn to the boundary between what was right and what was.

Three years later I graduated from seminary with no more sense of vocation than when I had entered it and took a secretarial job at Candler School of Theology, less than a mile from my parents' home. While I probably should have been humiliated by that career move, I was not. The people were kind, I was at least serving those who served the church, and typing for a living meant that I still lived by words. I also had a great deal of freedom, so when I saw an ad for a summer writing institute, I enrolled on the spot. I began writing short stories and falling in love with poets. I rented a garret. The following winter I was accepted for a month's residency at Yaddo, the artist's colony in upstate New York where the ghosts of Flannery O'Connor, John Cheever, and Katherine Anne Porter still linger. I built a file of rejection slips from the best magazines in print. I never sold a story.

Around the same time, I was invited to preach for the first time at the downtown church where I worked on the weekends — not a proper sermon from the pulpit but a short homily from the pew, for some poorly attended service during Holy Week. *Sure, I said, I'd be glad to.* There were about ten people there, as I recall. I had worked at least ten hours on the homily, and could feel the sweat running down both sides of my body as I delivered each dense word from my wilted manuscript. Afterwards, someone asked if I would make her a copy. *Sure, I said, I'd be glad to.* It was not until I was driving home that I realized I had just sold my first story.

In this way I found my vocation, which involved wedding my two old constants — love and words — with my newer love for the word of God. I became a preacher instead of a short story writer, although not without some deep claw marks along the way. I never intended to live such a public life. Nor did I intend to serve such a public cause. My plan had been to follow my own vision wherever it led without asking anyone else whether my interests were acceptable or not.

Instead, I entered the service of God's word in community, which involved submitting myself to a vision that did not belong to me. That vision — described in scripture, interpreted through the ages, revealed by the spirit, guarded by the church — that vision belonged to God and to the people of God. For Christians, the kind of life it made possible was summed up in the life of Jesus, and while there were certain things one was allowed to imagine about him — such as his height or hair color — I learned the hard way that there were many other things one was not supposed to imagine about him, such as his feelings toward Mary Magdalene or his qualms about his own identity. I could, perhaps, imagine those things on my own time, but when it came time for me to speak within the community of faith, no one was looking for some brand new word from me. My job was to proclaim *The* Word — God's Word — freshly and creatively, to be sure, but not overly inventively. One day as I listened to Ralph Vaughan Williams's "Variation on a Theme by Thomas Tallis," I discovered a helpful metaphor for my own work. My task was not to write an original score but to provide ornamentation for a melody that was already well known. My job was to produce a "Variation on a Theme by Matthew," or Paul or John.

It was and is a great privilege to preach — a privilege so often abused by many of us who do it that it is a wonder anyone is still willing to listen — which is why I felt more than a little guilty when I would pick up a book of Anne Lamott's and envy her dreadlocks, her salty language, her ability both to have and write about raising a son whose father she did not marry. Or when I would behold Brad Pitt in *Fight Club* and be wrecked by the speech he gave to a bunch of angry, underemployed men in the basement where they made meaning with their fists. A speech about the spiritual desolation of our money-glutted culture that I ached to quote in church, only I would have had to change all the R-rated language to PG-13 at least and so rob it of its sting.

Meanwhile, church people came to see me during the week about all the R-rated things that were going on in their lives — not only family violence, extramarital affairs, and the abuse they suffered for being gay or lesbian, but also religious questions they would not dream of raising with other Christians. In some cases, the questions concerned what they could no longer believe about God. In others, the problem was some very real experience that did not fit with any of their beliefs — a burning bush where no respectable burning bush should have been, for instance, or a being of pure light who hovered over their beds in the middle of the night and changed everything. Only how was that possible? And what were they supposed to *think* about it?

My knowledge of Updike and O'Connor turned out to be as useful on these occasions as my knowledge of Matthew and Luke, or to put it another way, the language of beholding turned out to be as helpful as the language of belief. What I had always loved about poetry, fiction, and drama was precisely the way that it *did not* preach. Whatever the writers of such works may or may not have believed, communicating those beliefs directly to me was not their concern. They observed the first commandment of creative writing: *show, don't tell.* Their concern was to increase my capacity for beholding life on earth in all its glorious and terrible reality — to make a kind of sling for my chin with the web of their words so that I could not look away — never telling me what to think about what I saw but showing me so much with so much clarity that I had to think for myself: Is this right? What needs to happen here? If it were me instead of him or her, what would I do?

When I worked that same way with the people who came to see me, they could almost always answer those same questions for themselves. All they really needed was someone to behold their lives with them, someone to hold their own chins so they could not look away, until wisdom rose up inside of them to meet what they saw. At best, my job was to say back what I heard them saying so that they could hear it too — sometimes to offer a new name for what they beheld, or to place a frame around it so that it was not so overwhelming to them at first. But never was my job to disqualify the beholding on the basis of belief or to trim away what did not fit in the name of loyalty to God. In my line of work, you meet lots of people who come to church to flee life, instead of to find it. Plenty of them are clergy, too, but whoever they are, it can be very difficult for them to accept that faithfulness to their own embodied lives on earth might be a prerequisite for any kind of faithfulness to God.

Almost seven years ago now, I left full time parish ministry for college teaching, at least partly because the language of belief had become too contentious for me. Both at home and in the news, Christian faith seemed to be more and more a matter of defending theological positions instead of washing dirty feet. The old short story writer in me cringed when people waved the Bible to support their various causes, freeze-drying foundational stories of the faith into rounded tablespoons of exclusive doctrine. Context, plot, character, and dialogue — all those vital details that some writer worked so hard to capture, all those rich sources

9

of earthy complexity and divine paradox — were chucked in the mining of pure convictional gold. I found myself wanting out of the answer business and back into the question business. I wanted to reopen closed files and read banned books. I wanted to seek the kind of faith that has nothing to do with being sure what I believe and everything to do with trusting God to catch me, though I am not sure of anything.

Now I am a religion professor, which is sort of like being a preacher except that I get to give grades. I also write, almost therapeutically at this point, as I try to find my way back into the language of beholding that I once knew so well. There is plenty to behold, too, since I slipped my leash. Every semester I take students in my world religions classes to the Drepung-Loseling Center for Tibetan Buddhist Studies in Atlanta as well as the Atlanta Masjid of Al-Islam. Swami Yogeshananda, the 80-year-old Ramakrishna monk who keeps the Vedanta Society of Atlanta going, invited me to speak to his small community one Sunday morning last year, where I ran into a former parishioner from a church I once served.

"What are *you* doing here?" I asked her.

"You first," she said.

I have put so much time and energy into learning the boundaries of the language of belief that I still jump at the alarms that go off, both inside of me and in my listeners, when I go past them. But I have found that if I can just keep walking, there is a whole crowd of people out in the sweet grass who want to know where I have been — and why it took me so long to get there. Like me, they have not stopped believing things. They have just decided to let God challenge and refresh their beliefs on a regular basis by attending to all that God has given them to behold.

Some of them learned how to do that in Sunday school, incidentally, where many of the first stories they learned began with the word, "Behold!" What followed that word in both testaments were things truly beyond belief — not only the aforementioned burning bushes but also split seas, bread from heaven, guiding angels, immaculate conceptions, miracle-working messiahs, and physical resurrections from the dead. The Nicene Creed did not come up for them until third grade at least, and by then it was too late. By then, they knew that God colored outside the lines all the time — as a matter of divine principle — and there was no going back.

What saddens me these days is how many Christians I meet who identify themselves as "heretics" — jokingly if they are still in churches and defiantly if they are not. For some, the issue is that they believe *less* than they think they should about Jesus. They are not troubled by the thought that he may have had two human parents instead of one, or that his real presence with his disciples after his death may have been more metaphysical than physical. The glory they behold in him has more to do with the nature of his being than with the number of his miracles, but they have suffered enough at the hands of other Christians to learn to keep their mouths shut.

For others, the issue is that they believe *more* than Jesus. Having beheld his glory, they find themselves better equipped to recognize God's glory all over the place, including places where Christian doctrine says that it should not be. I know Christians who have beheld God's glory in a Lakota sweat lodge, in a sacred Celtic grove, at the edge of a Hawaiian volcano and in a Hindu temple during the festival of lights, as well as in dreams and visions that they are afraid to tell anyone else about at all. These heretics not only fear being shunned for their unorthodox narratives; they also fear sharing some of the most powerful things that have ever happened to them with people who may ridicule them.

Given the history of Christians as a people who started out beholding what was beyond belief in the person of Jesus, this strikes me as a lamentable state of affairs, both for those who have learned to see no more than they are supposed to see as well as for those who have excused themselves from traditional churches because they see too little or too much. If it is true that God exceeds all our efforts to contain God, then is it too big a stretch to declare that *dumbfoundedness* is what all Christians have most in common? Or that coming together to confess all that we do not know as we reach out to one another is at least as sacred an activity as declaring what we think we do?

Clearly, this is a work in progress. I have no idea where I am going either as a writer or a preacher, but I mean to stay in the beholding business as long as I can, following the same good advice that God seems to use on me: *show, don't tell.* Hold the chin. Direct the gaze. Trust the vision. Find the Perfect Word.

And to seek out communities like this one, where the boundaries between the languages of belief and beholding are so beautifully blurred, where the invisible bread of our communion together is not any creed we can say in unison but our love for the Word that breaks each of us open in a different way.

KATHERINE PATERSON

....

Image and Imagination

⸻

Tonight I promised to talk about the imagination, but like many writers, I have a sort of spooky feeling that if I start dissecting the creative process to see what makes it hop, I may very well end up with a dead frog. As the years have gone by, I've had to do more and more talking about what I do, but it still makes me feel uneasy to do so.

What I will not do, truly cannot do, is talk about a book when I'm in the midst of writing it. But eventually the book is published, and I have to figure out a way to talk about it. When my last novel was due in the bookstores any day, I heard that dreaded question — "So, what's your new book about?" — and could no longer avoid an answer.

"Well," I snapped, "I guess I have to start talking about it sooner or later." Now what should I say that didn't make my beloved book sound totally stupid?

"Okay," I said finally, "I guess I can tell you where it came from."

My questioner had perked up with great interest, so I went on: "I had this image of a child tumbling off the back of a wagon, and nobody comes back to look for him."

"Oh," she said brightly, "there's another book that starts just like that."

I froze. Another book that began just like my dear, fragile, unborn one. How could that be? She searched around in her mind for the title.

Pecos Bill, she said finally. "Doesn't it begin just like that? The child falls off the back of the wagon, is rescued by coyotes and raised by them?"

At least there were no coyotes in my book. But that's the sort of thing that happens when you try to talk about a book. "Just read the book," I want to say. "Don't ask me about it. What do I know?"

This evening you'll have to bear with me as I take a writer's approach. And not just any writer's approach, this writer's approach. I'm going to do this by talking about some images of God and relating them to my own imaginative experience. The writers of the book of Genesis give us more material than we could explore in a lifetime, but for tonight I want to look at four images of God that can be seen in the first book of the Hebrew Bible: God the artist-creator, God the judge, God the wrestler, and God the maker of story. Do not pretend for a moment that these four images have exhausted the portrait of God in the book of Genesis. I have chosen them quite arbitrarily as models for the imaginative experience as I understand it.

The book of Genesis gives us two quite different pictures of God the artist-creator: the majestic creator of chapter one by whose word the light breaks and separates from the darkness, and the literally down-to-earth maker and shaper in chapter two. James Weldon Johnson manages to capture both images in his poem, "The Creation," which concludes, as you remember,

> Up from the bed of the river
> God scooped the clay;
> And by the bank of the river
> He kneeled Him down;
> And there the great God Almighty
> Who lit the sun and fixed it in the sky
> Who flung the stars to the most far corner of the night,
> Who rounded the earth in the middle of His hand,
> This Great God,
> Like a mammy bending over her baby,
> Kneeled down in the dust
> Toiling over a lump of clay
> Till He shaped it in His own image;

Then into it He blew the breath of life,
And man became a living soul.
Amen. Amen.

I read the first chapter of Genesis, and God sounds like a poet. I read the second chapter of Genesis, and God sounds like a novelist. I can't push this comparison too far, for certainly concrete imagery is necessary to poetry. But there is a difference in the raw material of the poet and that of the writer of fiction. As Flannery O'Connor explains, "The fact is that the materials of the fiction writer are the humblest. Fiction is about everything human and we are made of dust, and if you scorn getting yourself dusty than you shouldn't write fiction. It's not a grand enough job for you." O'Connor says "dust" — I prefer the image of the mud by the creek bank that James Weldon Johnson evokes. Either way, it is in writing with the dust or clay of human character and experience that we fiction writers get into trouble, especially those of us who write for children, for our critics believe that somehow we should be fashioning our tales out of a finer material. I suppose sooner or later most poets and writers of fiction get around to asking questions about the creative process through poetry or fiction. Looking at my own books, I see that I have done this several times, mostly in bits and pieces. But it was in *Come Sing, Jimmy Jo* that I asked myself what it meant to be given the gift to create. Scientists may try to dissect the process, but I think for most of us, the process of the imagination has an element of mystery which we must acknowledge with awe.

James Johnson, the protagonist of my story, is a singer. But in writing about him, I've really written about what it feels like to be a writer.

When James got to the mike Friday night, he said, "This here's a new song that my daddy wrote for me, and I'm singing it for him." And he did, putting into the song all the pain of the ride to West Virginia and the joy of their time there together. His father's eyes were bright with tears.

It was funny how he didn't seem to mind the fans that night. In fact, it was as though he was standing in a glowing circle. He smiled at each one and signed their autograph books and scraps of paper. They weren't greedy and grabbling, but sad and lonely, their faces almost hungry. *Don't be sad. Don't be hungry.* He wanted to reach out to them all and heal their hurts. How rich he was. How full of good things. Jerry Lee had written a wonderful song, and James had opened his mouth, and the song had come to life. He had been possessed by it, as though it were a magic spell. The enchantment had poured out from his body through the air — all the way to West Virginia. Maybe Grandma would call. He hoped she would, although he didn't need her to say that he had been good.

She did call, but all she did was cry, the puppy yowling with dismay in the background, until they both had to laugh. He went to bed without talking to anyone. He didn't want to talk anymore. He just wanted to lie there in the darkness, holding inside his body the fierce sorrow of the music. His fingers, his head, his chest, even his toes rang with it, and he could not hold it in. He had been swallowed by the hugeness, the greatness of it — like Jonah in the belly of the whale. The vastness filled him with wonder, but he was not afraid. This must be how it feels, he thought, this must be how it feels to have the gift.

This brings us to the third chapter of Genesis and the second image I want to talk about: God as judge. The image of God as judge is not confined, of course, to this one chapter. I'm deliberately avoiding the picture of the angry God who sentences the creation and nearly all of its creatures to death in the flood. There are surely times when artists destroy in anger what they have made. In a *Fraser* episode, Fraser and his brother Niles meet a J. D. Salinger kind of writer, who wrote one great book and then disappeared. By a kind of coincidence, confined to situation comedy and Shakespeare, the brothers have a chance to surreptitiously read the author's long awaited second book as the author is on his way to give it to the publisher. They are astounded by it. It is better than the first — which was a masterpiece of nearly legendary proportions. When they are caught in the act of reading the book, the writer demands their opinion. At first they are tongue-tied. Then to make up for their first inarticulate response, they become increasingly lavish in their praise, showing how the book brilliantly mirrors certain passages in Dante's *Inferno*. The writer is furious. "See!" he cries, "Why did I think I have anything to say. It's not original! It's just a cheap imitation of Dante." And with that he rushes out onto the balcony of the high rise and throws the whole manuscript out into the air, where the pages fall down into the rush of traffic many stories below. Yes, sometimes artists do in anger destroy their work. But even in a sitcom it is hard to laugh. We look on such destruction as an aberration, like a mother committing infanticide.

How Noah's ark became a favorite story for children I shall never understand. Any thinking child's imagination is sure to stray from the animals marching two by two up the gang plank to all those left gazing wistfully from the shelter of the trees — not to mention the men, women, and children who aren't even aware that those first rain drops mean deluge. No, I will leave the problem of the nearly merciless judge of the flood story, the artist who destroys his masterpiece to older, braver minds. Then there's the judge of Abraham's complaint: "Shall not the Judge of all the earth do what is just?" But in the dialogue with Abraham, this judge behaves more like the mysterious wrestler of Jacob than the implacable judge of Noah's time or even the God of the earlier chapters who both condemns Cain and sets a mark upon the murderous forehead to protect him from human judgment.

I want to move back in the story to the creator who gives abundance along with boundaries: "You may freely eat of every tree of the garden, but of the tree of the knowledge of good and evil, you shall not eat, for in the day you eat of it, you shall die." The creator, it would seem, gives everything to the man and woman he has made including meaningful labor, except the knowledge of what is good and evil. The man and woman may enjoy all God's good gifts, but they may not judge what is good and what is evil — for judgment is the prerogative of God alone.

I don't imagine there is a soul in this room that does not know what happens next. Disobedience falls hard on the heels of prohibition. The third chapter of Genesis is more important to the writer of fiction even than the first two. Nor do I have to tell you what happens next. The fruit is eaten, the unwelcome knowledge comes, the curses, the separation, the garments of skin made by the Lord himself to cover the nakedness of the man and woman. "Then the Lord God said, 'See, the man has become like one of us, knowing good and evil, and now he might reach out his hand and take also from the Tree of Life and eat. And live forever.' Therefore the Lord God sent him forth from the garden of Eden to till the ground from which he was taken."

Why are these words so important to the writer of fiction? Let me pose a question: is fiction possible where there is no fall? I don't think that it is. Isn't it the broken image, the damaged image of God in human-kind, that is the stuff of fiction, whether we're speaking of *Peter Rabbit* or *Anna Karenina?* And not only is fallen humanity vital to the substance of story, the consequence of humankind's disobedience is necessary for the crafting of story. You have to be as a god, knowing good and evil, before you can construct a fictional narrative.

I don't think that you could say that without sin there is no creativity. If that were true, there'd be no creation. Even human creativity is not dependent on eating the forbidden fruit. Surely, the pure heart can paint masterpieces, compose heavenly music, write great poetry. I can see angels doing any of the above.

But novelists must deal with the brokenness of the human condition. They must write about people as they are. Though I may get an argument here, I believe that, however they may love their characters, novelists must pass moral judgment on the creatures they have brought to life. They must be able to show in the life of the story the human behavior that tends toward wholeness and holiness, and that which further bends, breaks, and destroys the divine image. As far as the world of their novel and the characters in that world are concerned, surely novelists must be as gods, knowing good and evil.

There's another phrase in Genesis chapter three that, I'm amazed to acknowledge, I had never really taken in until I was preparing this talk. Here is the sentence again: "Therefore the Lord God sent him forth from the garden of Eden to till the ground from which he was taken." This is what Flannery O'Connor was saying about the task of the novelist: we must till the ground from which we were taken and if we scorn getting ourselves dusty, then we shouldn't write fiction. We have said traditionally that the difference between God's creation and our own is that God creates *ex nihilo,* out of nothing. I wonder if we can really say that. We know now that the raw material of creation is energy. So perhaps it is more accurate to say that God creates out of God's own spirit, out of God's own energy. Because God is good, all that God creates is good. We also create out of ourselves, out of the earth from which we were taken. But that perfect creation is spoiled, bent, and broken.

There's a third image of God in Genesis which speaks powerfully to me as a writer of fiction. It is the image of the wrestler. Here again scholars may want to argue with me about the choice of this image. But certainly for Jacob and for me, it was God or, at the very least, God's angel messenger that was involved in that mysterious wrestling match beside the brook of Jabbok.

> Then Jacob was left alone, and a man wrestled with him until daybreak.
>
> When he saw that he had not prevailed against him, he touched the socket of his thigh; so the socket of Jacob's thigh was dislocated while he wrestled with him.
>
> Then he said, "Let me go, for the dawn is breaking." But he said, "I will not let you go unless you bless me."
>
> So he said to him, "What is your name?" And he said, "Jacob."
>
> He said, "Your name shall no longer be Jacob, but Israel; for you have striven with God and with men and have prevailed."
>
> Then Jacob asked him and said, "Please tell me your name." But he said, "Why is it that you ask my name?" And he blessed him there.
>
> So Jacob named the place Peniel, for he said, "I have seen God face to face, yet my life is preserved."

In Robert McAfee Brown's book on the liberating power of fiction, entitled *Persuade Us to Rejoice,* he devotes a chapter to Elie Wiesel which he calls, "The Human Obligation to Question God." Jews have always recognized that the Bible is as much a book about men and women questioning God as it is about their obeying God. We Christians in some misguided definition of faith have seemed fearful of acknowledging this. Listen to some of the questions in Genesis alone: "Am I my brother's keeper?" "Shall I indeed bear a child, now that I am old?" "Shall not the Judge of all the earth do what is just?" "What is your name?" As we go through the Bible, the questions become more anguished. Job, Jeremiah, the anonymous singers of the Psalms. Jesus himself, wrestling with the angel in Gethsemane and crying from the cross the question of all who have trusted and not seen their deliverance, "My God, my God, why have you forsaken me?"

One reason I love to write for children is that many of them are still asking these questions. Why? How can these things be? How long? We who are older, especially I fear, we who have grown up in the church, have stopped asking these questions, at least aloud. And when, in times of deepest distress, we find the questions simply torn out of us, there is the danger that some well-meaning friend of Job will seek to hush our cries with pious platitudes. But in the scriptures, God's friends wrestle with God. As Brown writes of Elie Wiesel, Wiesel, this modern prophet, shows us over and over again, that "it is the questions, not the answers, that are important." We may never know the answers, but quoting Wiesel himself, "we can keep refining the questions and refusing to surrender them to easy speculation."

When our son David was eight years old his best friend, a bright, funny little girl, was struck and killed by lightning. Now how is any rational human soul to make sense of this tragedy? Should we not cry aloud to God when such a thing happens? Should we not wrestle with the scandal of a world in which children die, whether by the unfeeling hand of nature or by the cruel and careless hands of other humans? Aren't we less than the souls God intends for us to be if we view such monstrous events with passive pseudo-piety? When I wrote *Bridge to Terabithia,* I thought I was writing a story to make sense for myself of a child's senseless death. But before long I was forced to recognize that the book was not simply about David and Lisa. I was writing the story after Lisa's death, to be sure, but it was also the year of my own bout with cancer. I know that by writing *Bridge to Terabithia,* I was wrestling with my own angel of death.

Not long ago, I had the wonderful chance once again to be part of the chorus for Brahms's *German Requiem.* We'd been practicing the requiem all fall, and everytime I sang it I marveled. The *German Requiem,* as you probably know, uses the German of Luther and is not your standard day-of-wrath-and-judgment requiem. It doesn't even pray for the souls of the dead. It is a work of enormous comfort and incomparable beauty, and it has been written for the living. It heals my soul to sing it, even if Brahms did like to keep his sopranos stuck in the stratosphere of high Gs and As, longer than any normal voice should attempt those heights without oxygen. In the third movement of this wonderful cantata, a baritone soloist sings, and the chorus echoes, the words of Psalm 39,

> Lord, make me to know the measure of my days on earth,
>> to consider my frailty, that I must perish.
> Surely all my days here are as an handbreadth to thee and
>> my life time is as naught to thee.
> Verily, mankind walketh in a vain show, and their best state
>> is vanity.
> Man passeth away like a shadow. He is disquieted in vain,
> he heapeth up riches and cannot tell who shall gather them.

Then, in his grief for the fragility and the apparent meaninglessness of his life, the psalmist cries out, "Now Lord, only what do I wait for?" Brahms piles up this universal cry of the human heart through anguished repetition from soloist to every part of the chorus. There is an abrupt moment of silence. Then the answer comes, at first *piano,* then crescendoing into *forte,* crashing like great waves upon the shore: "My hope is in thee." That is what *Bridge to Terabithia* was about. It was not about Lisa's death and David's loss. It was about me. I was Leslie who must die, as we all must. I was Jesse who had to learn how to live with most unwelcome death. I'm not the biblical writer, nor am I Brahms, but in my little story, I've spoken of the gravity, the frailty of life, the fear that life may be in vain and death victorious. And then I have heard the soaring affirmation of hope.

The fourth image of God in Genesis that I want to remind you of is found almost at the end of the book. You may consider it far-fetched and indeed the construct of a writer of fiction, but I do believe it is there. It is vital both to faith and to fiction. In the last thirteen chapters of the book, we are given the long narrative of Joseph and his brothers. The plot twists and turns until finally all is well. Old Jacob has been brought down to Egypt, where he dies surrounded by all his sons. After his death, Joseph's brothers get nervous: "What if Joseph still bears a grudge against us and pays us back in full for all the wrong we did to him?" The guilt-ridden brothers approached Joseph with what we can only take to be a self-serving lie:

> "Your father gave this instruction before he died. 'Say to Joseph I beg you forgive the crime of your brothers and of all that they did in harming you.' Now, therefore, please forgive the crime of the servants of the God of your father." Joseph wept when they spoke to him. Then his brothers also wept, fell down before him and said, "We are here as your slaves." But Joseph said to them, "Do not be afraid. Am I in the place of God? Even though you intended to do harm to me, God intended it for good in order to preserve a numerous people as he is doing today. So have no fear. I myself will provide for you and your little ones."

Here is God, the maker of story, the one who will determine the outcome of the plot. This is not the hapless writer whose characters just run away with the story. This is the maker of story who, while remaining forever true to the nature of his characters, has the end firmly in hand. The outcome is invariably a revelation of the grace that has been there, though often unseen, at every twist and turn of the plot. In "Last Visit in Three Voices," Stanley Wiersma wrote a dramatic poem about his father's final illness and death; as the title implies, it is a poem in three voices: his own voice, his father's voice, and his mother's voice. The poem ends with his mother's voice . He has included here, apparently the only poem that his mother wrote in her life. She wrote it the night before she died:

> Amen, Father, on your planning.
> Amen for you'll see us through.
> Amen when the cross weighs heavy.
> Amen everything you do.

That's true Calvinism, the Calvinist acknowledging the maker of the story of her life.

Those of us who write stories for the young do not sneer at plot. We know how important the meaningful construction of narrative is. If you want to ask me a hard question, don't ask me where I get my ideas. Ask me where I get my plots. One idea, as I often say to school classes, one idea doth not a novel make. Not even *Jip*. I started with the boy tumbling off the back of the wagon, but then I had to figure out why such a thing should happen. When I began working on *Jip*, I had the hope of writing an adventure story. It seemed to me that, when I had on my critical hat rather than my writer's, there was a dearth of really good adventure stories around these days. So I went back and read the classics: *Huckleberry Finn, Great Expectations, Treasure Island,* and finally, *Kidnapped*. It was *Kidnapped* that absolutely drove me back to my own book. What a story! Stevenson really knew how to do it. For days I floated about, inflated with Stevenson's language, pacing, characterization, wild high on setting. I was little more than a Stevenson wannabe. But then, I came thudding back to earth — I was not Robert Louis Stevenson. Surprise, surprise. I could not write like him. Nor, in truth, did I want to.

As much I admired *Kidnapped,* I didn't want to rewrite it. I wanted to write the book that only I could write. I wanted to set my book in the hill country of Vermont, not the Scottish highlands. I wanted to bring to life that child who rolled off the wagon, the child that no one had come back to search for. Who was he? Why had he been abandoned? And why did he seem so precious to me? As I wrote I learned more about him, his almost mystical way with animals and people in need, his common sense, his hard working nature. And then reading for setting and atmosphere I met another person so compelling that I knew his story and Jip's were meant to entwine. I was reading a town history of Hartford, Vermont, when I came across a paragraph about a resident of Hartford's poor farm, a man named Putnam Proctor Wilson. Wilson was one of two lunatics for whom the town had built wooden cages. These men, the writer said, were

> raving crazy most of the time and there, caged up like raging beasts in narrow filthy cells, I often saw them in their pitiable condition, was impressed with the conviction that the inhuman treatment to which they were subjected was sufficient of itself to make lunatics of all men. Poor old Putnam had some rational moments and was always pleased to see children to whom he would sing

the old song, "Friendship to every willing mind," as often as requested.

I had that chill that goes up and down your spine, and so I took poor Putnam Wilson, named him Put Nelson, and gave him a new song and my already beloved boy. I knew Jip would give Put not just pity, but genuine love and friendship. For a long time I worked doing more research than actual writing, still unable to figure out where Jip had come from and thus what must happen to him for the mystery of his beginnings to be solved.

One morning I woke and I knew. At last, I had a plot. You'd think I'd rejoice; actually, my first reaction was irritation, almost anger. How dare that be the explanation? That would ruin the rollicking adventure story that I so longed to write. The solution my subconscious presented me with was suspiciously close kin to the kind of story I always seem to end up writing. I struggled against the revelation and then finally gave up. People think writers have infinite choices to make when constructing a book. My experience is that we have very little choice. Usually the choice for me is whether or not to complete the book. I chose to write it; I was too much in love with Jip and Put to let them go. Nearly always when I'm talking to children, I say that life often doesn't seem to make sense, but a story has to or no one will put up with it. And because stories make sense, they help us to make sense of our lives. As a child of the creator God, it is an enormous source of hope to me to believe that not only my life, but our times are in the hands of the master maker of story.

Those are my four Genesis images: artist, judge, wrestler, and maker of story. I see as I have talked about them that I have reversed a miracle, turning the heady wine of Genesis into tap water. But it seemed to me that unless I showed you how these images affected my imagination, there would be no excuse for me standing up here tonight, taking up your time. But I have one more image, and I cannot leave without it, an image that overarches the whole biblical story: the image of the parent whose steadfast love endures forever.

Twenty years ago, when our four children were young, my husband and I were asked to be temporary foster parents. We have four children, two adopted and two homemade. Since our daughters are adopted, we were already certified "genuine okay" parents, so we were supposedly qualified to serve in this emergency situation. The request was that we take in two brothers for two weeks. Four kids, six kids, two weeks — no big deal. As the two weeks stretched into months, I began to learn things about myself that I didn't necessarily want to know. Up until then, I had rated myself C+, maybe even some days B-, as a mother. But I had to realize that, as a foster mother, I was flunking. When I began to ask myself why, I was horrified. Because I tend to ask my life-shaping questions in fictional form, I wrote a story called *The Great Gilly Hopkins.* She is an eleven-year-old foster child bounced from house to house since she was three, and she has declared war on a world that has no real place for her.

This is a story that many of my critics wish I had written differently. But, friends, you can't write about a lost child and make her a role model. "If she just didn't curse," one of my good Christian friends said, "it would be such a lovely book." A child who lies, steals, bullies the handicapped, a child who is viciously racially prejudiced does not tend to say "fiddlesticks" when she is frustrated. Her mouth must somehow reflect and match her behavior.

Some years ago in Philadelphia, a woman approached me at a gathering for teachers and librarians. "I work," she said, "in a juvenile correction facility. The children in our institution are not runaways or shop lifters. They are children who have committed violent crimes. I cannot tell you how much your books mean to them."

"The other day," she went on, "A girl brought a copy of *Gilly Hopkins* back to the library. 'This is me,' she said."

"Tell me," I said. "I get so many protests about Gilly's profanity. If she hadn't cursed, would your children find her believable?"

She looked at me as though she thought I'd lost my mind. "Of course not!" she said. Then, I told myself, it's worth it. If a single child in a corrections facility can see herself in Gilly, there's hope that she may find someone who will be Trotter for her.

I was being led away to speak at a meeting in Mississippi several years ago when a young woman grabbed me. "Wait," she said, "I have to ask you a question. I'm doing my doctoral dissertation on southern settings in children's literature at the University of Chicago, and I have to know: who is Mamie Trotter?" Now there was a woman leading me to the platform, and she was not happy that we were being arrested midway to the podium and began pulling me by the arm in the other direction. So I called back as I was being dragged away, "God." I couldn't tell from the expression on the graduate student's face if they believe in God at the University of Chicago, but I was sure that they didn't believe that she spoke with a southern accent.

But Mamie Trotter is an image of God, modeled shamelessly after the father of those two lost boys: the prodigal and his poor, dear, dutiful, equally lost brother. Trotter is the foster mother to end all foster mothers, the expiation for my sin. Back when I had been briefly a foster mother, I had heard myself thinking, "Well, we can't deal with that problem — they'll only be here a few weeks. Thank heavens they'll only be here for a weeks." Now do you hear what I was doing? I was acting as though two human beings, persons created in the image of God, persons God loved every bit as much as he loved me — I was treating them as if they were disposable. That's why crimes are committed. That's why wars are fought. That's how holocausts can happen. Because one person or one group of persons thinks another person or another group of persons is disposable. But in the economy of heaven, no one is disposable. Indeed, if we are to believe the scriptures, Jesus himself means for us to discover in the least and the most miserable of our human race God incarnate.

A year ago last October, my husband John and I went to Kentucky for a very special event in the life of our family. Our son David, with the composer Steve Liebman, had adapted *Gilly Hopkins* for the stage, and it premiered at Stage One in Louisville. Now I'm somewhat familiar with the story. I had read David's script several times. I had already heard all of Steve's wonderful music. But seeing the play was a totally unexpected experience. I suppose it was as close as a writer could possibly come to reading your own book for the first time. I saw three performances of *Gilly* and was more affected each time. It begins a brief Broadway run the week after Easter, and I plan to go and cry my way through it still another couple of times.

The scene I want to share with you occurs fairly early in the play as well as in the book. Trotter has asked Gilly to read aloud to her neighbor who is old, blind, and African-American. Gilly's first reaction to Mr.

Randolph has been offensively negative, but now she just can't resist showing off how well she can read.

"'You want the Wordsworth one, Mr. Randolph?' Trotter asked. 'Or do you have that by heart?'

"'Both,' he answered."

There then begins a spoken Wordsworth duet with lines alternating between the sullen, angry child and the beautiful old man:

> There was a time when meadow, grove, and stream,
> The earth, and every common sight,
> To me did seem
> Apparell'd in celestial light,
> The glory and the freshness of a dream.
> It is not now as it hath been of yore; —
> Turn wheresoe'er I may,
> By night or day,
> The things which I have seen I now can see no more. . . .
> Our birth is but a sleep and a forgetting:
> The Soul that rises with us, our life's Star,
> Hath had elsewhere its setting,
> And cometh from afar:
> Not in entire forgetfulness,
> And not in utter nakedness,
> But trailing clouds of glory do we come
> From God, who is our home.

At this point in the play, the spoken duet turns into a haunting melody. Gilly and Mr. Randolph sing together the final stanza:

> Thanks to the human heart by which we live,
> Thanks to its tenderness, its joys, and fears,
> To me the meanest flower that blows can give
> Thoughts that do often lie too deep for tears.

Steve Liebman is the composer I first met when Stephanie Tolan and I asked him to write the music for our stage adaptation of *Bridge to*

Terabithia. When someone in the audience says to Steve afterwards that they've enjoyed the play, he says, "You were supposed to say: I laughed, I cried, it changed my life." Steve is only half teasing. That is what art is supposed to do: help us experience the spectrum of human emotion, and somehow to make us richer, more compassionate, wiser human beings in the process. From time to time, people ask me why, with all my theological training and religious background, I don't write Christian books. But you see, I think I *do* write Christian books. I think of the child in the correctional center and the librarian she trusted and am deeply grateful for the stories that God has allowed me tell. For I believe that stories truly told can give us a key to unlock for each other those thoughts that "do often lie too deep for tears."

I look at *Jip,* the story of a boy who tumbled off the back of the wagon, and once again, I see there a tiny echo of the same glorious theme I have known for so long in the Bible, the theme of the steadfast love of God, the work of grace. Like God, the word "grace" cannot be exactly defined. When speaking of it, we are always reduced to simile, to metaphor, to story. So when I write for children, it is in the hope that the works of my imagination will somehow reflect the image of a God who creates in beauty, judges in mercy, wrestles with those in puzzlement or anguish, shapes the end by steadfast love and unfailing grace. People want me to teach moral values in my stories — and believe it or not, I am all in favor of morality — but I do not think a writer can choose what the reader will learn from reading her book. A writer doesn't write a novel in order to teach something, she writes in order to learn.

As I write, I cannot tiptoe about trying not to step on the toes of nice people. I have to write as truly as I can about our human experience because if I falsify that experience, how can children find hope and encouragement in what I say? But most importantly, I want to share the grace I have been given in the twists and turns of the narrative of my own life. I want, however haltingly, to speak a word of hope in a world that is harsh and fearful for most of the children I know. To tell, as truthfully and beautifully as I can, a story that might bring comfort to a discouraged or even despairing child. To mirror, however dimly in my own stories, the healing life of the one story which is the revelation of the Word made flesh, full of grace and truth.

FREDERICK BUECHNER

. . . .

The Eyes of the Heart

On the evening of that day, the first day of the week, the doors being shut where the disciples were for fear of the Jews, Jesus came and stood among them and said to them, "Peace be with you." When he had said this, he showed them his hands and his side. The disciples were glad when they saw the Lord. Jesus said to them again, "Peace be with you. As the Father has sent me, even so I send you." And when he had said this, he breathed on them and said to them, "Receive the Holy Spirit. If you forgive the sins of any, they are forgiven; if you retain the sins of any, they are retained."

Now Thomas, one of the twelve, called the Twin, was not with them when Jesus came. So the other disciples told him, "We have seen the Lord." But he said to them, "Unless I see in his hands the print of the nails, and place my finger in the mark of the nails, and place my hand in his side, I will not believe."

Eight days later, his disciples were again in the house, and Thomas was with them. The doors were shut, but Jesus came and stood among them and said, "Peace be with you."

Then he said to Thomas, "Put your finger here, and see my hands; and put out your hand and place it in my side; do not be faithless but believe." Thomas answered him, "My Lord and my

God!" Jesus said to him, "Have you believed because you have seen me? Blessed are those who have not seen and yet believe."

John 20:19-30

There was a great teacher of the Old Testament at the seminary where I studied for the ministry years ago, and one thing he told us that I have always remembered is that we really can't hear what the stories of the Bible are saying until we hear them as stories about ourselves. We have to imagine our way into them, he said. We have to imagine ourselves the Prodigal Son coming home terrified that the door will be slammed in his face when he gets there, only to have the breath all but knocked out of him by the great bear-hug his father greets him with before he can choke out so much as the first word of the speech he has prepared about how sorry he is and how he will never do it again, not unlike the way you and I say in our prayers how sorry we are and how we will never do it again. We have to put ourselves in the place of the good thief, spread-eagled in the merciless sun, saying to the one who is dying beside him, "Jesus, remember me when you come into your kingly power." The way at the heart of every prayer we have ever prayed or will ever pray, you and I are also saying it in one form or another: *Remember* me. Remember *me. Jesus,* remember.

I don't know of any story in the Bible that is easier to imagine ourselves into than this one from John's Gospel because it is a story about trying to believe in Jesus in a world that is as full of shadows and ambiguities and longings and doubts and glimmers of holiness as the room where the story takes place is and as you and I are inside ourselves.

It is the evening after the Resurrection, and all but one of the disciples are gathered together in this shadowy room. The door is bolted tight because they are scared still that the ones who seized Jesus in the night will come and seize them next. Every sound they hear — the creaking of the house, the stirring of air through the trees, a dog barking — becomes for them the dreaded sound of footsteps on the stair. If they speak at all, you can imagine them speaking almost too quietly to hear. The room is small and crowded and the air acrid with the smell of their fear. That morning just after dawn, Mary Magdalene told them that she had seen Jesus alive again, but even the ones who believed her were not much comforted because he was not alive again with them there where they needed him. Then, suddenly, he *was* there: "He came and stood among them," John says, and Jesus spoke to them.

"Shalom," was what he said — "Peace be with you" — which was of all words the one which in their un-peace they needed most to hear. But the way John tells it, is as if they were too stunned to understand what they had heard, even to know who had spoken. So Jesus had to show them what had been done to his hands and to his side, and it was only then that they recognized him. "As the Father has sent me, even so I send you," he said, and then he breathed on them.

Can we imagine ourselves into that part of the story, I wonder? Can we put ourselves into their place as they took his breath into their lungs, his life into their lives? I think that we are often closer to their experience than we believe we are. I think that Christ dwells deep down in all of us, believers and unbelievers both, and that again and again, whether we realize it or not, he brings us healing and hope. I think that there have been moments for all of us when the hand we reached out to another's need was not our hand, but Christ's, and moments when the tears that have come to our eyes at another's sadness or joy, or even our own sadness, our own joy, were Christ's tears. "Receive the Holy Spirit," he said to them there in the shadows, and I think we have all of us received more of that spirit into our own shadows than we dream.

The one disciple who wasn't in the room when Jesus appeared was Thomas, of course, although he was as much a friend and follower of Jesus as any of them. As far as Thomas knew, Jesus was dead and that was the end of it. He was aware of what Mary Magdalene claimed she had seen, and now, that evening, his friends were claiming the same thing, but Thomas himself had not seen him, and the words he spoke when they told him about it have the ring of unvarnished truth. "Unless I see in his hands the mark of the nails and place my finger in the mark of the nails and place my hand in his side," he said, "I will not believe."

Thomas is called the Twin in the New Testament, and if you want to know who the other twin is, I can tell you. I am the other twin. And, unless I miss my guess, so are you.

How can we believe that Christ is alive when we haven't seen him? I believe the sun rose this morning because there it is in the sky above us. I believe that you and I are alive because here we are looking at each other. But when it comes to this central proclamation and the holiest mystery of Christian faith — that after his death, Jesus returned to live and is alive to this day — how can we believe that?

There are lots of other things we *can* believe about him. We can believe that of all good people, he was the goodest. We can believe that no one else in history embodied the love of God so movingly and unforgettably. We can believe that, although down through the centuries endless follies and barbarities have been committed in his name, the beauty and holiness of his life remain somehow untouched. That of all the great saints the world has produced, he remains the loveliest and the one most worth following. But when Thomas says that unless he sees Jesus with his own eyes he will not believe that he is actually alive the way you and I are actually alive, I think we all know in our hearts what he is talking about.

What we have to remember is that our eyes are not all we have for seeing with, maybe not even the best we have. Our eyes tell us that the mountains are green in summer and in autumn the colors of flame. They tell us that the nose of the little girl is freckled, that her hair usually needs combing, that when she is asleep, her cheek is flushed and moist. They tell us that the photographs of Abraham Lincoln taken a few days before his death show a man who at the age of fifty-six looked as old as time. Our eyes tell us that the small country church down the road needs a new coat of paint and that the stout lady who plays the pump organ there looks a little like W. C. Fields and that its pews are rarely more than about a quarter filled on any given Sunday.

But all these things are only facts because facts are all the eye can see. Eyes cannot see truth. The truth about the mountains is their great beauty. The truth about the child is that she is so precious that, without a moment's hesitation, we would give our lives to save her life — if that should somehow ever become necessary. The truth about Abraham Lincoln is a humanness so rich and deep that it is hard to stand in his memorial in Washington without tears coming to our eyes. The truth about the shabby little church is that, for reasons known only to God, it is full of holiness. It is not with the eyes of the head that we see truths like that, but with the eyes of the heart.

Eight days after Jesus' first appearance to the disciples, John says, Jesus came back to them again. This time Thomas was with them. Again, Jesus said "Peace" to them. Then, he turned to Thomas and spoke only to him, as if there was no one else in the world just then who mattered, and there was nothing more he could say, nothing more he needed to say. Can we imagine ourselves into that part of the story? Have we ever even come close to seeing the truth of Jesus the way Thomas did just then?

I believe we have, more than we know, and I believe that, in the last analysis, those glimpses more than anything else are what bring us to church Sunday after Sunday. I believe we have glimpsed the truth of Jesus in the faces and lives of people we know who have loved him and served him, and let each of us name their names silently to ourselves. I believe we have glimpsed him in the pages of the Gospels when, by some miracle of grace, those pages come alive for us, and it is as if we ourselves are the ones he is speaking to when he says, "Come unto me, all you who labor and are heavy-laden, and I will give you rest." I believe we have caught sight of him in works of art that have been created to honor him, like the *St. Matthew Passion* of Bach or the flaking, faded frescoes of old European churches where he moves like a dream across the walls.

I believe we have seen him once in a while even in our own churches, especially when there is a pause in our endless babbling about him and for a moment or two he is present in the silence of waiting and listening. I remember how once when the minister was administering the chalice to me, he made my heart skip a beat by calling me by name and saying, "The blood of Christ, Freddy, the cup of salvation." I saw suddenly that Christ not only remembers us, but remembers each one of us by name as surely as he remembered the good thief. He welcomes us to his table not in some sort of impersonal, churchly sense, but as if the party wouldn't be complete without every last one of us. The same way the father in Jesus' story threw his arms around the Prodigal and welcomed him home.

I believe we have seen him in those rare moments when, moved by his spirit alive within us, we have been able to be Christs to one another — as well as at those moments when we have resisted his spirit within us and turned away from each other, full of a kind of dimness and sadness.

Most of all, I believe we have seen him in our endless longing for him, even when we don't know who it is we are longing for.

"Have you believed because you have seen me?" Jesus asked Thomas, our twin. My guess is that Thomas believed not because of what his eyes had seen, but because of what his heart had seen. With his eyes, he had seen only Jesus the son of Joseph and Mary, a man much like other men — so many inches high, so many pounds heavy, hair this color, eyes that color. But with his heart, he saw, maybe for the first time in his life, the one he was destined to love and search for and try to follow as best he could for the rest of his days when Jesus was no longer around for him to see with his eyes — any more than he is around for us to see with ours.

The last thing of all that Jesus said to his disciples that day was, "Blessed are those who have *not* seen and yet believe," and I think that among others he meant you and me. We have not seen him with our eyes the way Thomas did, but precious as that sight would have been, I wonder in the long run what difference it would have made. What makes all the difference in the world is the one whom from time to time, by grace, I believe we have seen with our hearts. The one who is there to see always if we will only keep our hearts peeled for him.

To see him with the heart is to know that, in the long run, his kind of life is the only life worth living. To see him with the heart is not only to believe in him, but little by little to become bearers to each other of his healing life until we become finally healed and whole and alive within ourselves. To see him with the heart is to take heart, to grow true hearts, brave hearts, at last.

That is my dearest hope and prayer for all of you and also for me.

DORIS BETTS

. . . .

Whispering Hope

W hen Flannery O'Connor was asked before one of her Southern audiences, "Why do you write?" she promptly answered, "Because
I'm good at it." People recoiled; in our region, modesty is thought to be
automatically transmitted with the X chromosome. But Miss O'Connor, a
committed Catholic, was not being arrogant. She hastened to add that
she took seriously the parable of the talents in Matthew 25, so if she
wrote fiction because she was "good at it," that answer grew out of her
conviction that every person's talent was a gift, that each of us has a responsibility for using that gift as well as we can and by that use returning
it to the Giver at least as large as ever — possibly larger if service has
helped it to increase.

Though this Presbyterian agrees with Miss O'Connor on the why of
writing, we differ on the how. She wrote in "The Fiction Writer and His
Country" that if a writer can assume that her audience does not share
her beliefs, she may have to make her vision apparent through shock: "To
the hard of hearing you shout, and for the almost-blind you draw large
and startling figures." That is certainly one method, but I — like many
mothers and kindergarten teachers — have found that the whisper can
also be effective. There's quite a range between characters like
O'Connor's startling Hazel Motes in *Wise Blood* and Ann Tyler's quiet Ian
Bedloe in *Saint Maybe;* as there's a range between times when Jesus in-

35

veighed strongly against a "generation of vipers" and other times when he might stoop and silently scratch words in the ground.

In O'Connor's world, the road to Damascus runs straight through south Georgia, where God's grace gets thrust almost violently into people's lives; in Walker Percy's world, some awkward pilgrim will set out, of his own free but uncertain will, on a quest to determine God's very existence. Graham Greene works with apparent moral failures like the whiskey priest of *The Power and the Glory*. C. S. Lewis extracts a whole pre-Christian novel *(Till We Have Faces)* out of 1 Corinthians 13. In Susan Ketchin's collection of writer-interviews, *The Christ-Haunted Landscape*, novelists as different as Lee Smith, Reynolds Price, Harry Crews, and Will Campbell express their talents in very different styles.

If, in O'Connor's stories, the Grandmother recognizes the Misfit and then perishes, or Mrs. Turpin gets called a wart hog in two different ways, or the Holy Ghost continues, implacable, to descend from a ceiling stain, my own characters don't seem to earn such direct intervention. Like the descendants of Job's second cousins once removed, they struggle through a long weekday process that includes losses and boils until in the end God does not so much answer their questions as silence them, simply by being there, so that my characters end by saying — or maybe whispering — "Mine eye seeth Thee." Some of them might add, "That is You, isn't it?"

Neither a shout nor a whisper spoken by a believer who thinks she distinguishes a dim gestalt of the Holy Spirit operating in this world will convince a non-believer. Answered prayer is the easiest of all experiences for an atheist to explain away — until he has one answered himself. I work mostly with characters who gradually, sometimes reluctantly, become alert to the possibility that human life is more than meets the eye. Being alert to possibility is, after all, the way most writers generate stories. Metaphor, simile, symbol suggest meanings beyond the concrete objects from which they arise. The "seeds" for stories that Henry James described seem to arrive as mere coincidence.

My most recent novel, *Souls Raised from the Dead,* got underway because on my daily commute to the University of North Carolina–Chapel Hill, I came upon a chicken-truck wreck beside the highway. Seventy-five hundred capons, raised in houses heated and lit by electric current —

chickens that had never set foot to ground before — were loose from the overturned poultry truck. They flew; they hobbled with bloody wings, banged into passing windshields. Neighbors were catching some in tow sacks for lunch and dinner. Imbedded in this scene, with wounded chickens flapping past his head, a state trooper was trying to bring order out of chaos in a tableau both horrible and funny. And the look on his face? Pure existentialist despair. If Jean-Paul Sartre had lived in Chatham County, North Carolina, he would have recognized this as Page One, though perhaps we would have written different paragraphs at the end. In my case, that chicken-truck wreck opens a novel in which a highway patrolman longs to protect his daughter from all harm at all times, to rear her as perfectly as if she could be kept in unnatural isolation like those chickens. But of course, there is no way to give children a perfect or a perfectly safe life. There will be wrecks in their lives, too. There will be escapes, freedom. And in time there will be injury.

As I was starting the novel, Harold Kushner, a Massachusetts rabbi, published his 148-page book in memory of his son who had died at age 14, *When Bad Things Happen to Good People.* Here he brought traditional Judaism to wrestle with the old question of undeserved suffering in a world he believes to be ruled by both a good and a powerful God. Kushner never pretended that people get what they deserve in life; he did not accept the premise that God sends pain for testing or improvement, nor that either God or ourselves are to be blamed for the cancer, the avalanche, the drive-by shooting. What he did choose to do was what my own characters must: cope with grief and loss, struggle for hope, help one another. In my novel, the survivors, not the sick child, are the "souls" that are to be raised, raised from despair.

Not until the novel was done did I notice that its structure had taken the shape of an anecdote Kushner tells, an old Chinese tale about a woman whose only son had died. In her grief, she went to the holy man and said, "What prayers, what magical incantations do you have to bring my son back to life?" Instead of sending her away or reasoning with her, the holy man said, "Fetch me a mustard seed from a home that has never known sorrow. We will use it to drive the sorrow out of your life." At once the woman set off in search of that magical mustard seed. She came first to a splendid mansion, knocked at the door, and said, "I am looking for a

home that has never known sorrow. Is this such a place? It is very important to me!" They told her she had certainly come to the wrong house,
and began to list all the tragic things that had befallen that family. Since
she had been through misfortune of her own, the woman decided she
might be the best person to help these wealthy people, so she stayed to
comfort them. Later she continued her search for a home that had never
known sorrow, this time going to a shack, next time to a city slum. But
wherever she turned, from palace to public housing to country club, she
listened to one story after another of sadness and misfortune. Ultimately
she grew so involved in ministering to other people's grief that she forgot
about her quest for the magical mustard seed, never realizing that it had
— in fact — driven the sorrow out of her life.

At the end of my first chapter, I could see that a young girl was going
to have a life-threatening illness. In her name, Mary Grace Thompson, I
managed to whisper both "Grace" and the surname of a poet named
Francis, and lift an invisible hat to a Flannery O'Connor character as
well.

But what should the illness be?

A friend and rather literary doctor at the U.N.C. Medical School, Bill
Blythe, was the obvious adviser. His father, LeGette Blythe, had published many biblical novels, *Bold Galilean* being the best known. His son,
a former student of mine, is now an editor at *Esquire*. Could Dr. Blythe
suggest some fatal illness? (Not leukemia: that's been done; and not that
obscure literary ailment that kills off the girl in *Love Story,* what we usually call "Ali McGraw Disease.") Dr. Blythe suggested kidney failure because, he said, "We can cure almost everything else."

Immediately the moment of the chicken-truck wreck turned trans-
parent and permeable; I went falling through it like Alice into the whole
territory of medical ethics — those questions our grandparents seldom
raised in Sunday School. What about organ transplants, heroic deathbed
measures, surrogate parents, euthanasia, abortion, genetic manipula-
tion? I began to be homesick for O'Connor's "Greenleaf" with its unam-
biguous bull that would drive a horn straight into Mrs. May on the last
page.

And how to tell this medical story? O'Connor's "large and startling
figures" could easily be transformed into melodramatic actors on some

38

TV "Disease of the Week" program with soaring background music and Tylenol commercials. Should it be written in cool and clinical prose? Or should I assign to the state trooper a bookish narrator-friend who reads theodicy on the side? And if the daughter died, how could the story be anything but morbid and depressing, as even the Gospel story would be if it stopped short on Good Friday or Holy Saturday?

Anton Chekov's story, "Grief," which is also about a father's loss of a child, confronts all these risks of being melodramatic, sentimental, overdone. On a cold, winter night in St. Petersburg, the driver of a horsedrawn cab is transporting passengers back and forth through the swirling snow, to parties and back, to the opera, the cafe; and tonight the job is very hard for him because his son has just died. All evening, he tries to tell his passengers about that death and about his grief, but they're too busy to hear. They talk with one another about the magnificent overture, about the velvet gown their hostess wore, about the quality of the evening's wine. At the end of the long, cold night the cab driver goes through the falling snow and down to the stable where he tells his grief to his horse. "Listen," he says, "suppose your colt died and you lived on? That would be sad, wouldn't it? Yes, that would be sad."

For Chekov, what keeps that moment full of sentiment but just short of sentimentality, is its brevity and understatement played out against the snow, that whirling frigid snow that cools the moment, that holds it in tongs like a specimen.

In North Carolina we lack blizzards, so I set out to balance a story about illness and death against — not cold snow — but the warm counterpoint of life and laughter. One axiom of storytelling is that if a character is to die in a way that moves the reader, that character must first be made fully alive; otherwise no more emotion will be generated than when strangers' names appear in the obituaries.

But writers turn into foster parents themselves, and once I concentrated on bringing Mary Grace to life as a normal, funny adolescent, I was in the same position as her trooper-father. I did not want to lose her. When Charles Dickens was publishing *The Old Curiosity Shop* in installments, it's said that when the sailing ship bearing the latest chapter came into Boston Harbor, people were waiting on the docks, shouting, "Did she die? Did Little Nell die?"

Nobody was waiting to hear hard news from me. I ran head-on into a wall that was half theodicy, half writing-block.

When in *The Brothers Karamazov,* Ivan debates how God can be both all-good and all-powerful, considering how much the innocent suffer — especially the innocent children — he becomes enraged at injustice. He offers to give back his ticket to life because, if God is good but not all-powerful, then he can't intervene against cruelty; but if he's all-powerful and simply unwilling to intervene, then how can he be good?

When Caroline Gordon, in *How to Read a Novel,* cautioned against the "novel of ideas," my translation is that it's better for novelists to get to metaphysics via a chicken-truck wreck than the other way around. Stories, like lives, give rise to questions naturally. To start from philosophical premise risks constructing a tinker-toy novel, a paint-by-number portrait, a Barbie doll sculpture, in which all content is a means to an end and a means with the life wrung out. Students in writing classes can easily be paralyzed by the question I once heard a teacher ask: "Do you really have anything to say?" Only allegorists start from that end and work backwards. Most writers set out to tell a story, knowing that who they are and what they believe will whisper its way in just as they do in one's daily life; their personality and beliefs will sink below the word-surface like a stain; they will be inside events the way the peach seed grows inside the peach.

Despite my first assumption that I was writing a medical novel, I saw that its pages had been whispering religious implications all along — that from the first glimpse of that poultry-truck wreck the subject matter partook of Jesus' lament over Jerusalem in Matthew 23:37 and Luke 13:34.

That's how "The Hound of Heaven" by Francis Thompson got into the plot, because I did not hold the same theological position as Rabbi Kushner. I was not even in the exact position of that Chinese lady who sought the magical mustard seed, since I knew a different mustard-seed story. Kushner's book lifted the ceiling off the Old Testament and flooded that view of Yahweh with the light of mercy and compassion, but it still wasn't the same as the New Testament.

Beyond this block of metaphysical seriousness came the psychological one of refusing to let Mary Grace die. I invented several miraculous cures, brought in European specialists. I wrote splendid sky-descriptions. Many minor characters entered the book and most of them made exits.

Then Czeslaw Milosz, Nobel prize poet, came for one semester to the Chapel Hill campus where I teach. Awestruck, I could not think of any conversation to make with a man who had survived the Nazi occupation of Poland, had written so many memorable poems, and had called tragedy "awareness of the philosophical deep, over which — and thanks to which — science and technology have erected their flimsy palaces." But the great man proved accessible, humorous, a devout Catholic whose wife grew up in eastern North Carolina. By then I had already entitled the novel *Souls Raised from the Dead,* but now stumbled across its thematic epigraph in a poem Milosz wrote in memory of his mother who had perished in World War II. In the poem, at Mass, after hearing the morning's scripture, the speaker of the poem says:

> A reading this Sunday from the Book of Wisdom
> About how God has not made death
> And does not rejoice in the annihilation of the living.
> A reading from the Gospel according to Mark
> About a little girl to whom He said: Talitha, cumi!
> This is for me. To make me rise from the dead
> And repeat the hope of those who lived before me.

Discovering this poem, like the chicken-truck wreck, seemed fortuitous, seemed lucky. It seemed like grace.

All my novel had to do was to repeat that hope or, as T. S. Eliot would have said, to "redeem the time." The soul to be raised was not that of Mary Grace from death, but the soul of her father from despair — the ultimate death. And the end of the novel does not shout about Heaven, does not draw large and startling pictures; it only whispers. In the end Mary Grace Thompson does die and her father's heart is broken, but he makes a start toward hope in divine mercy. Hope may even be whispered so softly that not every reader will notice that there are fathers and Fathers in the final paragraph.

Would I describe it as a "Christian" novel? That durable noun first used to name the saints at Antioch seems to spoil to a rancid adjective with a slight whiff of the Pharisee. Between Pittsboro, where I live, and a neighboring town there's a gas station with a sign: WE TITHE. BUY GAS FOR JESUS. I drive on by.

Yet at the end of the novel, my bereaved state-trooper father is entering the state George MacDonald ascribed to one of his own characters, an elderly Anglican priest named Thomas Wingfold, who has spent his entire life serving the church. Now Wingfold is old; his doubts have awakened again; he is afraid of dying. Also, he wonders if his life has made any real difference or had any meaning at all. Wingfold ends with a version of the Pascal wager, hoping eternal life is true, choosing it even if he can never be absolutely certain. In his diary, Wingfold writes these words:

> Even if there be no hereafter, I would live my time believing in a grand thing that ought to be true if it is not ... Let me hold by the better than the actual, and fall into nothingness off the same precipice with Jesus and John and Paul and a thousand more, who were lovely in their lives, and with their deaths make even the nothingness into which they have passed like the garden of the Lord.

BRET LOTT

....

Why Have We Given Up the Ghost?
Notes on Reclaiming Literary Fiction

———

My name is Bret Lott, and I believe in God the Father Almighty, Maker of heaven and earth. And in Jesus Christ his only Son our Lord, who was conceived by the Holy Ghost, born of the Virgin Mary, suffered under Pontius Pilate, was crucified, dead, and buried; he descended into hell; the third day he rose again from the dead; he ascended into heaven, and sitteth on the right hand of God the Father Almighty; from thence he shall come to judge the quick and the dead. I believe in the Holy Ghost; the holy catholic Church; the communion of saints; the forgiveness of sins; the resurrection of the body; and the life everlasting. Amen.

That's where I'll start today.

I'd also like to say that this won't be a sermon, but an examination of my own story as a writer, and why the question of why we have given up the ghost continues to haunt me, no matter how many books I have written.

What is "literary fiction," really? I've always known it to be fiction that doesn't sell very well, but when my students ask me point blank what the difference between popular and literary fiction is — and they ask this question a lot — I tell them that literary fiction is fiction that examines the character of the people involved in the story, and that popular fiction is driven by plot. Popular fiction is meant primarily as a means of escape, one way or another, a kind of book equivalent of comfort food. Literary fiction confronts us with who we are and makes us look deeply at the human condition. Henry James said that it wasn't "the rare accident" — the plot — that made a story worth our attention, but the "human attestation" to that plot: how people deal with their histories, rather than those histories in and of themselves.

I have started this talk with the Apostles' Creed because I do believe in Christ's divinity and resurrection, and in His being precisely who he claimed to be. That is, I believe in a supernatural God, one who loves us and cares intimately and deeply for us, so deeply that he gave his only begotten Son to die for us. And I believe in a supernatural God whose wrath, as my life's reference book, the Bible, tells me, will be inflicted upon this world so fully that John saw in his revelation:

> ... the kings of the earth and the great men and the commanders
> and the rich and the strong and every slave and free man, [hide]
> themselves in the caves and among the rocks of the mountains;
> and [say] to the mountains and to the rocks, "Fall on us and hide
> us from the presence of him who sits on the throne, and from the
> wrath of the Lamb; for the great day of their wrath has come; and
> who is able to stand?"

That is the God I believe in: the loving God who loves us on his terms, and his only.

And now begins the rub of this all: I may be preaching to the literary choir here at the Calvin Festival of Faith and Writing — and despite the fact that perhaps the choir here is made up of vast and even disparate literary-musical traditions, from Gospel to Southern Baptist Hymnal to Gregorian Chants to Contemporary Praise, even perhaps some a capella Churches of Christ in here too — I feel pretty certain some of you out there must be asking yourselves right now, does he really believe in the supernatural? Does he really believe that, today, God asserts himself outside of our hands, outside our control, outside of our concepts of time and space, to actually show himself to us?

Yes. I believe in a God who works outside of us all.

Let me tell a story now. Or two. Maybe three.

44

A few years ago I worked my way through the book *Experiencing God,* by Blackaby and King — and already I can bet I have fallen in the eyes of many out there. You're thinking, next thing you know he'll tell us he's read *The Purpose-Driven Life.* But I'm afraid it's even worse than that: I am an adult Sunday school teacher at East Cooper Baptist Church, a Southern Baptist church in Mt. Pleasant, South Carolina, and I *taught The Purpose-Driven Life* last year.

The fact is, I am about the squarest person you will meet. I was a cubmaster for seven years, assistant scoutmaster for three; I was an assistant soccer coach for eight years too. I play baritone sax in my church orchestra — not in the hip and cool Praise Band, but the orchestra. Until a year or so ago I ran our church's Wednesday night supper. To reach even further back, and to see perhaps how mundane my faith story really is, I was born again after a Josh McDowell rally when I was nineteen years old and a freshman at Northern Arizona University, and I met my wife — we've been married for nearly twenty-four years now — in the college and career Sunday school class at First Baptist Church of Huntington Beach/Fountain Valley in Orange County, California. We are talking square here.

But one day, *Experiencing God* instructed me to pray for an opportunity to share Christ in some way. I was told to pray specifically for an opportunity and then to keep my eyes and ears open for that opportunity, rather than simply to pray it and forget it.

Later that day, in my office at the college where I teach, I received a phone call. It was from one of my students, a genuine slacker who hadn't shown up for class that day, a kid I had written off weeks ago. I don't dislike any of my students — I love them. Really. But there are certain kids who let you know by their actions how they feel about your class, and you begin to adjust your own views of them to reflect theirs of you. This wasn't a kid with whom I would have gone out of my way to build a relationship. He was simply marking time in my class, and so I was simply marking time with this phone call.

He was calling to say he was sorry for missing class, offering some lame excuse. I leaned back in my chair and put my feet up on my desk, rolling my eyes.

And then he said it: "Mr. Lott," he said, "if I were to read a book from the Bible, which one would it be?"

Just like that. Out of the bluest blue you can imagine, me already shining this kid on, rolling my eyes, marking time with him.

I sat up, then stood, hit square over the head with the two-by-four of God's answer to my prayer that morning. Sadly, I had just about dozed off at the wheel, but I recovered in time to begin to talk about the Gospel of John, but also about the Book of Acts, my favorite. Oh, and James, too. But John. The Gospel of John.

And I saw, because I had been caught unawares, that this prayer wasn't about my giving the message of grace to someone whom I had signed off, but about my having signed him off: it is the *being ready* that mattered, I saw. The message of salvation saves in and of itself; if we are awake, opportunities to share it abound every minute.

It is being ready to do so that matters.

Of course, the enlightened among us will chalk up the outcome of that story to chance, to coincidence. Maybe even to a conniving kid who knew, as most every kid on my campus does, that I am a Christian and thought he had found a way to appeal to my forgiving side. Don't think this hasn't occurred to me.

But I see, finally, that none of that matters. What matters is that that morning I prayed for something — an opportunity, and an awareness — and was provided with both when I was least expecting it. That kid had no idea that I was praying for this, and though I have to this day no idea if he read John or not, he was given an opportunity by a willing messenger: me.

That willingness is all God asks.

And this opportunity was a supernatural act, God's answer to prayer.

But here are the other two stories.

I have been on church missions trips to the eastern European country of Moldova twice now, first with my older son Zeb to help build an orphanage for kids in the town of Telenesti, the second time with Melanie and both our boys to help run a Bible camp for kids in the same town. Moldova, formerly an industrialized Soviet-bloc country, is now the poorest country in Europe — the average income there is thirty dollars a month.

My job this last visit was to be the camp activities director. Here was my Cub Scout expertise come back to haunt me. My job, given me by acclamation, was to herd 140 children ranging in age from four to eighteen into four groups, and then to entertain them for four ninety-minute blocks each day for a week — all in translation, either to Romanian or Russian, depending on the age of the kids. I and my team organized games and sports for them all. We'd brought our own supplies — clothespins, empty soup cans, jump ropes, all sorts of arts and crafts supplies, everything from Polaroid film to T-shirts — 140 of them — for the children to tie-dye the last day. The mission group — there were sixteen of us, all from East Cooper Baptist — spent an afternoon one week before we left parceling out all these supplies evenly so that no one was overburdened. There were entire sets of Old and New Testament flannelgraphs, too, for the nationals to use once we got to the camp in Moldova, all parceled out.

In one of the relay games we played, each kid was supposed to run to a paper bag, put on a pair of garden gloves, reach into the bag to pull out a pack of chewing gum, extricate a stick of gum from the pack with the gloves on, put the stick in his mouth, take off the gloves and run back to tag the next person on his team, until everyone was done.

The problem we faced all week, though, was the kind of problem we all wish for: there were simply more kids than we had been told would be allowed to participate. Simply too many kids. The first day we opened up, in a ruined school building that, in America, would have been featured on national news for the scandalous fact its broken and filthy shell still housed classes, 170 kids showed up.

I'd packed only enough gum for 160 kids, thinking that twenty extra pieces — we were told there would only be 140, remember — was in fact planning ahead. So that on that last day, going into the relays, I knew we didn't have enough gum. I knew it. But there had been no place to buy more, and so we simply went ahead with the game.

Zeb and Jake, my younger son, served as monitors, helpers for the smaller kids once they were down at the bags and trying to put on those gloves. Late in the day, once we were working through the last batch of kids, Zeb hollered out to me, "Dad, we're going to run out of gum!"

I hollered back to him the only thing I knew to do: "Pray!" I said, and prayed myself, that somehow there might be more gum, that this would work out.

47

Zeb prayed, too. As did Jacob, and Skip McQuillan, the other dad along, and his two sons, Sam and Mac. We all prayed there, on the spot, that somehow there would be more gum, enough for all of them.

And there was enough gum. To a child. At the end of a frantic day spent playing crazy games to entertain kids who were being brought the Gospel message elsewhere in the school by the nationals for whom we were helping with this camp.

It is with a kind of wonder and joy that I tell you this story, no matter the cynic in me — Satan, actually — who rationalizes that perhaps not every kid participated that last day, and maybe not every kid did the relay. But there were more kids that day than any other, and they all did the relay.

And if a kid had come up to the bag and found there was no gum for him, where would God have been, finally?

I believe in a supernatural God.

One last story, this from that same trip. There's a little fact I left out of all this: two of our team lost their luggage altogether, traveling from Charleston, South Carolina, where we all live, to the capital city of Moldova, Kishnau. So that though we had spent all that time parceling out all our various supplies, it didn't really matter: we didn't have enough of what we needed.

Sure, the crafts director, Debi McQuillan, Skip's wife, had brought some extra Polaroid film, more than she'd passed out to us all, and there were plenty of ice cream sticks for the frames they would make for those photos. There was enough glue and glitter, enough of that Dayglo plastic string to make lanyards for them all. We made do with a couple of softballs and a baseball bat less than we had planned on.

But the big craft event the last day was the tie-dyeing of T-shirts. We'd packed 140 shirts, enough for the number of kids we'd been told would be there. Some of those had been lost with the luggage. There wouldn't have been enough, not by a long shot, even for the number of kids we'd planned for.

And here's what we did: we prayed over the shirts, and then stepped boldly into that last day's craft activities, faithful that somehow we would have enough T-shirts, though we knew we had less than we needed.

And at the end of that long day of messy crafts (imagine, to begin with, trying to guide that many kids at dyeing T-shirts twisted and rubber-banded into knots, and then not being certain who would get one and who wouldn't), there were precisely enough shirts — one each for over 170 children.

In the book of Joshua, God instructs Joshua to choose twelve men from the tribes and to have each one carry a stone from where they crossed the Jordan and place it where they were camped on the other side. "Each of you is to take up a stone on his shoulder, according to the number of the tribes of Israel," Joshua instructs them, "to serve as a sign among you. In the future, when your children ask you, 'What do these stones mean?' tell them that the flow of the Jordan was cut off before the ark of the covenant of the Lord. When it crossed the Jordan, the waters of the Jordan were cut off. These stones are to be a memorial to the people of Israel forever.'"

These stories I have just given you are three of my own standing stones. They are reminders to me and to those who come after me — you listening to me — of the supernatural power of God. Because I cannot explain to you how we got the right amount of gum, or why a kid called me to ask what book of the Bible he should read on a day when I'd written that kid off, or how we got enough shirts to make each kid feel a part of that camp at the end of a week in which they were presented the Gospel message.

In the town of Telenesti, in the country of Moldova, there is no running water. There are no flush toilets. Needless to say, there is no Wal-Mart to which we could repair and purchase bundles of T-shirts to save the day. But in Telenesti, there were orphans, kids whose parents had left them outright simply to go somewhere else and try to live. And at our camp, there were also kids who lived with their parents, who showed up unannounced and unplanned-for.

And not one of them went wanting. No one was missed.

I can only tell you that these standing stones point to a supernatural God, one I can't explain by logic or rationalization. I can only bear witness to him.

And now, finally, we come to the thin ice of my own believability as a human being, and at the same time the concrete foundation of what it

49

means to have faith. Do I really believe that God reached out his hand to us and, as those five thousand people who'd gathered at Bethsaida on the shore of the Sea of Galilee were given food from five loaves and two fish, gave us some extra gum and a big wad of T-shirts?

Yes I do. Count on it.

For if I, as a believer in Christ as God on earth, can find a way to explain away a phone call or a pack of gum or those T-shirts, then what is the point in my believing in the resurrection of a dead man? Plain and simple.

But I do believe it. Plain and simple. Our God is a supernatural God.

I have a friend who is a surgeon. Like me, he is a believer, and told me one time that he has to be careful about talking about God and God's role in his life when he is around other surgeons. No matter your skills, he told me, no matter what schools you went to, where you did your residency, no matter how long you've been saving lives, once your colleagues smell on you a belief in something outside of yourself, you will be thought of as a loose cannon, a nut. A surgeon's hands are his to maneuver, a doctor is taught, and to believe that there is any sort of supernatural element involved in your being a successful surgeon is to admit into the operating room an unaccounted-for entity, and hence the possibility for error. It is to admit a vulnerability.

I believe the same thing happens in the world of literary art. We have become so primed to believe in the self that there is no room for anything else, that it seems preposterous to have characters whose lives are altered by a supernatural God. James Joyce took that word "epiphany" — the "shining forth" or revelation of God to man in the person of Jesus Christ — straight out of the church to stand for his notion of the moment in a story when man's humanity, as it were, shines forth on himself, or on the reader. Ever since, when it comes to stories, that term "epiphany" has meant a kind of psychological reckoning of characters to themselves and their world.

Regrettably, we have no choice but to admit that literary fiction as we know it today is a product of the Enlightenment. In Kant's landmark essay, "An Answer to the Question: 'What is Enlightenment?'" he writes:

Enlightenment is man's emergence from his self-incurred immaturity. Immaturity is the inability to use one's own understanding without the guidance of another. This immaturity is self-incurred if its cause is not lack of understanding, but lack of resolution and courage to use it without the guidance of another. The motto of enlightenment is therefore: *Sapere aude!* Have courage to use your own understanding!

This definition sounds downright inspiring, employing as its assumptions — its beginning points — language that ties inextricably a dependence upon the guidance of another with immaturity, with cowardice and irresolution. Who wants to be immature, cowardly, indecisive? Who among us wants to be thought of as anything but a thinking, courageous, understanding person?

But of course the Enlightenment led from one thing to another — and I am fully aware of the historical leapfrogging I am doing here — with each succeeding movement a movement, in the world's eyes, forward, until we have arrived here, today, at a moment when existentialism — whether optimistic or pessimistic or simply refusing to choose sides — has yielded an age in literature in which God isn't just dead, but nonexistent. According to the *Oxford Dictionary of the Christian Church,*

> The Enlightenment combine[d] opposition to all supernatural religion and belief in the all-sufficiency of human reason with an ardent desire to promote the happiness of men in this life. . . . Most of its representatives . . . rejected the Christian dogma and were hostile to Catholicism as well as Protestant orthodoxy, which they regarded as powers of spiritual darkness depriving humanity of the use of its rational faculties. . . . Their fundamental belief in the goodness of human nature, which blinded them to the fact of sin, produced an easy optimism and absolute faith of human society once the principles of enlightened reason had been recognized. The spirit of the Enlightenment penetrated deeply into German Protestantism, where it disintegrated faith in the authority of the Bible and encouraged Biblical criticism on the one hand and an emotional "Pietism" on the other.

It is this notion of reason-centered pietism, as it were, that I believe rules the day in the world of literary fiction, pietism that is reliant solely on the manifestation of what we have come to know as compassion, a word sorely misused for years as a kind of secular stand-in for fact of grace.

Flannery O'Connor writes in her essay "The Grotesque in Southern Fiction,"

> It's considered an absolute necessity these days for writers to have compassion. Compassion is a word that sounds good in anybody's mouth and which no book jacket can do without. It is a quality which no one can put his finger on in any exact critical sense, so it is always safe for anybody to use. Usually I think what is meant by it is that the writer excuses all human weakness because human weakness is human. The kind of hazy compassion demanded of the writer now makes it difficult to be anti-anything.

Further, in her essay "Novelist and Believer," she puts her finger exactly on what the believer ought to know is the difference between "hazy compassion" and the making of excuses for human behavior. She writes,

> The Christian novelist is distinguished from his pagan colleagues by recognizing sin as sin. According to his heritage he sees it not as sickness or an accident of environment, but as a responsible choice of offense against God which involves his eternal future. Either one is serious about salvation or one is not. . . .

Oh, how I miss Flannery O'Connor.

What she said nearly fifty years ago is not one thrown electron less true today. Compassion is the new and ultimate religion of the writer of literary fiction. Compassion is wisdom, is love, is genuine heart — all virtues we none of us will disdain for fear of being accused, as Kant did of those who depended on the guidance of another, of being cowards in the face of human reason.

But I'd like to cite a different text for a moment here, one a lot older than either O'Connor's or Kant's, one that speaks of the folly of such notions as the preeminence of man's reason. Get a load of this:

For although they knew God, they neither glorified him as God nor gave thanks to him, but their thinking became futile and their foolish hearts were darkened. Although they claimed to be wise, they became fools. . . .

Therefore God gave them over in the sinful desires of their hearts to sexual impurity for the degradation of their bodies with one another. They exchanged the truth of God for a lie, and worshipped and served created things rather than the Creator. . . .

That's Paul, by the way, in the first chapter of Romans. Oh, and Paul again, in chapter 3 of 1 Corinthians.

Do not deceive yourselves. If any one of you thinks he is wise by the standards of this age, he should become a "fool" so that he may become wise. For the wisdom of this world is foolishness in God's sight.

Francis Schaeffer, in *The Great Evangelical Disaster,* comments on these passages from Paul:

What is involved here is the way men think, the process of reasoning, thought, and comprehension. Thus "their thinking became futile and their foolish hearts were darkened. Although they claimed to be wise, they became fools." When the Scripture speaks of a man being foolish in this way, it does not mean he is only foolish religiously. Rather, it means that he has accepted a position that is intellectually foolish not only with regard to what the Bible says, but also to what exists concerning the universe and its form and what it means to be human. In turning away from God and the truth which he has given, man has thus become foolishly foolish in regard to what man is and what the universe is. Man is left with a position with which he cannot live, and he is caught in a multitude of intellectual and personal tensions.

These tensions that Schaeffer points out as being the logical end of a world fooled into believing in itself as God are what we've wound up calling "angst," a word that, like "epiphany," was first used in a religious sense. Kierkegaard, in reaction to Hegel's proposed happy universe of Reason and Reality as the sole and ultimately unifying principle, employed the word "angst" to describe the anxiety felt deep in man's heart when faced with the uncrossable chasm between God and our broken world. But then the existentialists took up the word in the twentieth century to stand for the feeling of being backed into a corner, without, it seems, recognizing that it was ourselves who were doing the backing up, until we'd hit the hard corner behind us of our own illegitimate deification.

One need only look at the way in which these two words — "epiphany" and "angst" — have been abrogated by the world, only to end up being diminished in their meanings by a world bent on proving God doesn't exist, to see the loud echo off the iron of Paul's words — "their thinking became futile and their foolish hearts were darkened. Although they claimed to be wise, they became fools." Once stolen, these words moved from the shining forth of Christ to the shining forth of man — and from the sense of fear and trembling we must daily feel as we work out our salvation to the sense of fear and trembling felt at a purposeless and pointless life.

The thesis of G. K. Chesterton's *The Everlasting Man,* published in 1925, is that "those who say that Christ stands side by side with similar myths, and his religion side by side with similar religions, are only repeating a very stale formula contradicted by a very striking fact." The fact, of course, is Christ's role in history as God made flesh, and Chesterton's book serves up beautifully and intelligently why man's foolishly believing in the power of himself leads to the dead-end of himself, and why man's shining forth on himself leaves us to this day with the angst we know, and have come to accept as part and parcel of our lives. In it, he writes,

> Certainly the pagan does not disbelieve like an atheist, any more than he believes like a Christian. He feels the presence of powers, about which he guesses and invents. St. Paul said that the Greeks had one altar to an unknown god. But in truth all their gods were unknown gods. And the real break in history did come when St. Paul declared to them whom they had ignorantly worshipped.

The substance of all such paganism may be summarized thus. It is an attempt to reach the divine reality through the imagination alone; in its own field reason does not restrain it at all. It is vital to the view of all history that reason is something separate from religion even in the most rational of these civilizations. It is only as an afterthought, when such cults are decadent or on the defensive, that a few Neo-Platonists or a few Brahmins are found trying to rationalise them, and even then only by trying to allegorise them. But in reality the rivers of mythology and philosophy run parallel and do not mingle till they reach the sea of Christendom. Simple secularists still talk as if the Church had introduced a sort of schism between reason and religion. The truth is that the Church was the first thing that ever tried to combine reason and religion. There had never before been any such union of the priests and the philosophers.

And so here, finally, is where I can begin, I believe, to talk about reclaiming literary fiction. We must see that, as with the fact of our being forgiven, the work of reclaiming has already been accomplished: Christ's insertion into history combined once and for all story and logic, imagination and reason. We, like those thinkers Paul warns us against, have been foolishly fooled into believing in a literary aesthetic that holds as its assumptions, its prejudiced beginning points, a schism between imagination and philosophy, between story and supernatural meaning; and we have believed as well — and again foolishly — that to believe the twain shall meet requires a kind of cowardice on our parts as believers in the need for guidance from another, no matter that the good shepherd whose voice we recognize is that guide.

That is, if we are believers in Christ, we must recognize that we are frolicking in the sea of Christendom, and not swimming upstream in either of the twin rivers of imagination or philosophy. We have been saved.

We, as believers, must see that there is no one save Satan who stills our fingers over a keyboard when we come, with fear and trembling, to begin to write of our "human attestation" to the role of grace in our lives.

But.

But, you may say.

Let's be realistic. The world of books is run, by and large, by the notions of money, and how much can be made. One gatekeeper — let's just call it New York — is by and large uninterested in the supernatural save in the bankability of the supernatural's demonic sense. The other gatekeeper, Christian publishing — mysteriously like its evil twin New York — is by and large uninterested in the supernatural save in the bankability of the supernatural's ability to comfort the already convinced. Christian publishing in this way, it seems to me — and I do not say this lightly, nor to condemn — is undoubtedly even more uninterested in art than New York. We must admit as well that this leaves us with no other conclusion to draw than what Christian publishing is most interested in — and again mysteriously like its evil twin, New York — is how deep the pockets are of the choir to which it already preaches.

Please know, again, that I do not say this lightly, nor do I say this to lay blame for the lack of good writing that wrestles not with the contrivances of plot but with the contrivances of the human heart anywhere but at my own feet. Again, no one save Satan stills my fingers at the keyboard when it comes to my creating art that is Christ-centered. No one; and I believe, as Christ told the Pharisees who wanted him to quiet the crowds calling out "Blessed is the king who comes in the name of the Lord!" on his triumphant entry into Jerusalem, that if we keep quiet even the stones will cry out.

But even so, you, if you are a writer of fiction that has no genre but that of the human heart, have every right to ask, how do we write literary fiction that is built upon a supernatural God, in a world that doesn't want to hear it?

And you wouldn't be the first to ask that. I said earlier that I so miss Flannery O'Connor. I do more and more every day. Truly. Let me pause here and quote a few passages from her, because this is ground she trod a long time ago, and which she wrote about so very much clearer than I ever could.

Here she is, in her second letter to a friend known only as "A," written in August of 1955:

> One of the awful things about writing when you are a Christian is that for you the ultimate reality is the Incarnation, the present re-

ality is the Incarnation, and nobody believes in the Incarnation; that is, nobody in your audience. My audience are the people who think God is dead. At least these are the people I am conscious of writing for.

And this, again from the essay "Novelist and Believer":

> It makes a great deal of difference to the look of a novel whether its author believes that the world came late into being and continues to come by a creative act of God, or whether he believes that the world and ourselves are the product of a cosmic accident. It makes a great difference to his novel whether he believes that we are created in God's image, or whether he believes we create God in our own. It makes a great difference whether he believes that our wills are free, or bound like those of the other animals.

And this bright indictment of us all from the same essay:

> Ever since there have been such things as novels, the world has been flooded with bad fiction for which the religious impulse has been responsible. The sorry religious novel comes about when the writer supposes that because of his belief, he is somehow dispensed from the obligation to penetrate concrete reality. He will think that the eyes of the Church or of the Bible or of his particular theology have already done the seeing for him, and that his business is to rearrange this essential vision into satisfying patterns, getting himself as little dirty as possible. . . .

And finally this, from the essay "Catholic Novelists and Their Readers," a passage which brings us, ultimately, right back to this notion of marketplace, and of value:

> St. Thomas Aquinas says that art does not require rectitude of the appetite, that it is wholly concerned with the good of that which is made. He says that a work of art is a good in itself, and this is a truth that the modern world has largely forgotten. We are not

content to stay within our limitations and make something that is simply a good in and by itself. Now we want to make something that will have some utilitarian value. Yet what is good in itself glorifies God because it reflects God. The artist has his hands full and does his duty if he attends to his art. He can safely leave evangelizing to the evangelists. He must first of all be aware of his limitations as an artist — for art transcends its limitations only by staying within them.

It seems to me that, if we look either to Christian publishing or New York for our venue, for our outlet, for our income, as it were, from writing about the human being in relation to a supernatural God, then we have missed the point of creating in God's name entirely. If we are asking this question — Why have we given up the ghost? — for any reason other than a desire to better serve God, then we are no better — I mean this — than the silversmiths under Demetrius at Ephesus, craftsmen who were more interested in the income off their silver shrines of Artemis than they were in the good news Paul proclaimed.

But allow me, if you will, one last faith story. One last story of our supernatural God.

I was born again after a Josh McDowell rally when I was nineteen. Then I ended up in a creative writing classroom for no good reason other than that it was an elective. I had a good time, though I'd never in my life thought of being a writer.

A couple of years later, me a newlywed and getting ready to head off with my wife to study writing at grad school in Massachusetts, I decided to begin sending out my stories for publication.

I bought a little plastic file box in order to keep my rejections — the ones I knew would be on their way — and to house as well my own filing system of what I had sent where.

But before I sent out my first story, I sat down at the small table we had in our apartment in Long Beach, California, and wrote out this verse, and then prayed it:

Proverbs 16:4: "Commit your works to the Lord, and your plans will be established."

Here's the piece of paper right here — you can still see the remnants of the yellowed Scotch tape I used to tape this to the inside lid of that filing box. To this day, I keep this scrap, written in my 21-year-old hand, taped to the wall above my desk.

I now have in my box 596 rejections — I have kept all but one (that's another story) since that day in 1980. This does not count the number of rejections of my novels and story collections. There are perhaps forty of those.

But also to this day, before I begin writing, I commit, in prayer, my works to the Lord, so that my plans will be established.

What I continue to learn through my life as a writer — through all those rejections and successes, past, present, and yet to come — is that the plan I want established is not to succeed in the world's terms, but in terms of the loving God who loves us on his terms, and his only. I continue to learn to relinquish my plans for success, and simply plan to do, as clearly as the Holy Spirit can lead me, God's will, and not my own.

And here I am today, a writer, because of the supernatural intervention in my life of a loving God — the only true God. Certainly God's answer to my prayer wasn't as quick as the one we got on a hot summer day on a playground in Moldova, when we called out for gum, and certainly not as mysteriously achieved as the appearing of the right number of T-shirts for kids who had just had given to them the good news of Jesus Christ.

But it is supernatural all the same, that I would be given the blessing of being able to speak to you all today, twenty-four years after I'd scrawled that verse on a piece of paper. Which leads to the end of my long-winded plenary kick off of the Calvin College Festival of Faith and Writing.

I want to ask, in closing, Do you believe in a supernatural God?

Do you believe in a God who provides, in love, T-shirts and loaves of bread? In gum and oddball phone calls and the atoning work of a Son he gave to die for us?

Do you believe that if we don't cry out, with our art, that the rocks will proclaim, "Blessed is the king who comes in the name of the Lord"?

And if you do, I have to ask, then how can you write with any eye whatsoever on the foolishness of a world that tells you that the truth, rather than setting you free, has caged you in its self-induced and pointless angst, and that the shining forth of Christ is a myth, to be replaced by the feeble shining forth of man on himself?

For whom do you write?

And are you willing?

KATHLEEN NORRIS

··

An Interview by Linda Buturian

LINDA BUTURIAN: Kathleen, I'm struck by the kind of community that you create in your works. Even in *Dakota* and *The Virgin of Bennington*, which are memoirs, your voice is one of many: a fourth century monk, a little girl in a schoolhouse, a neighbor in Lemmon. In a way, each book is like an elaborate dinner party where you're the hostess. You're adept at bringing out the best in your guests.

KATHLEEN NORRIS: That's a wonderful image. I'll take that with me. When I started writing memoir, I was conscious of not wanting it to be just my own voice. I had stories people told me or I'd overheard, and experiences with children I had worked with over the fifteen years I was artist in the schools in North and South Dakota. They were part of my life and I was part of theirs, and it didn't seem right to just write about myself. It is a kind of community that I deliberately try to create in my books.

Strictly first person memoir works, but there is the pitfall of the narcissistic eye. Once I judged a non-fiction contest for memoirs; the books were steeped in narcissism. And even though people had interesting experiences, I couldn't get in the books. Maybe I went overboard in not doing that with my memoirs. One of the reviewers of *The Virgin of Bennington* called it an "un-narcissistic anti-memoir," and I want to send that person a prize.

LB: One of the strengths of your essays is that you can shuttle between, say, a discourse on virgin martyrs from an earlier century to the current plight of marginalized women, to a memory from Bennington College, to a line from a hymn, and you do it in a way that is seamless to the reader. How do you do that?

KN: It's what used to get me in trouble when I was in elementary school — I have a very messy mind, and it will jump around. But I think that is the nature of the poet: our greatest joy is connecting things that aren't supposed to be connected. It's what metaphors do. When I spot something like the fact that the stories of the virgin martyrs from the early church reminded me of what I was reading in the newspaper about the abduction, rape, and murder of young women, I thought "you know, there is a connection here and I'm going to explore that." To me, writing is all about making those connections.

LB: This connection that you make extends out to the reader as well. In a sense, we are also invited to the dinner party, and lots of us have showed up. In the preface to *Amazing Grace: A Vocabulary of Faith,* you say that you "persist in your hope that you have something to say to people who can't believe you joined a church, as well as those who wonder what took you so long." Rhetorically, that's a tall order.

KN: I had skeptical writer friends who didn't think I could connect these worlds of religion and writing and art. My ultimate week was when I was interviewed by *Christianity Today,* who chose *Cloister Walk* as the top religious book of the year, and the Vatican radio. Now that's a nice stretch; that's flexibility. Some of the questions were similar, and that's what I really like.

My Jewish editor, Cindy, has been very helpful, especially as my books — *The Cloister Walk* and *Amazing Grace* in particular — got more specifically Christian. As a person from another tradition, she will ask me questions in an extremely helpful way. It forces me to explain what I mean more clearly than if I were writing for a strictly Christian audience.

I remember I had slipped in a little Christian jargon, "the living Christ," and Cindy wrote a penciled note in the margin, "Do you mean that Christ is someone who once lived, or someone who lives now?"

"Well," I said, "I mean both."

And she replied, "Then you're going to need to unpack that phrase and explain what you mean." It's been both fascinating and gratifying to me, the variety of people who have found ways to use my work.

LB: I'm one of those people. I moved to a small town in rural Minnesota and have lived there for about seven years. I recently reread *Dakota* like it was a map, like it was essential to my orientation in the world. Sections of it are unflinching in your assessment of the dynamics of a small town. You even have a chapter called, "Can you tell the truth in a small town?" Can you — and continue living there in the fullest sense of the word?

KN: You can if you know what the price is, and if your ultimate goal is not to punish people, get revenge, make your point at the expense of someone else, but to do it in such a way that you can keep living together. I think that's what happens in small towns — we know we're stuck to-gether out there, and so we have to get along. It sometimes means having to confront things directly and to tell the truth. It's all in how it's done. Of course in my small town, they knew my grandparents and know my mom. I've got standing there. I didn't just bluster in to make my point, but did some sitting around and seeing how things were working and be-ing deliberate and careful about how to tell the truth.

I began writing *Dakota* because the farm crisis was disrupting churches, schools — all the small town institutions. I was hearing horror stories from some teachers and pastors. The last chapter I finished was "Hope Church," which was the ultimate positive one for me, but it was quite a process from that negative stuff to work my way through to the more positive.

LB: What sort of comments did you get from your neighbors?

KN: Oh, it was wonderful because everything I said about gossip was confirmed by my experience. Many people have pointed that out to me. At the time, I was on a book tour, and *Dakota* was a little slow to actually arrive to Lemmon. But people were hearing about it from relatives in Boston or New York. All these wild rumors were being spread — that I had named names and that it was awful and that I had done a terrible disservice to the town. I got a phone call from a good friend, and she asked, "What have you done?" Turned out she had gone to a coffee group, and everyone was very upset. But then she told me, "I got so mad because when I asked them, 'well, who's read the book?', no one had. They were just spinning out this crazy stuff."

I was glad I was out of town.

When people got the book and started to read it, they realized the rumors weren't true and that I had tried to give a more balanced picture. And since I haven't moved away after my success — and that's the normal pattern — and I love the place that was reassuring to people, too. It took a while, but I think most people are quite happy with it, and the Chamber of Commerce is now selling it on Main Street. In the tourist information, they promote Lemmon as the "Hometown of Kathleen Norris." They actually get people driving Highway 12 coming through Lemmon just because they read *Dakota.* So I'm good for business.

LB: A parallel sort of question for *The Cloister Walk.* How was it received by the monks and the sisters?

KN: Again, because I had known Benedictine men and women for about fifteen years by the time that book came out, I guess the main reaction was that people were so relieved to be human beings and not romanticized in the book. Sometimes people write about monasteries, and they're all "Gosh, this is heaven on earth." A monk or nun reads it and thinks "if they only knew." This is community, this is living with other people, and it's never easy. They thought I painted a fairly accurate picture for someone who was definitely an outsider, but still knew them pretty intimately.

LB: I've met a fellow Catholic here at the conference who was saying that for years he's gone on retreat with the Trappist monks at their monasteries and lately they've been booked. I think this is a phenomenon —

KN: And you blame me as part of the problem?

LB: It's a nice kind of blame, but yes, how does it feel to be responsible in part, for this phenomenon?

KN: I'm not really responsible because that was starting to happen in the seventies, especially with Protestants, more than Catholics, taking advantage of monastic retreats. Whenever I would go to a monastery, I would run into all sorts of Protestants — a variety of people — so I'm not going to take total blame for that. I think it reflects a real need in our culture for silence and prayer, and for communities that are practicing day in and day out. In some ways, this total immersion in scripture all day long is the ultimate Protestant experience. It's indicative of a really deep need.

LB: I've had the good fortune of going on retreat, and it makes such a difference in part just knowing the Carmelite nuns are praying for us. The challenge is bringing that contemplative spirit back to my daily life. That's why I appreciated this little book, the *Quotidian Mysteries,* subtitled "Laundry, Liturgy, and Women's Work."

KN: That was given as part of a twenty-year-long lecture series at St. Mary's College in Notre Dame, Indiana. As the first Protestant woman who was invited to do this lecture, I was honored. This was my interim book between *Amazing Grace* and *The Virgin of Bennington. Quotidian Mysteries* is a meditation on spirituality in everyday life. I once gave a retreat based on the subtitle, and one of the women remarked, "I came because the word 'laundry' was in the title, and I thought if someone can connect spirituality and laundry, I gotta hear about this." I was glad to get that kind of response because how we do everything reveals our spirituality. How you give a baby a bath can teach a lot about honoring the body as a created being, or you can just dunk the kid and rub and be irritated and distracted. It is a very ancient Christian idea that thoughts matter: monastic people thinking about definitions of good thoughts and bad thoughts later get turned into virtues and sins.

LB: My mom, Rita, a devout Italian-Catholic, fell in love with your books and claims that in your interpretations you're more Catholic than she is. I mean, for Pete's sake, you wrote a book called *Meditations on Mary.* But she wondered why you haven't converted.

KN: A lot of people ask me that, and it's just not there. I'm a fairly conservative person in that I respect my roots — which are extremely Protestant. We have a lot of ministers in my family. My grandfather and great-grandfather were both Methodist pastors, circuit riders. On my father's side, one of the people that we trace back to at the time of Henry VIII is a man who had been a Catholic priest and became an Anglican priest. So I have deep roots in the Protestant tradition and that's something that I haven't felt compelled to set aside. It's just one of those internal things. If it happens some day, it will surprise me. I've got a Catholic side and a Protestant side, and if I can keep them in balance, then I'm okay. *The Cloister Walk* is kind of Catholic; *Amazing Grace* is kind of Protestant, more Protestant than a book about the liturgical year.

LB: Years ago, I had this moment of insight when I was playing tennis with a friend. It started to mist and we kept playing. Then it started to drizzle, but we were enjoying it, so we kept playing. Then it really started to rain, and we continued. We were slipping on the court and an arc of water would follow the ball. But when two people came out on the court next to us, however, I thought, "Now what would possess people to come out in the rain and play tennis?" In that moment I realized, "That's how I feel when people convert to Catholicism. What would possess them to come out in the rain?"

KN: A lot of people think of it as finding a home. When people have a serious religious conversion or commitment to a Protestant or Catholic church, there's usually some interesting story behind it. They're seeking and finding something, so you have to honor that.

LB: Your writing has helped me to understand why they would.

KN: My husband was raised Catholic, and since he was about 12, he hasn't wanted to go near it. As an outsider, it was easier for me to see what was good there.

LB: This morning you alluded to the monastic practice of *lectio divina,* a kind of holy reading that you write about in *Cloister Walk.* You discussed how the poems that you were writing in response to the scripture were a form of *lectio:* a way of reading that, in the words of a 4th-century monk, "works the earth of the heart."

KN: *Lectio divina* is writing as a spiritual process, where the poems are wiser than you are. This has happened to me a great deal, and I think it happens with a lot of writers: that you look at something you wrote a few years ago and all of a sudden you realize what it's about. You weren't conscious of it at the time, but maybe you were working towards something. That is part of the process of writing, where the words and poems that come out know more than you do. Poetry works well for *lectio* because it is usually written in that state of going slowly and trying to evoke things, rather than to grab and hold onto them. The writing becomes the conversion itself.

Poet Denise Levertov wrote a beautiful essay about her experience. Her father had been an orthodox Jew and became an Anglican priest, and her mother was Welsh. I mean talk about a recipe for a poet. She was writing a poem, and she thought, "So many composers have written masses and done so much with the liturgy, why not a poem that is a mass?" As she began writing it, she was basically agnostic with religious roots; by the time she got to the *agnus dei,* she was a believer. Writing the poem and working with the mass had converted her.

Writing has that kind of power. The term, *lectio divina,* sounds so mysterious. It's just a very slow process of reading. You're not reading for information, you're reading with the heart. If a word or phrase stops you — and this is especially powerful with the Bible — you say, "Oh, he shall wipe away every tear from their eyes. Let me just think about that. All day." It helps when you turn on the TV news and you think, "He shall wipe away every tear from their eyes." That becomes a powerful play with the world. The Word and the world, in you, working out something.

LB: In *The Cloister Walk,* there's this inherent tension between academic or theological discourse and poetry. You called Emily Dickinson "the patron saint of biblical commentary in poetic mode." Who are other writers who have wedded the theological with the poetic?

KN: Emily Dickinson is the prime example, partly because she knew the Bible so well. Poet Scott Cairns would be a good example. He has a fairly sophisticated understanding of the early church and saints and modern commentary. It's kind of unusual. You find a scholar like Walter Brueggemann who writes very well and in an accessible way, and his scholarship is great. He doesn't write in that dry academic style. Roberta Bondi has a doctorate from Oxford in the ancient church, but she writes like a human being; she engages in real story telling. I look around for people who are solid scholars but also have a real style.

LB: Why don't we move to poetry. Let's talk about the poem "Little Girls in Church."

KN: "Little Girls in Church" is the title poem of my book that came out in 1995. For a while, I was haunted by little girls in church. Whenever we'd go to a worship service, there would be little girls doing something interesting. I think you can see how this poem was a part of my own conversion. It is a transitional poem because at that time I wasn't sure I could pray — for myself or for anyone — so that's why the poem ends: "I will pray for you, if I can." It is a prayer, in a sense, but I still had that huge area of doubt and agonizing. It is kind of wimpy when you think about it, but that's what I was capable of at the time, so it felt more honest to leave that poem as it was.

LB: I have a three-year-old, and I have to decide what to do about church. The last line where you write, "The great love within you, star-like and wild. As wide as grass, solemn as the moon." I didn't find a lot of that in church. And yet, partly why I have faith today is because of that time I spent in church.

KN: Sure, you were raised in it. When I'm in Honolulu, I attend an Epis-copal church, and I love what they do with children. The kids have Sunday School and miss out on the stuff that would bore them, which is the readings and the sermon. Then they have their own procession where they bring the gifts up to the altar. Two of the children have white robes and are usually barefoot or in flip-flops, and they're carrying their own cross. The majority of them come in and sit with their parents, right when we're going to do the Eucharistic prayers. One little boy has this rit-ual: he comes in and hugs his mother, then his father, then his baby sis-ter. It's like "Wow! This is Eucharist. This is worship." They fidget and make a little noise, but that's when you want a little noise, some celebra-tion.

By the time the kids are in eighth grade or high school, they're having struggles. Some churches have figured out ways to give these kids a solid tradition in joyful worship, music, and prayer. That's something that they'll keep with them, whether or not they drift away for a while. Teen-agers are asking difficult questions, and they need something — maybe their own worship service — besides. Rather than making them memorize a lot of things and do things by rote, we need to answer why we do things in worship. Because they're curious. Give them good answers about why we light candles or don't, or why we have the cross where it is, or why we sing hymns. I think that's a significant part of the formation as a Christian.

LB: How do you decide whether something's going to be a poem or a poetic piece of prose?

KN: I usually know pretty quickly because if it's a poem it starts out as a kind of wordplay. Some little phrase will stick in my mind. I'll spin it around and gradually write it down. A piece of prose often starts out as a story I want to tell or an idea that I want to get across. Some of the chap-ters in *Dakota*, especially the sections about the farm crisis, seemed too big a subject for my poetry. So it's usually in the origin — where it comes from. And sometimes they switch places, too.

LB: You quoted Jean Cocteau: "Poets, like monks, are useless but indispensable."

KN: My husband says that about himself: "I'm useless, but indispensable." I am very glad that there are these communities around the globe that are praying all the time, 24 hours a day. I like knowing that.

One of the most marvelous things is when I'm in a monastery choir, especially with young monks or sisters, and I realize that these people have been doing this for 1700 years. And before that, it was the Jewish Psalm tradition of morning and evening prayer. That is really ancient, and we're still doing it. It's not the new and improved model, it's not for sale on TV. It's something much more significant and powerful and truly ancient.

LB: In *Dakota* you state, "Gossip done well can be a holy thing. It can strengthen communal bonds." And your children's book is called *The Holy Twins*. What do you mean by the word "holy"?

KN: When I said that about gossip, I was reflecting the history of the word, which originally meant someone present at a baptism. A gossip was a godparent. I looked it up in an etymological dictionary and it said "gossip: see holy." And I thought, "Whoa. I don't think so. Now how has that word changed from being something holy to being something unholy?"

So I guess "holy" as in whole and hail and hearty. When something is right, righteous and healthy, we know it, that's what makes it holy.

At the Presbyterian church in South Dakota, when we have our joys and concerns, it really is a form of gossip. Some of the people go into great detail about operations and recovery — we're learning more than we need to know — but it's all for the purpose of prayer. Afterwards, if you visit another church member in the hospital, you gossip: "This is who we prayed for in church this morning and this is why." And you tell them about the operation and the recovery.

Knowing what people are up against in a small town can sometimes be very useful. Like when I'm working in the library and somebody comes in and I've just heard they are in the middle of a messy separation and an impending child custody battle. I may not say anything directly about it, but it's good to be aware of it. That's what I mean by the holy use of gossip. I've had a lot of responses — teenagers especially — who say "Gossip is horrible. There's nothing good about it," but I would argue with that. I think we can reclaim that as a holy word.

LB: In *Dakota,* we get a sense of both the strength and fragility of Hope Church, and if it isn't thriving, it feels like somehow all of us are diminished. The readers end up having a vested interest in Hope Church.

KN: Hope Church is doing well, but that is only because another small country Lutheran church closed. We're talking about the frontier where everything, including boundaries, are a little different. What happened was all the Lutherans decided to join the Presbyterian church, rather than let another country church dwindle. The Lutherans who were living close to Hope Church became Presbyterians and it's been a seamless transition. After I wrote about Hope Church, it was down to 30 members. Now it's back up to around 50.

When my editor visited me, one place she definitely wanted to go to was Hope Church. We had car trouble on the way back and she joked, "This is what happens when a nice Jewish girl goes to church." But car trouble at Hope Church meant we had all sorts of help. We were rescued along a country road by a church member. It's a remarkable and hospitable place in this sea of land.

LB: Let's talk about celibacy. I was speaking with a single Protestant woman and she liked what you had to say about celibacy in terms of hospitality — that resonates with her experience.

KN: I've noticed with monastic people that their celibacy has a lot to do with how well they listen and respond to you. That's one of the reasons all sorts of people go to a monastery — because they can sit and be listened to. Some of the nuns have explained to me, "This is our form of intimacy, it's a part of our hospitality. We want to be open to everyone — not just to a wife or a husband."

The Orthodox tradition makes a lot of sense. The clergy are often married or not. It's their choice. But the monastic communities are always celibate because if you're trying to have a religious community and you have people pairing off, it doesn't work so well. When you have these exclusive or intensely sexual romantic relationships, then the community suffers.

LB: This woman wondered about the implications of celibacy for Protestant men and women, given that there isn't really a community supporting celibacy.

KN: I think community is the key. The current crisis in the Catholic Church with the priestly abuse of their role and their authority doesn't have to do with celibacy, per se. It's a factor of the loneliness of the diocesan priest, someone who's out there without a community, trying to be celibate. These people get extremely lonely, and they stop praying. It's a difficult situation. I talked to a Benedictine, and he said, "If I had to be out there alone in a parish, I couldn't do it."

If you want to be single and celibate and Protestant, I think you have to be very aware of getting a support system, having friends of both sexes and being deliberate about not letting yourself be isolated from human affection. I think that friendships would become extremely important. And you would need to avoid not just isolation but also the big danger in thinking "because I am celibate I am holier than the people who aren't." That can get all twisted. If you're doing it because you're repressed, then that's going to kick you in the rear in the long run.

LB: I think many here would like to know, how did you cultivate the permission to write about the big things like incarnation, trinity.

KN: You know, that was funny. While I was working on *The Cloister Walk,* I started writing these passages about words, and finally my editor and I agreed that there were two different books emerging. I decided I wanted to call the other book *Scary Words,* but my publisher said, "No, no, you can't do that." Still, I started tackling words that had troubled me the most when I was trying to make my way back to church. Or simply words I had learned something about that I wanted to share, like "perfect" as in "Be perfect as your heavenly Father is perfect." That's a bad translation; it really means "ripe" and "mature" and "fulfilled" and it's a much richer word than "perfection."

But it was comical because I would think, "Oh my God, I have to write about judgment. Ugh." I would come in from working intensely, and I would say to my husband, "David, be nice to me — I've been writing about hell all morning." At times I would think, "Why me, Lord? Why am I doing this to myself? Why am I tackling sin, judgment, hell" —

LB: Antichrist.

KN: Antichrist. Oh yes, what a fun subject. I was inwardly driven to do that book. I think it's obvious when you read it. I guess because I'd been a poet so long, I had some nerve. Poets really do rush in where angels fear to tread, so that makes us either poets or fools or both.

WALTER WANGERIN JR.

Glory into Glory

As a writer, I think it is my job to seek God in the common things; indeed, to believe that God is already in the common things ahead of and outside of me. This happens in three ways: first of all, to see the glory of God in the world, to perceive it, to find it, sometimes to be stunned by the discovery of it when I hadn't been looking well enough. Second, having perceived it, to acknowledge it, to salute it, to be aware of it, to know it, to dance with it, to think about it, to engage with it — and having engaged with it, to give that glory back to God. The third part involves writing — or maybe I should say praise. Ultimately, it is my job to praise.

Psalm 19 embraces much of what I just told you and almost everything else I'm going to tell you. It's in the fourteenth verse that you will find me, the writer, crouched down and waiting. This is a poem which is filled with the language of languages; it's filled with talk about speech. It's filled with what we do when we fool around with words, only it starts at a place before we are involved.

The heavens declare the glory of God
And the firmament shows his handiwork.

"Declare," *kaphar* in Hebrew, means to make account of or to write up in an accounting book. That is, the heavens want to be sure that the glory of God is recognized and recorded throughout the universe. The word for "shows" is *nagad*, which comes from *nagod*, storytelling. The heavens tell the story of the work of God's hand. This is language.

> Day unto day utters speech,
> And night unto night reveals knowledge.

The presumption here at the beginning of this psalm is that the heavens themselves are perpetually in song, singing of the glory of God. In fact, instead of "speech," the word in Hebrew would be *'omer,* talking. Talking gushes forth like a fountain, day after day. Isn't that amazing? We are surrounded by the language of God in the creation of God. The earth itself is gushing forth.

> There is no speech nor language
> Where their voice is not heard.
> Their line has gone out through the earth,
> And their words to the end of the world.

Writers, what do we do? We deal with language, and when it is well with us, even the voices of the heavens find place in what we write. That is a marvelous thing.

In the psalm's second part, the poet draws upon an image that the Greeks and the Hebrews would understand: the sun, coming like a living thing. In Greek mythology, of course, the sun is a god. Here, the sun is something that God asks to work or serve. How specifically does the sun do this? The psalmist gives us this picture. God has "set a tabernacle for the sun which is like a bridegroom coming out of his chamber, and re-joices like a strong man to run his race." Picture that sun on the far east horizon, "its rising is from one end of heaven in its circuit to the other end." You can see it trembling to break out of its tent, trembling to begin to rise and soar in the heavens, singing. This image of the sun is a power-ful one, one that makes me want to exclaim, "O God, let me be like the heavens. O God, let me be like the sun that rises in the day."

Though the third section is parallel, it focuses on another kind of a language all together. It's narrower than the whole of creation by describing the utterance of God to a people of God. Listen to the goodness of this:

> The law of the Lord is perfect, converting the soul.
> The testimony of the Lord is sure, making wise the simple.
> The statutes of the Lord are right, rejoicing the heart. . . .
>   The judgments of the Lord are true and righteous altogether.
> More to be desired are they than gold,
>   Yea, than much fine gold;
>   Sweeter also than honey and the honey comb.
> Moreover, by them your servant is warned
>   And in keeping them there is great reward.

We begin to approach the writer now and the appropriate attitude we should cultivate as we prepare to write:

> Who can understand his errors?
>   Cleanse thou me from secret faults.
> Keep back your servant also from presumptuous sins;
>   Let them not have dominion over me.
> Then I shall be blameless,
>   And I shall be innocent of great transgression.

Finally, the concluding verses — the pleading I do unto God:

> Let the words of my mouth and the meditation of my heart
>   Be acceptable in your sight,
>   O Lord, my strength and my redeemer.

The "words" here are the very same 'omer — talking — as that fountain of language that breaks forth day to day. But the opposite is here too: the Hebrew for "meditation" is the equivalent of mumbling; even that's a part of our writing.

One October, my wife Thanne and I were driving from Fairbanks down to Anchorage and then to the Kenai Peninsula. I had been invited to Alaska, first of all, to lead a seminar, and then, after that, somebody had a really good idea. It was suggested that I should go to all those small places where big name writers don't come, and read and talk and listen and preach. It would not have been my choice to drive in October because the weather changes suddenly. I'm going to tell you straight up — as we were driving, I thought we were going to die. I was driving someone else's car, a very old four wheel drive Jeep. A fellow in Homer had loaned it to me, so that I could tool around. I'd never driven a four wheel drive before in my life, and that was one of the reasons I thought we were going to die.

But maybe the most important reason for my fear was that it was snowing — a wet, icy snow. With wilderness left and right, the road was above the muskeg, and it was freezing. I had in my mind this picture of us sliding off the side of this road, down into the muskeg — and nobody finding us because it's Alaska, it's the wilderness. My knuckles were white on the steering wheel, and sitting next to me was Thanne, praying out loud. Every once in a while she would say, "You're doing fine, Walt. We'll be fine."

After about two and a half hours of driving, we came over a rise and like magic — for the first time in all of the time we were in Alaska — the clouds drew back, the sky was blue, and we saw Denali, standing up with a scallop of white snow. I relaxed. We were not going to die. We drove through Anchorage, and by evening, just as the sun was going down, we stopped to eat in the little town of Kenai. While we were eating, someone came in and said, "The whales! The whales are breeching!" Everybody jumped up and ran out to the coastline.

Now the reason I told you this whole story is for what happened next. When we ran out, we were looking directly west at a great bay, Cook Inlet. To my left, the land rose all the way up, until you could see the bay sweep around. To my right, the land sank and was about the same level as the water of the bay. I was standing on a very high precipice that must have been sixty or seventy feet straight above the water. I scanned the water, but I saw no whales whatsoever. Other people started mumbling to one another, and seeing no whales either, they peeled off and went back to the restaurant.

Before I turned to go back to the restaurant, I looked down low on the horizon, and, perhaps a mile away, I saw an eagle flying in my direction. It flew right along the edge of the precipice, rising as it came. I fixed my attention on that eagle. It never veered to the right and over the sea, nor did it veer to the left and over the land. The closer it came, the more I saw how it is that an eagle flies: that its head makes a thrusting and rocking motion; that its wings don't just go up and down, they come forward. It was as if the eagle were rowing the wind. I was entranced.

The closer the eagle came, everything else fell away. I heard those wings strike the wind, as if I'd never heard it before. I know I'd heard the little tiny flutters of birds' wings, but I'd never heard that tremendous roiling of the air as the eagle came closer. My heart stopped — it was coming exactly to me, now no more than ten feet off the edge of the precipice. Just as it came to my level, when I could have reached out my hand and felt the tips of its primary feathers strike me, just then, something happened that transfixed me forever. In that single moment, it was as if everything froze while everything else went on.

The eagle looked at me.

Suddenly, in a flash, it was as if that black pupil of its eye, surrounded by its yellow iris, was as huge as a rainbow, broken free of the earth and filling the sky itself. A tumult of feelings rushed through me, but I can't speak to you about the sweetness of the delight without also mentioning the awe-fulness. In that glance was Alaska, in that glance was Denali, in that glance was the snow storm that could have killed me. In that glance was the sunlight which was our freedom, when I did not die after all and when grace had come down like light itself.

But in that glance too, and this is terribly important, was fear. I was scared. I was scared in the midst of everything else. And the only thing I can say now, looking back at it, is that it scared me because I suddenly realized that I existed. When you are looked at by things that you didn't expect had the capacity to look at you, suddenly you are different from what you were. You are here — and it sees you. It's as if it called your name. That's frightening.

What do we do with the eye of the eagle? As one who lives in this universe, who was suddenly called to account, I was suddenly called *to be.* Have you ever noticed when you casually cross in front of traffic, and, for some reason or another, somebody beeps at you. Have you noticed how your whole gait changes? It's harder to walk suddenly because you know somebody's looking at you, especially if you looked at the beep, and it was nobody you knew before. You can't walk casually. What happened? Somebody called your name. And when you know that you are known, you're not the same anymore. What, then, do we do with that eye of an eagle? Praise.

Near the end of his life, Rainer Maria Rilke said that the most important thing that a poet can do is praise. What would his response have been? Earlier, he would have watched the eagle as clearly as he possibly could. And he would have seen the eagle so well that when he wrote the poem about the eagle, the eagle itself would seem to take up space and residence in the poem. When you read his poem, you would see the world through that eye of the eagle.

Later in his life, he comes to something different. He writes:

> O tell me Poet what you do? — I praise.
> But the deathly and the monstrous,
> How do you accept them, bear them? — I praise.
> But the nameless, the anonymous,
> How, Poet, can you still invoke it? — I praise.
> Under every costume, every mask of us,
> What right have you to be true? — I praise.
> Or that the calm and the impetuous
> Should know you, as star and storm? — Because I praise.

What he means by praise is that not only does he get it right in his poem, as he might have done earlier, but he gives praise back unto the world. He gives it back to the eagle itself in a way that he says is more spiritual and eternal. He magnifies the things that he sings about. In fact, he says in another place, "Praise is all there is."

So far, so good. But then he suggests that when the poet praises something it is transformed into song and that song is made immortal. What the poet does there is elevate himself almost to the godly realm because he is the one by whose praise immortality is conferred. That step I can't quite take.

Another individual whom I appreciate very much is "Mad" Christopher Smart, so-called because he had the unfortunate habit of praying. As they said about him, if the man was taken by a desire to pray in private, nobody would have noticed. But "Mad" Kit Smart would pray wherever he felt like it, dropping to his knees and involving everybody else in his prayers. What he said he was doing was praising God, and for that they locked him up in the lunatic asylum.

As a poet, he believed that all of creation exists for no other reason than to praise the creator, and that it was his job to recognize it and to give voice and word to the mute praise that everything else gave. Thus, if he had seen that eagle, he would have rushed back into the restaurant, stood up on a table, dropped on his knees and asked everybody to pray with him in joy. Then, he would have put that eagle in a poem. In fact, he actually did. In his writing, he climbs on the back of the eagle and the two of them together soar in song unto God. I like the extraordinary quality of Smart's poetry, which ultimately was not crazy. By the way, if you commit yourself to praise and to somehow thinking the deity has anything to do with your writing, expect someone to think you're crazy too.

There are things, however, that Smart misses. First, all of his praise is joy, and he thereby misses the difficult things. Second, he only recognizes the creation praising — thereby missing humans.

What, then, shall we do with the eye of the eagle?

This is what I do. I remember the passage in Isaiah 6 where Isaiah heard something equivalent to the eye of the eagle when he saw the curtain torn open and witnessed divinity. Here's how he begins: "In the year that King Uzziah died, I saw the Lord upon a throne, high and lifted up and the temple was filled with the hem of his garment." It is very possible that Isaiah was either part of or had access to the priesthood, so perhaps he was performing some priestly duty at that moment. It could have been that this was New Year's Day, Rosh Hashanah, when the gates of the courts around the temple and the very doors of the temple itself would be opened up. At a certain point, the sun would pierce its way over the top of the Mount of Olives, and the rays of the sun would rush forward into the darkness of the temple with a brightness that was shattering and surprising.

If you were Isaiah, kneeling about your holy sacramental business when, by the grace of God, the sun rises up and shoots into the temple in front of you with the altar's incense putting up its smoke, you can see how the sunlight would hit that smoke and begin to *become* the hem of the garment of God. Above God are the sparks of the fire itself, whirling.

Smoke and sparks are common, except when every once in a while, they become evidence of the glory of God in the world. Those sparks become the "burning ones," the seraphim, with six wings each.

> With two he covered his face, with two he covered his feet,
>> and with two he flew.
> And one cried to another and said:
>> "Holy, holy, holy is the LORD of hosts;
>> The whole earth is full of His glory!"

Terrible word, "holy," *qadosh* in Hebrew. It means "other, other, other is the Lord of hosts." Different, different, different. Unapproachable and unknowable. The holiness divides us completely.

This comes as a fearful grace. The whole earth, all of creation under the singing heavens, is filled with the glory of God. If holiness brings glory into the world, where are you going to look? You're going to look at the cockroach, you're going to look at the ground, you're going to smell the air, you're going to look at absolutely everything — because in almost any common thing, the glory of God may strike forth and call your name.

Of course, you know what Isaiah's response is: it's fear. He's scared. And why? Notice what he focuses on: "Woe is me, I am undone! For I am a man of unclean lips, and I come from a people of unclean lips." We don't say things right. We obscure, we obfuscate, we lie, we become proud.

But one of the seraphim goes to that altar of incense, takes a coal with the tongs, and in a baptism of fire, touches the writer's lip. You are clean. Forgiveness is part of the process.

Then a voice says, "Who will go for me? Who will talk?"

The pitiful, little writer who has just seen the eagle fly says, "Uh . . . me?"

What is that glory, that *kabod?* The image behind this Hebrew word is weight, heaviness. Like what we say when someone walks into the room: "he throws his weight around." That's what glory is — it's the authority of God, made present in all that God created. All things reflect God's authority as the creator.

How do we see that glory? How do we recognize it? I'm going to tell you the simplest thing right now, something that comes directly out of dear Kit Smart: "When nature does what God commanded it to do, nature in its obedience shows forth the glory of God. When anything within nature does what God created it do, the authority of God is reflected in the sweet and speechless obedience. Seek obedience."

I have to take one step, though, beyond Kit Smart who only looked at nature. When human beings, consciously or unconsciously, find themselves sweetly in the midst of obedient response unto God, there is the glory of God. Where are you going to look? Please. Where do you think you cannot look? Where do you think you will not find anything? It's nowhere. It's the looking, not the thing at which you look, that will find the glory of God.

What's the final step? I want to go beyond Rilke, even beyond Kit Smart, to my friend Melvin. Like me, Mel was sent away to a Missouri Synod Lutheran all-male prep school (which no longer exists) in Milwaukee at the age of thirteen. In my shyness, I had very few friends, but two doors down from me in the dormitory was a fellow who had the odd habit of making tea in the evening and drinking it, something I'd never known anyone else to do. I became friends with Mel, nevertheless. Every one of his brothers and sisters had gone off and had gotten jobs as pastors or teachers within the church. Of course, Mel was going to follow in their footsteps.

Mel was from a dairy farm north of Milwaukee, so he would take me home. I rejoiced in what I could see with him on the farm. It was beautiful, called in those days "Real Lane" because of the tree-canopied lane that went out to the meadow where they kept their cows.

I came to love Mel's mama, Gertrude. His mother, a short, German woman had a great, round face and was a powerhouse for speaking German. Mel used to invite me to help her sell vegetables at the Farmer's Market in Milwaukee. Folks would come and try to buy potatoes from me — and try and get them cheap because I couldn't speak German as fast as they could. But when Gertrude stood beside me, we always won. She liked me, and I became something of her son. She cooked when I went, and I had my own bed upstairs, since the other siblings had left the farmhouse. I spent many wonderful times in that place.

A few years ago in October, I went to visit Melvin. I don't see him very often, maybe once every seven or eight years. His dad had died, and he had had to quit college. He was the only one who had stayed home on the farm. The area was now being taken over by subdivisions, and so the way in which Melvin was able to take care of his mother and the farm was to sell their property off, bit by bit. Now they were down to five acres.

It was a bright day, the sky high blue. There was a winey smell on the wind from the apples that lay on the ground under the old apple trees. I knocked on his door. Melvin, looking lean and so wise, opened the door and smiled.

"Wally," he said. "Good to see you."

I smelled apple pie. "Melvin!" I exclaimed, "Your mother has made me a pie."

"Oh no," he said and ducked his head, always shy. "No, I see to the necessary things now.

"Come on in. Let me show you mom." We went into the kitchen, through a little hallway, and entered what was always called the parlor. When we were younger, we were very seldom in there — that was the special room for guests. When I walked in, I saw that there was now a bed with its head to the wall on the right, and a chair on the left. Melvin pointed and said, "That's where I sit at night when I read because I have to watch Mama."

I saw Gertrude — the woman with such power to sell potatoes, who was my mother for a while — sitting up in bed and smiling. Then Melvin did an odd thing. He walked to his mother and said, "Mother, be pleased to meet my friend, Walter Wangerin. He's a writer."

I was surprised — I'd known her for years and years. "Be pleased to meet my friend, Walter." I walked forward, and I saw that she raised her hand as if I would shake it. When she did that, I understood. Gertrude's face was as large as ever, but it was as shining and empty as a plate. Her skin was as white as if it were powdered in flour. She never looked me in the eye, never raised her eyes. But she raised her hand, and when I reached to shake it, I took hold of something like dough. She didn't know me. Gertrude didn't know me. I glanced at Mel, and he nodded and said, "I see to the necessary things now."

He reached for a dish of prunes on the sideboard and gave them to his mother. She began to chew them and smiled at us as we left.

We spent the afternoon walking under the trees. Melvin so wise, so blameless — he could school presidents and priests and kings with his wisdom, if they would only listen. Do you remember what the psalmist said? Just as nature obeys God, so when human beings know the law of God, there is an obedience that shines forth the glory of God. One of those laws is that remarkable commandment, "honor your father and your mother." You must understand that the word "honor" in Hebrew is related to *kabod,* to glory, to weightiness. Thus, what the commandment means is that you honor your parents not when you are little and because they can make you obey if they wish. Obedience has nothing to do with honor. Instead, it means that when they are older and there is no honor in them, when they are no longer honorable to themselves, you grant unto them weight and gravitas, so that they take up a weightiness in your life. When you honor them, they therefore have honor.

I ate Melvin's cooking, and I drank his tea. We ate his pie, and I went to bed. I woke up at about two o'clock in the morning to a high-pitched sound that I could not understand. It scared me.

"Yaaaaaah, la, la, la, la." It woke me up, like cold in my blood.

"Yaaaaaah, la, la, la, la." It was coming from downstairs. I got up and, without thought, put on my coat since I didn't have a bathrobe. I went downstairs in the darkness, and I came into the kitchen. I saw through the hall that there was a light in the parlor.

"Yaaaaaah, la, la, la, la." I stopped right in the parlor door. The chair was empty, the light was on over the chair, but Melvin was kneeling next to the bed. It was his mother. She had thrown her head back, and at the top of her lungs, his mother was crying out as loud as she possibly could, "Yaaaaaah, la, la, la, la."

I would have withdrawn because it looked like Melvin knew what he was doing. But he saw me, and he smiled that lean, gentle smile and pointed at the chair as if to say, "Sit."

I sat. And I watched. And I came to understand what was going on downstairs. What Melvin was doing. I smelled it. Melvin was changing his mama's diapers. He was washing her clean. That's not all. Melvin was also singing to his mother in her own native tongue. Softly, softly, I heard the son singing to his mother a lullaby, an evening hymn.

I swear to you she was singing back. That's what she was doing. In that music, in that old song being sung unto her, I have no doubt that she was young and beautiful as an Easter morning. The voice of the song in her own mouth now was "Yaaaaaah, la, la, la, la."

Melvin was honoring his mama. Melvin was giving glory back unto God. Melvin had found glory where glory wasn't. And in that moment, I was the author who was able to sit and watch the eagle's eye one more time, to write this story and to tell you the story now and to invite you to participate.

Glory into glory. But Melvin knows that glory is more than the *kabod;* he also knows the glory of the New Testament *doxa* — which isn't weight anymore, it is light. If you follow very carefully the glory of the New Testament, you see one more additional characteristic, mercy. Certainly mercy is evident in the Old Testament as well, but it is characterized in Philippians 2 thusly; writers should have a mind as follows:

> Let this mind be in you which was also in Christ Jesus, who, though he was in the form of God, did not count this authority, this equality with God, a thing to be grasped. But made himself of no reputation, taking the form of a bondservant, and coming in the likeness of men. And being found in appearance as a man, did not count this powerful thing, but he emptied himself and took upon himself the form of a servant.

Where is the glory of God now? "Being found in human form he humbled himself." Christ humbled himself unto death, even death on the cross.

This is the final word about glory. You will find God in the places where human beings are lonely or sad or dying. But you won't find God in those places if you yourself don't also empty yourself and make of your observation a genuine participation in the lives of other people. Change their diapers.

As Thanne and I were being driven in West Africa, I saw ahead of us, a donkey, lying on the right side of the road. As we drove by, I gasped and I held my breath at what I saw: the donkey's haunch was flayed, the skin peeled back, and flies covered the blood-red areas. The Norweign woman who was driving us explained, "There is a disease that literally eats the flesh of the donkey, and the flies come. It will die soon."

About a week and a half later, we drove back the same way. I saw the donkey again. It was still lying on the ground, but now birds were landing on the haunch, and they were pecking at the flesh, the tips of their beaks red. "How can they eat the living blood of this thing," I thought. "It's dying."

When we arrived in town, the image of those birds and that donkey was still in my mind, and I mentioned it to one of the Africans.

"How can they do that? How can they kill the donkey?"

He smiled broadly at me and replied: "No, they're not killing the donkey. They are eating the maggots. They're cleansing it. They're saving the donkey, When they are done, the donkey will heal. And the donkey will live."

If you seek the glory of God, you will at some time have to walk into the wounds of the nation. If you do it wrong, it will look as if you're feeding off other people's sorrow. But if you do it right and you're willing to look with absolutely clean and clear eyes at what exists among human beings, if you're willing not to lie to yourself about the maggots, you will come with healing in your wings.

WILL CAMPBELL

Writing as Subversion

When I was called some months ago and asked to state a title for my remarks, I said off the top of my head, "What about 'Writing as Subversion'?" The more I thought about that, the better it sounded. But today, I had second thoughts about that because subversion has become increasingly difficult in this technological concentration camp in which we have placed ourselves. It's a very difficult thing — any kind of subversion — where even here, in the guest house, you have a little card that you push across to get in the door. I'm told that that not only lets you in, but it records the person who is entering the building and at what time they enter it.

How do you make a political statement anymore, really? I was able to make one not long ago. I was coming from somewhere, and I was a little out of sorts. I'm always somewhat peeved by the security system, which doesn't really do any good. I walked through those security uprights with my cane, when this fella, who has great authority vested in him now with a badge and a gun, said, "Now go and put your cane back on that roller where you put your bags through."

I walked back through, and when I got to the other end of the long roller, I put my cane on the roller and continued to stand back there. He kept motioning, "Come on down here and get your cane."

"No, I have done what you have asked me to do. Now would you bring the cane back to me."

"Can you walk without the cane?" he asked.

"Wait, a minute now," I said. "I pay someone else to pass on the state of my health. That's not your job. You just bring the cane back."

Of course, by then people were backed up behind me, clearing their throats, going to miss their airplanes. He stood there, and I saw that he wasn't going to give.

So I said, "Okay, I'll come and get the cane."

I got down on my hands and knees and, very feebly, crawled all the way down. Then I reached up and got the cane and started on down the terminal — and then gave the cane a little twirl.

"Why do you do that?" my wife asked.

"For only one reason and that is to say that I am not a robot, that I am a human being, capable of understanding rationality. This makes no sense."

"But it's the rule," she replied.

"I know it's the rule and that's why I'm breaking it."

It is only in ridiculous forms, in ridiculous things, that we can be subversive and that we can question the status quo. Now I think the cartoonists are on to something. They are able to do this better than those of us who deal with words. I remember a cartoon by Jules Pfeiffer showing a warden, a chaplain, and black man, with a noose around his neck.

"Nothing personal, Sam, it's a deterrent," says the warden.

"What does it deter?" the black prisoner asks.

"It deters you from committing any more homicides," the warden responds.

"Would it deter me if I was white?"

"Don't confuse justice with racism, Sam."

"Would it deter me if I was rich?"

"Don't confuse justice with anti-Americanism, Sam."

"Would it deter me if I wasn't black and poor and could afford a good lawyer?"

"I don't know where you got all those weird ideas, Sam."

"How many white, middle-class murderers you heard of on death row, warden?"

DROP.

And then the warden says, "So goes another enemy of free enterprise," while he is followed by a pious little priest reading scripture.

A number of people in the South — I happen to be one of them — work passionately against the death penalty, but I doubt if all of us combined can make the case quite so succinctly or convincingly as just this image.

There are others, certainly song writers, who have, I think, captured this spirit of subversion. This is not a how-to lecture on subverting the steeples or the academy or anything else. I can only, at best, speak in the spirit of this subject. But it seems to me that some of the country songwriters have caught this. I know quite a number of them but when I sit down and try to talk to them about this, they don't seem to know what I'm talking about. It's in their bones and their genes. Merle Haggard, for example, probably would not be eligible to be president of this college or even to teach sociology here, but he wrote and sang this song called "Mama's Hungry Eyes," addressing the problem of poverty. Many other songwriters too are writing similar things — songs of ethics, songs of subversion, songs about social change — and all come out of a thorough Christian milieu.

Now as a something of a wordsmith, I must confess that I fear that we have not been as successful as the cartoonists and the songwriters in capturing the essence of trying to effect social change. I assume that that's what any kind of subversion is all about — that when we write, we're trying to say something. We're trying to change people's minds, if even for an instant. Of course, it becomes a little more difficult, I think, when we're talking about literature. But what is literature? Is literature simply good books? And how good does a book have to be to qualify as literature? Who decides? How long does it take a good book to become literature? Is it dependent on the critics? (My God, I hope not.) And of course, what is Christianity? That covers a lot of territory. From three criminals hanging on crosses outside the city of Jerusalem, who Karl Barth said formed the first Christian community, to Pat Robertson and Jerry Falwell. Certainly, we would all agree that Falwell and Robertson are trying to effect social change, but does that make their words really subversive?

A book, in and of itself, does not, cannot effect social change. The words may influence people, inspire them, even compel them to various kinds of actions, but just the words on a piece of paper alone are not going to do it.

Behind literature is an authority. When we're talking about subversion, we must always be careful: what is the authority? Who's made you the troubler or the dissembler? One of the earliest bits of written words that went on to become important literature in anybody's book and to effect social change was when Moses sat down with Pharaoh and said, "We've got to have some changes. Let my people go." It was not the words, but what prompted the words that was important. It was not art for art's sake, but words growing out of an experience that Moses had. Moses had a story to tell — he had something to say, something to write about.

Now you all know the story. Moses worked for his dad-in-law and was out moving sheep from one side of the pasture to another, and he saw a bush on fire. Nothing particularly unusual about that in this arid countryside where they had a lot of fox hunters. Moses thought it might have been a campfire, and the hunters were out there waiting for the hounds. Then he saw that it was not a campfire, but it was a bush on fire. Nothing particularly unusual about that. In this dry country, some little Philistine kid thunked a roach over there, and it flamed up. (Could have happened that way — I don't say it did, but it could have.) Now Moses' life up to that point hadn't exactly been cruising down a river on a Sunday afternoon, but he was mildly daunted by a talking bush on fire, especially when the voice said, "Now Moses, ole buddy, we've got to make some changes in society. Things aren't right, and you've got to do something. My folks over in Egypt are slaves. They're being brutalized, tortured. We're going to do something about it. I want you to go over there now. I want you to go and get them out of there."

Moses, I'm sure, was just standing there lapping this up, but then he said, "Wait a minute. What if they ask me who sent me? Who told me to tell them all these things? Who do I say sent me? What is my authority?"

And the bush on fire said the most ridiculous, outrageous, absolutely nonsensical thing: "Just tell them I AM has sent you."

Moses, even more bewildered, said, "Now look, Mr. Bush, I can't tell them that. They'll send me to Menningers and shoot me full of thorazine. I've got problems enough. You're kidding."

And then Moses, being an old fox hunter and familiar with the vernacular, added, "No, now, Mr. I AM, whoever you are. It's time to pee on the fire, call the dog, and go home. I can't tell them I AM sent me."

"No, no," the voice said, "just tell them I AM who I AM sent you."

Subversion by the absurd, the utter ridiculous. I AM — come on! But thus began changes which continue to unfold to this very day.

The literature was there, and no literature so lusts after change, whether for good or evil, as religious literature because of who the authority is. Something so mysterious and awesome as to identify itself as I AM. No book of literature has ever influenced the literature that followed as much as what began when Moses began this process of negotiation with Pharaoh. Much of it violent literature, much of it highly subversive, but all of it directed at affecting what goes on within the community — not the community of believers, not our co-religionists — but in the community of humanity.

Of course, the stories of the Bible are numerous. So far I don't think any of us have tried to equal them. Whether we agree with the stories in the Bible or not, they are there and they are numerous. We think of this little fella named David. Just a little fella. Played for the Ephrathite Pee-Wee league. He had seven big brothers who played professionally for the Israelite Lions. When the Israelite Lions had a big game against the Philistine Bears who had a big defensive tackle named Goliath (I think they called him the Fridge), it was this little peewee who talked the coach into letting him into the game. He'd never been in a game like that before — played down with the little fellows — but he talked the coach into letting him into the game and said that only he would hit the Fridge. Which he did. Killed him. Cut his head off. And before he did, he invoked the same I AM, by saying "I have come against you in the name of the Lord of Hosts, the God of the army of Israel which you have defied. The Lord will put you into my power this day. I'll kill you and cut your head off and leave your carcass and the carcasses of the Philistines to the birds and the wild beasts. All the world shall know that there is a God."

The literature developed and grew and was passed on and added to. It was taught in the manner that I learned down in a little rural Baptist church called East Fork Baptist Church in south Mississippi. Mississippi, when I was growing up, was not exactly notorious for its social radicalism. But I learned from these stories a lot of important lessons, and they came in strange and subversive ways.

We were galvanized by the story of Jael and Sisera in the book of Judges. We had a wonderful old Sunday school teacher called Aunt Donie. She wasn't anybody's aunt that I know of, she was everybody's aunt. We lived down close to the Louisiana line, close to bayou country, and Aunt Donie — very colorful, fine imagination — thought Jael was a Cajun, and she told us that Jael was a cheerleader for the Ragin' Cajuns down in what used to be called Southwest Louisiana Institute in Lafayette.

You remember the story: Deborah had sent Barak and the Israelites, heavily outnumbered, out to fight the Canaanites, and Barak had put them to rout. Sisera, the commanding officer of the Canaanite forces, did what a lot of head officers do: he got his pipe and his braid cap and said, "I shall return." He bailed out. In any case, Sisera made his way to Jael's tent and Aunt Donie, as she told the story of what happened next, would skip and priss around and roll her eyes and turn around and shake her geriatric booty and talk in her Cajun accent, "Hey, big boy, come on over to my tent there. I'm going to give you something like you ain't never had before."

General Sisera, crusty old Army man that he was, thought he'd already had everything he thought you could catch — except leprosy, perhaps — so he went on in the tent.

"Now, now, baby. I'm pretty washed out right now, but I tell you what. Let me take a nap and rest up a little and we'll see."

That was all right for Jael because her agenda was not what the general thought it was. And anyway she had a headache. He was soon to have one too. A permanent one. She covered him up with an old Army blanket that she had bought at the Army surplus store and stuffed one of her husband's old T-shirts under his head, the one that said "Caesar's Palace: Gomorrah" or "See Mount Sinai," and rubbed his back and gave him a drink of buttermilk. She told him to get some rest and that she'd tell anyone who inquired that he wasn't there.

"Now you go nighty-night, baby," she cooed.

Highly subversive, you know.

When he started snoring, Jael took a ball-peen hammer and a long tent peg and drove it through his eardrums. Pretty graphic. The Holy Bible tells us that his brains oozed out on the ground, his arms and legs twitched and spasmed and he died. As well he might! This pretty little cheerleader had nailed that booger to the floor. In the name of the Lord.

We all grew quiet and attentive, knowing that all night we would toss and turn with the image of that big general lying there with a number eight spike driven through his sweetbreads, as Aunt Donie read that beautiful Song of Deborah coming immediately after this.

> For the leaders in Israel,
> for the people who answered the call, bless ye the Lord!
> Blessed above women be Jael,
> Blessed above all women in the tents.
> He asked for water, she gave him milk.
> She offered him curds in a bowl, fit for a chieftain.
> She stretched out her hand for the tentpeg,
> her right hand to hammer the weary.
> With the hammer she struck Sisera.
> She crushed his head, she struck and his brains leapt out.
> At her feet he bowed, he fell, he lay;
> at her feet he bowed, he fell;
> where he bowed, there he fell down dead.

Now there was no quesiton in anyone's mind where our sympathies lay, yet we could sense a kind of motherly empathy as Aunt Donie continued, a kind of worried look on her face.

> The mother of Sisera peered through the lattice, through the window she peered and shrilly cried, "Why are his chariots so long in coming? Why is the clatter of his chariots so long delayed?"

Well, we knew the answer, but we wouldn't say. We wouldn't say "I know, Aunt Donie — 'cuz Jael drove a tent peg through his eardrum." For you see, we knew that Aunt Donie had lost a son in the First World War, and she knew the feeling of the general's mother, wrong though he might have been. But she went on, "so perish all thine enemies, O Lord, but let all who love thee be like the sun rising in strength."

The point here is that the literature that has so influenced us all is literature rooted in great violence and in ambivalence and all kinds of subversion. There's nothing new about our talking about writing as subversion. The beautiful Song of Deborah was inspired by a tent peg through an army general's head. And the little David who would leave the Fridge with the last spasms of life spurting blood all over the East Fork Baptist Church floor was also the sweet singer of Israel, the original country picker, I maintain. Writer of beautiful country love songs and songs of praise and victory and grace.

Certainly, I would hope that our subversion will not be quite so decisive as Jael's, but you get the point. I have been involved in one social movement or another all of my adult life — but I've always been suspicious of them. I never trusted any of them. We must be ever careful that our subversion, if it is in the name of this social movement or that social movement, is done correctly. When we talk about writing as subversion, it must be in the presentation of a kind of aura, of a mood, of an attitude.

It's not that we know the answer to this question or that. God knows, I don't. What we write *about* is not the authority out of which we write. It is not I AM. What we *write* is not the authority. It may be the spirit out of which we come, but we don't have the final word: I AM is I AM. My books are not I AM. If our writings and if our writers do not reflect this, if they are not writing out of the mystery and awe of I AM, they are blasphemous.

Now the story of Jael and Sisera can be used by warmongers, or it can be used by militant feminists. One may be evil, the other may be good. But neither one is I AM. I AM is I AM.

Augustine's *City of God* is certainly an important piece of literature to us. But in that great book, among other things, he said, "He to whom authority is delegated is but the sword in the hand of he who uses it and is not himself responsible for the death he deals." Of course, as others have said, on that basis, Eichmann should have been declared innocent. And would you agree that Augustine lays the foundation for the Lutheran position that there is an earthly authority, and we shouldn't mess with it very much? We now have to ask whether Lutheranism paved the way for Hilter's jihad. All that to say, be careful when you try to effect social change.

Yet we must try. Not on the basis of certainty, not on the basis of conduct, not on the basis of creed or even belief, but on the basis of faith. And faith is not belief. So when we, with word or action, subvert, it can never be because of something we believe. It can only be in this aura of faith. Any words that come out of belief, of certainty, are tractarian and not literature.

This would seem to be a contradiction — because belief is passive and faith is active. Yet it seems to me that the only definition one can find in the New Testament, the one in Hebrews, makes the point stand: "faith is the substance of things hoped for, the evidence of things not seen." Creeds and doctrines are based on belief, not on faith. To write in defense of creed and doctrine or theology is tractarian and is never literature. To write in faith is to try and reflect the way to be, in our day, followers of the Way. Such writing leads to discipleship.

Christ had no methods that people could adopt and put to definite use, had no clearly formulated conditions upon which one could enter the kingdom of which he spoke, never demanded of the people who wished to follow him that they must first know this or that — the nature of the Trinity, the plan of salvation. Now that, ladies and gentlemen, is heresy because the role and duty of the steepled institutional church is to formulate, teach, and defend — by force if necessary — creed, doctrine, theology. In my judgment (though I've always reserved the right to be wrong about anything, including that statement), the role called the "vocation of the writer" is to subvert the steeples, as I call the structures of the institutional church. Or to subvert some institution. Because all institutions are inherently evil because all institutions are after my soul. My soul belongs not to creed, not to doctrine, not to theology, but to I AM.

Quite by accident, I ran across a book by Edith Hamilton, a woman I had only known through her fine work in antiquities and mythology, which she wrote late in her life, called *Witness to the Truth*. I want you to listen to her words. I think they're important. Forty years ago, she wrote:

> The great church of Christ came into being by ignoring the life of
> Christ. The fathers of the Church were good men, often saintly

men, sometimes men who cared enough for Christ to die for him, but they did not trust him. They could not trust the safety of his church to his way of doing things, so they set out to make the church safe in their own way. Creeds and theologies protected it from individual vagaries, riches and power protected it from outside attacks. So the church was safe, but one thing its ardent builders and defenders failed to see: nothing that lives can be safe. Life means danger, and the more the church was hedged about with confessions of faith and defended by the mighty of the earth, the feebler its life grew until today it is hardly distinguishable from any other club.

The woman spoke an important truth, particularly for writers, certainly writers of literature. The steeples have their own scribes. They train them well, and they pay them well to defend the creeds and doctrines and theologies and confessions. No one pays the writer well, so he or she is in the shaky, but enviable, position of being free. She or he can be subversive, as Edith Hamilton was subversive, if you caught the impact of what she was saying. Because what she was saying was that the institutional church from the outset was a cop-out to keep us distanced from radical discipleship. Of course, that's a redundancy because all discipleship is radical. Edith Hamilton was subversive because she was talking not about a technological concentration camp, but about the ways that creeds and theologies and doctrines put us in *theological* concentration camps which keep us from being followers of the Way, in the spirit of I AM who I AM.

We as writers at least have that. We're free. We won't get paid much for it. Or I haven't. By what authority do we subvert the structures? By the authority of I AM who I AM. Not creed, not doctrine, not theology. And yes, like the church fathers, we as writers do love Jesus. But unlike the church fathers, if we are to reflect his story aright, we must also trust him because we are not called to build anything. That trust leads to freedom, a freedom that might lead to a cross.

ELIZABETH DEWBERRY

Writing as an Act of Worship

I've always struggled with the idea that "in the beginning was the Word, and the Word was with God, and the Word was God." As a child, I was taught that that Bible verse meant, very simply, that Jesus was the Word, who had been there from the beginning, that Jesus was with God the Father, and that Jesus was also God. Just substitute "Jesus" for "Word," and that's all you need to know. Jesus as Word made flesh meant that he is the mouthpiece for God and that whatever he says is God's Word because he is God. As far as it goes, this is somewhat informative. But at that point in my life — by which I mean my whole childhood — though I couldn't have articulated the circularity of the argument, it was not fully satisfying to me because it left the central question unanswered. *What* was the word that was there in the beginning? The idea of Jesus being *A* Word, *The* Word, especially when he came out of a culture in which the name of God was the only word that could not be spoken — or, for that matter, even written — left an unarticulated question unanswered for me. Why not, for example, "In the beginning was the light, and the light was with God, and the light was God"? How about, "In the beginning was love, love was with God, love was God"? Or, "In the beginning was grace, or truth, truth was with God, and truth was God"? You could have told me that Jesus was any or all of those things made flesh, and I would have said, "Okay."

But no, it's the Word. What does that say about the nature of God? And what does it say about the nature of words?

Flash forward to the end of this talk: those questions remain unanswered. I don't want to raise expectations that I'm going to solve a theological mystery that has haunted me for most of my life. But I do have a few thoughts on the subject, and maybe they won't explain what John meant when he wrote that Bible verse, but my hope is that they'll illuminate something I've come to understand about the importance of words. And of God.

When I was a child, it was widely believed, at least in my neighborhood, that language — words — were what separated us from the animals. What was so important about being separate from animals was our collective need for affirmation, in light of Darwinian theory, that we humans have souls. We're more than just highly-evolved animals. We're made in the image of God. Proof being: words.

But in the past fifteen or twenty years, scientists have become convinced that dolphins, whales, elephants, certain birds, and some species of apes also use language. If you take a crow from Florida and put him in Michigan, the Florida crow, who was able to communicate with other Florida crows, would not be able to understand the Michigan crows. They have that complex of a learned language, complete with dialects. Though this has yet to be scientifically documented, my cat, Eddie, knows about 75 words which he uses consistently and with feeling. One means "thanks for letting me in in a prompt and courteous manner." Another means "I've been out there meowing for twenty minutes, what does a cat have to do around here?" One means, "it's three in the morning and I can't sleep so why should anybody else?"

So it's not language that separates us from animals, or more importantly, proves we have souls.

But, to my knowledge, no animal has ever written a work of fiction.

There have been at least two collections of "poetry" by dogs, and it's really quite amazing that the word "doggerel" preceded those collections. Some dogs, it appears, can rhyme, but I defy you to show me a dog who can write real poetry, those two collections notwithstanding. Barbara Bush's dog, Millie, wrote a memoir, "as dictated to Barbara Bush," and of course the widely-circulated rumor is that Barbara used a human ghost writer, and Millie just signed off on the whole project in the end. So perhaps memoirs and verse. No animal, to my knowledge, has ever written a work of fiction. Or read one. So there we have it: fiction is what separates us from the animals.

I'm sort of kidding, but sort of not. Because if being different from animals proves we have souls, that, I think, is one of the primary values of fiction: it reminds us, affirms to us, that we have souls, that we have the capacity to connect to what is divine in the universe.

For as long as I can remember, I was always very conscious of words as a way of connecting to God. Through prayer, of course, and by reading the Bible. I loved hearing Bible stories — Adam and Eve, Lot and his salty wife, Noah and the ark, the parables. I believed the Bible was the literal word of God, transcribed as if off a tape recorder by the people who wrote it. One of the best things about God, in my opinion as I understood him at the time, was that he was a great story-teller.

My first novel happened the way I imagined the Bible to have been written: I felt the words were being given to me — they were tumbling through me almost faster than I could write them down sometimes. I don't mean to imply that I had illusions that I was writing "the word of God" — far from it — but I did feel that the words were being given to me. I was just trying to get them down.

It took a long time for me to identify God as the giver. At that point in my life, I was in a hopeless, abusive marriage, but I was determined to keep the vow I'd made before God to stay married till death did us part, even if it killed me. I was very angry — at my husband, but also at God — and I felt very guilty about feeling that anger. I had stopped praying because I didn't want to *lie* to God and the only things I had to say to him were things I didn't think he'd want to hear. Things such as, "I *asked* you if I should marry this man. I prayed for a good husband throughout my entire childhood" — I really did — "and I *thought* you told me to marry him, so *what?* Were you joking? Or did you *want* this for me? Did you *want* me to go through the rest of my life being abused and not being loved?" And though that was what I had to say to God, it wasn't my idea of what *anyone* should say to God. So I said nothing.

I was in graduate school at the time, studying for my orals, and when I had to read really boring books, I would reward myself with an M&M at the bottom of every page. At some point, I realized that I didn't deserve the M&M because although my eyes had passed over every word on the page, I hadn't taken in a one of them. I was hearing words in my head, and they were drowning out the words I was trying to hear on the page. I would run to the computer that I'd gotten to write my dissertation on and put down the words in my head — just dumped them there — so that I could focus on the words on the page.

Those words eventually became my first novel, *Many Things Have Happened Since He Died,* which is about a woman in an abusive marriage whose husband uses her faith against her. Unlike me, she gets pregnant from a gang rape, where one of the rapists is her husband, and gives the baby up for adoption. Unlike my husband, hers dies, and she tells her story into a Dictaphone as a way of trying to preserve her sanity. She gets very angry with God — indeed, cusses at him — which I would never have allowed myself to do in a million years. I didn't expect the novel to be published because everybody will be happy to tell you your first novel will be rejected, so I didn't worry about what other people would think about her anger with God — or the subsequent cuss words. I did worry about what God would think of it. I'm not sure what's a more accurate way of saying this: if I *decided* God would survive, or I *realized* it, or I simply took a leap that was based on the unformed, unarticulated idea that either God could handle this woman's anger and deal with it and maybe even allow for some kind of healing, or he couldn't. I allowed myself to be true to the voice in my head. After all, it was *her* anger, not mine. All I was trying to do at that point was to get it out of my head. I wrote what I thought was a completely fictional story about a woman who I convinced myself was very different from me: different level of education, different specific set of marital problems, different job, different apartment, different city. Though she did live in Birmingham, where I grew up. Went to the same kindergarten I did. Shared a few childhood memories with me. Still her husband had different hair and a different profession from my husband. That's what you call fiction.

I cannot tell you exactly when I first realized that writing that book had been an act of prayer. In fact, it was long after the fact of writing it that I was able to articulate it in those terms. I'm very reluctant to frame it in these terms because I've seen too many times when somebody says they've got the word straight from God, and it's this: give me your money, wear this kind of clothing, fight this battle, kill those infidels. But in a very private way, it was God speaking to me, through me, listening to my feelings, connecting to my soul, keeping me alive, though I had no idea that that was what was happening at the time. My marriage was as bad as ever and getting worse, and I still had it in my head that if God were going to intervene in my life, he would fix my marriage. That he would intervene in my life by communing with me — that had never occurred to me.

While I understood on some level that something extraordinary was happening, I didn't tell anybody, not even my husband, that I was writing a novel. I didn't even think of it as a novel. And when I "got" that voice, I never once stopped to figure out what was happening. Looking back, this strikes me as odd because I'm normally a very introspective person. The only reason I can imagine that I didn't think it out was that it was a little scary. It was a very powerful experience, and it didn't fit into my definition of what happened to normal, sane people.

The book got published, which put a strange new pressure on the marriage, partly because of the reviews. I remember one in particular that said the reviewer just wanted to shake the woman character in the book and say, "Get out! Now!" Suddenly I knew there were people out there who, if they knew my situation, would want to shake me and say, "Get out! Now!" I would go to readings and conferences, and during the book signings, women would tell me the most amazing stories about their lives, which paralleled my character's in one way or another. Sometimes they'd still be in their abusive marriages, sometimes they would have gotten out; sometimes they'd still have a relationship with God, sometimes they'd have given up on that; sometimes they'd still be church-goers, sometimes they would have found a way of worshipping outside the church. And I began to see in them a whole host of alternate futures for myself.

I still wasn't willing to leave my marriage, and I still didn't think of myself as a person who prayed. On the day that my book sold, I said a very heartfelt thanks to God, but basically, I still didn't believe that God would want to listen to what I had to say. In the Psalms, David complains over and over again, and quite eloquently, that he feels like God has

99

abandoned him. In Psalm 22:14 he writes, "I am poured out like water, and all my bones are out of joint: my heart is like wax; it is melted in the midst of my bowels." But by verse 22, eight verses later, he's praising God, and by verse 24, he says that when he cried unto God, God heard. To be sure, I felt that way, poured out like water, my heart melted. Where David pretty much gets over it after a paragraph or so, however, I'd been feeling that way for years. If I had thought that I could complain for a couple hundred words and then find myself saying — and meaning — that God had lifted me up, healed my wounds, and — why not? — even smitten an enemy or two, I would have started praying. I didn't see that happening.

I thought that God and I had reached a kind of truce. Whatever had gone wrong — whatever *was going* wrong — I wasn't going to blame him, I wasn't going to expect him to fix it, but I wasn't going to thank him for it either. Any praise I might have worked up would have been fatuous. Which left silence.

Or what I thought was silence.

After writing *Many Things Have Happened Since He Died,* I wrote one book that will never be published. Wrote the whole thing from my head, as an act of the will, not an act of worship, and the characters never came to life. I still didn't understand what had happened the first time well enough to understand what the difference was. I just knew it was different.

Then I started another novel, which was eventually published as *Break the Heart of Me.* This time I became aware of the process of writing as an act of communion. I still didn't think of it as communion with God. But communion with my characters, communion with the universe, or maybe the alternate universe in which my characters existed. But especially, communion with words. My narrator was very fragile, emotionally and spiritually. It was impossible to will her into being, she would crumble when I tried. And so I discovered, or re-discovered, that the most important element of writing fiction, for me, is listening. When you listen and don't hear anything — the computer screen is blank, and the words are not coming — you have to keep listening, which is an act of faith. I began to do that because my narrator required it, though I still didn't think of it as faith in God. I thought of it as believing in my characters, in the reality of their lives and their voices and the importance of their stories. I was vaguely aware that the only way in which fictional characters are real is in some transcendent way — their reality, if it exists, is not the reality of the words on the page. Their flesh, to the extent that they have it at all, is made out of words. Not the Word made flesh, but flesh made out of words. And though the literal things that happen to them — the events in their lives, their plots — remain fictional, they also have the capacity to transcend that literal truth and communicate universal human truth, truths of the human heart. In that limited sense, then, I was becoming more aware of the spiritual dimension of what was happening.

I purposefully put that in the passive tense — "what was happening," rather than "what I was doing" — because there is no tense that implies both, and though I was an active participant, the most important part of the process was one in which I felt that I was following my character's lead, learning from her how to tell her story, receiving a gift.

After I finished writing *Break the Heart of Me,* but before it was published, I remember making one conscious prayer. I had been to a conference. I was in an airport, changing planes, passing signs with planes going to Nashville, Mexico City, Los Angeles, Detroit; I would have preferred to go to any of those places than home. I wanted to get on a plane and go to a place, any place, where I could disappear and not live my own life anymore.

Instead I got on my plane, headed for Columbus, Ohio, where I was living at the time, and to keep from bursting into tears on the plane, I started praying. I said, "God, the Bible says that if a person seeks you with all their heart, they will find you. Well, maybe you don't think I did it with all my heart — obviously, you don't — and maybe I wasted my heart on something else, but I don't have anything left. I can't *try* any more. So now, if you want this to happen, you find me."

I still don't have as fast a turnaround time on my prayers as David did, but about a year later, my marriage pretty much collapsed in on itself — not violently, not dramatically, not even sadly. I've never kept vigil with someone who was dying a long and excruciating death, but it felt something like that to me. By the time it ended, I had already spent many years going through the stages of mourning: denial and isolation, anger, bargaining with God, and depression, and reached the final stage, acceptance. It was a loss, but it was also a relief.

I remember thinking at some point, nobody who loves me, including God, would want me to stay in this marriage. In that one thought, I realized that I had come to a new definition of love and a new understanding of God.

I felt like I had been hanging on by my fingernails to a concept of a mean, petty, and unforgiving God. I had believed for a very long time, indeed all my life, that if I chose to break the vow I'd made before God, I would be, in effect, divorcing God. But when I finally let go, I didn't experience the long and terrible fall into godless chaos that I'd once expected. Instead, I found myself in a place where I'd never been before. The amazing thing about it was that God — the same God who had been with me throughout the writing of my first two published novels — was still there. Love was still there. The possibility of connecting with other people, with God, with my own soul — it was all there.

This is starting to sound a little bit like a testimonial, which is not my intention at all. To quickly finish the story: I fell in love and got married again. It was only in that context that I was able to understand what had happened to me before as I wrote my first two published novels: as encounters with God, as worship. My point is not that I went from a bad marriage to a good one — that it's all about *men* — but I went from a relationship where there was no love to one where there is. And it *is* about love. It's about connecting to the other — the other person in the marriage, but also about moving through life as a writer connecting to the universe, connecting to God. God is love which is what connects us to each other.

Eight years passed between the publication of my second novel and my third, and during those eight years, I started writing plays. When I heard another playwright point out that plays had started out as acts of worship, people acting out Bible stories, and that she hoped her plays tapped into that tradition, something clicked for me. I was now in a loving marriage where I had been rebuilding my faith in love and therefore in God. I began to redefine worship in a much bigger way than I had before. Worship, at its heart, is about connecting with the divine. It's that simple — and that complicated. It can happen in church. But it can happen in a theatre, and it can happen in front of the computer screen as well.

Do you remember the passage in *Our Town* where Rebecca Gibbs says a preacher sent a letter to a sick child and addressed it to "Jane Crofut, the Crofut Farm, Grover's Corners, Sutton County, New Hampshire, United States of America, Continent of North America, Western Hemisphere, the Earth, the Solar System, the Universe, the mind of God"? I've always loved that passage, though I used to find it rather whimsical. But there are many legitimate physicists working today who think the whole field of physics is headed toward an understanding that the universe we live in is a projection of or is contained by some other, transcendent reality. Physicists are generally very reluctant to identify what that other reality is — some say it might be another universe with another set of dimensions. Virtually all of them agree that whatever it is, it's not limited by time and space, which suggests, to me, something eternal and omni-present. What if Thornton Wilder, speaking through Rebecca Gibbs, was right, and that transcendent reality that physicists are scrambling to figure out the mathematical proof for *is* the mind of God? Maybe that *is* where we all ultimately exist: in the mind of God.

I like to think so. It explains a lot. It explains where archetypes come from, for example, much more eloquently than saying they're part of the collective unconscious. It also explains where fiction — and all art, for that matter — comes from.

Jesus said that the greatest commandment was, "Love the Lord thy God with all thy heart, and with all thy soul, and with all thy mind." Though I can't summarize everything he meant by that, for fiction writers, or for me, anyway, it means, Be passionately engaged with the universe. Write with all your heart, from the depths of compassion and empathy that you can find for your characters. Write with all your mind: pay attention to structure and story and detail and craft. Write with all your soul: the place where God dwells and that therefore connects you, through him, to every other person in the history of this planet, to those people who lived long lives, to those who barely lived at all, to those who lived before you, to those who will come after you, and — I'm not trying to sound strange, but here's how I see it — also to those whose lives are imaginary, fictional, existing only in the minds of their writers and readers. He's known and loved them all, and when you are writing from that space, your soul, you have the privilege and the obligation to tell the stories that are given to you as truly and as well as you can, to use those holy and awesomely powerful things called words, to create flesh, flesh that, in the same way that John described Jesus, the Word made flesh, is full of grace and truth.

Understanding writing as worship, understanding that what I'm doing when I'm writing, at my best, is connecting at the level of my soul to the universe, to God, to everything else that is in the mind of God, including the souls of my characters and the souls of my readers — that is, for me, the basis for hope that my characters' individual experiences can transcend their specific realities of race and gender and ethnicity and nationality and religion to express universal human truth. If that weren't possible, if we were each stuck in our own skins, unable to enter into the lives of others, to understand their pain, to connect with their yearnings, to feel their humanity and touch their souls, I think we would eventually destroy each other. If we remain unable to realize our deepest connection to each other, we will, to that same extent, continue to go to war with each other and ignore each other's suffering, even when that suffering reaches the levels of famines and epidemics and genocides and holocausts. But I also believe that through fiction, through words, we can transcend the limits of our own individual existences and connect in profound ways, to each other, to the universe, to God. That is what makes words holy. That is how words are like God. It's what I hope and pray to do in my work. And it's what I hope and pray for this planet.

RON HANSEN

....

Faith and Fiction

K indergarten. Omaha. 1952. After morning recess, our Dominican teacher, Sister Martha, assembled the kindergartners in our dank basement classroom in Holy Angels Grade School and told us we'd be putting on a Christmas pageant for our parents. She then scanned our faces while reading from a sheet of paper that named whom we'd portray. Cynthia Bash, the prettiest girl, got to play Mary, and John Kocarnik, the tallest boy, got to play Joseph, choices I probably would have made if asked. But then three boys I found, at best, annoying were assigned the roles of Magi, who I knew got to wear the fanciest costumes, and a handful of girls were joined into choirs of angels, and finally my twin brother, Rob, and some trouble-makers and oafs were handed the no-line jobs of shepherds. And that was it. My name had not been mentioned. Of all the kindergartners at Holy Angels Grade School — and there were plenty in that age of baby boom — I was the only one without a role in the Christmas play. I felt ashamed that I'd offended God in such a way that he was forbidding me a part. And I was afraid that I'd flunked kindergarten as I'd seen some whiny and incontinent children do. Wanting to know for sure just how bad my situation was, I got the gumption to walk up to Sister Martha at playtime and while fighting off tears told her she'd left me out. To my astonishment, she was not irritated at me. She seemed, instead, embarrassed that she'd given a role to one of the Hansen twins and not the other. She probably had intended to be the one to recite the story of the nativity from the Gospel according to Luke, but on seeing my worried face she was inspired by pity to say, "Well, we'll need a narrator. You can be Saint Luke."

The last shall be first indeed. Classmates looked at me with jealousy when I confided to them about it, and even my folks seemed impressed and surprised that Sister had honored me with such a hallowed role. My kindergarten friends were each given little scraps of paper on which their lines had been printed out in order to practice them aloud with an older child or parent, but I handed over to my mother a full page of Indian-head tablet that was filled with handwriting I couldn't yet read.

We'd sit at the dining room table at night and she'd read a sentence from chapter two of Luke until I could repeat it, and then she'd go on to another sentence. I have a sense of the great language acquisition gifts of children when I recall how little we actually practiced those lines before I had them fast in my head. Meanwhile my father was proudly predicting that I'd perhaps be a great public speaker or politician one day. Dwight Eisenhower had just been elected president and one of his speeches was featured on television. My father pointed to Ike and said, "Maybe that'll be Ronnie when he grows up." All I could think of was that he meant I'd someday be horribly dull and bald.

On the night of the Christmas pageant, as a hundred people found their seats on folding chairs, I stood off to the side in a turban made from one of my sister's pink towels and in my own striped bathrobe from home, but unfortunately without the filthy charcoal mustache and beard that my friends who were shepherds wore, so my pleasure was incomplete. While the kindergarten girls sang "O Little Star of Bethlehem," I saw my folks grinning hopefully at their twin sons while my eleven-year-old sister Gini frowned at me in her Don't screw this up, I have friends here way. And then with the song finished, and Sister nodding me forward, I walked to the front of the audience and in the high scream of a four-year-old projecting his voice, I announced, "At that time, there went forth a decree from Caesar Augustus that a census of the whole world should be taken!" On and on I went, reciting sentences I didn't fully understand. "And it came to pass while they were there, that the days for her to be delivered were fulfilled. And she brought forth her firstborn

Son, and wrapped Him in swaddling clothes, and laid Him in a manger, because there was no room for them in the inn." When I finished I felt Sister Martha's sigh of relief that I hadn't forgotten anything, and I watched as my friends completed their histrionic pantomime of stargazing, childbirth, and adoration. The Magi sang, "We Three Kings" and we all joined together on "Hark, the Herald Angels Sing," and then it was over and the families applauded their own.

I frequently have been asked when it was that I first had the impulse to be a fiction writer, and I find myself often thinking of that kindergarten play and of those hundred grown-ups and older children who I knew weren't listening to me but to those fascinating and archaic words, "betrothed," "swaddling," "manger." I felt the power that majestic language had for an audience, that they'd been held rapt not just because of what Luke and I reported but because of the way we said it.

Luke is the most writerly of the Evangelists. Embellishing, adapting, and harmonizing, he does what fiction writers do to hook and hold his audience and get his message across. Even his impatience with other accounts of Christ's life is the sign of a genius whose own faith has found too little affirmation in the accounts of varying worth being offered at the time, for the first paragraph of Luke's Gospel makes it clear that it is a fusion of faith and historical narrative handed down to him by the followers of Jesus and those fervent heralds of the good news whom he calls "ministers of the word." Luke saw it as his vocation to be one of them, to examine what was being said, to "follow all things closely," and to put order and the hard eye of probability on what was possibly for him a frustrating hodgepodge of reminiscences, miracle stories, sayings of Jesus, a passion narrative, and theological interpretations, as well as hearsay, misunderstandings, and heretical fabrications.

A high order of craft and planning and mastery of the storyteller's art is plainly evident throughout all the Gospels, and yet though they are, like fictions, things made or formed (the Latin *fictio* means shaped or feigned), they have their foundation in a Christ whom their authors were willing to die for. Yet one need not have faith in Christ to be influenced by his story, for we have seen many nineteenth- and twentieth-century novels with no religious pretensions whatsoever whose trajectories imitate that of the life of Jesus of Nazareth.

We generally find in them an initiating incident or graced event that incites the protagonist to a quest for a higher goal. With the rising action of the plot, he or she often gathers friends who share in the quest, and ever greater successes are achieved, obstacles are overcome, enemies are sundered, until a final triumph seems assured. But there is a forbidding crisis in which the protagonist is offered the choice to go ahead in spite of the dangers, or to follow another path, and in that high noon of the soul, the protagonist faces the future abandoned and alone. And then, when all seems lost, by dint of the hero's force of will, a greater victory than seemed attainable is finally won.

Christ's story is so primary to our literature that the eyes of faith can find it in a thousand variations. Look at William Faulkner's *A Fable,* Harper Lee's *To Kill a Mockingbird,* John Irving's *A Prayer for Owen Meany,* and Tom Wolfe's *The Electric Kool-Aid Acid Test;* or, in film, *Mr. Smith Goes to Washington, Cool Hand Luke,* and *Shane.*

We look to fiction for self-understanding, for analogies of encounter, discovery and decision that will help us contemplate and change our lives. And so it was for Jesus himself as he formulated his parables. Each of them is Christ's symbolic way of telling us what has been revealed to him in prayer about the Mystery we call God, about Christ's ministry in the world, and of the Father's will for us all.

When we chance upon a metaphor or simile in our reading, we may not notice that we are first halted by the obvious falsity of the statement — the heavyweight boxer Muhammad Ali did not truly "float like a butterfly, sting like a bee" — and then are forced to find connections and similarities we may not have noticed. And because there is no real equivalence, no meshing of objects, our interpretation is never finished, only abandoned. And so it is with parables.

Whenever necessary throughout the Gospels, Jesus offers the faithful proverbs and ways of praying and rules of right conduct and signs of his healing power. But his favorite method of teaching seems to have been in parables because stories so well fuse the feelings of immanence and transcendence that are the two primary qualities of religious experience.

Often in Christ's familiar and very concrete parables there is an upsetting element — a harvest like no other, or homicides in a vineyard —

that skews quotidian reality to such an extent that we are obliged to undertake a new way of thinking, to find in our paltry circumstances occasions for surprise, revelation, and self-transcendence.

Even at his last supper, in the Gospel of John, Jesus teaches his friends wholly through metaphors and cryptic turns of phrase. Everything is obliquely stated; it is theology through conundrum. We can practically feel his disciples squirming in uneasiness and wonder. "Where I am going, you cannot follow me now; but you will follow me afterward." "I am the true vine, and my Father is the vinegrower. He removes every branch in me that bears no fruit. Every branch that bears fruit he prunes to make it bear more fruit." "A little while, and you will no longer see me, and again a little while, and you will see me." And finally, "I have said these things in figures of speech. The hour is coming when I will no longer speak to you in figures, but will tell you plainly of the Father."

Jesus was, in Max Weber's terminology, both an ethical prophet — one who outlines rules of conduct for his followers — and an exemplary prophet — one who presents his own life as an example to his followers. And he is never so exemplary as in his Passion. The hour comes when Christ says he will tell us plainly of the Father, but instead he offers us the mysteries of his crucifixion and resurrection. We are told plainly that he cannot hit the nail on the head, that the Word is inexpressible, that it is a burgeoning, a florescence, an opening out into further interpretation. Were the Gospels more biographical, our thinking about Christ would have been more confined, conservative, and hopelessly bound up in human predilections and prejudices.

We instead have a kind of myth, a history full of facts and truths but also a fiction formed with harmony, proportion, and beauty, and fully at ease with uncertainties, metaphor, and poetic fancy.

We have a tendency to separate heaven and earth, soul and body, mind and matter, the unseen and the seen. Myth unites them. Myth honors our intuitions, frees our imaginations, mediates between those things we can explain and those things we cannot explain but in our heart of hearts know. We fall in love unreasonably. We act on premonitions, inklings, and perplexing needs. Who among us have held time in our hands? And yet we know we are changed by it. Our lives are filled with mysteries and miracles, coincidence, hunches, and revelations, feelings that have no basis in anything we can put a finger on. Myth pays homage to those intangibles, acknowledging that they are as fully a part of our experience as the tulip glass of Veuve Clicquot we had the other night.

In the ninth of his "Eleven Addresses to the Lord," the poet John Berryman says of the Holy Being, "an old theologian/asserts that even to say You exist is misleading." Our fragile human language, attenuated by imprecision, overuse, and false associations, is not up to the hard task of talking about the infinite. Anthony DeMello has even adduced that any image we have of God is more unlike him than like him. We seem to be far better off if we try to determine who the Creator is by considering creation, by finding parables of holiness and grace in the world around us.

Saint Ignatius of Loyola was doing just that when, in his "Contemplation to Attain the Love of God" in the Spiritual Exercises, he urged retreatants to consider "how God dwells in creatures: in the elements giving them existence, in the plants giving them life, in the animals conferring upon them sensation, in man bestowing understanding. So He dwells in me and gives me being, life, sensation, intelligence; and makes a temple of me, since I am created in the likeness and image of the Divine Majesty."

In finding God in all things, Saint Ignatius was possibly inspired by the postresurrection appearances of Christ to his friends in which they so often mistook who he was: a gardener near the sepulcher, a vagabond on the road to Emmaus, a lone figure on the shore of the Sea of Tiberias offering the fishermen free advice about where they should cast their nets. Christ seemed to be teaching his friends that he will be with them always, as he promised, but in the world at large and in the faces of strangers.

A faith-inspired fiction has a fondness for humanity and finds cause for celebration in the beauties of the natural world. A faith-inspired fiction is ever aware that we are on holy ground. And at the same time that fiction shares in the communion expressed in the famous lines of Reverend John Donne, that "any man's death diminishes me, because I am involved in Mankinde; and therefore never send to know for whom the bell tolls; it tolls for thee."

In the finest of our fictions, whether it be Willa Cather's *Death Comes for the Archbishop* or Walker Percy's *The Moviegoer,* we have a sense of humanity functioning as it generally does, but at a higher and inspired level where harmonies are revealed, order is discovered, the questions that lie hidden in our hearts are given their just due. We think, if we are Christians, that this is what it is to live fully in the presence of grace. We glimpse, if only through a glass darkly, the present and still-to-come kingdom of God.

And it seems to me we have it as an obligation to witness to what God has revealed, holding to the testimony of Psalm 40, where it is written:

> I have told the glad news of deliverance in the great congregation;
> see, I have not restrained my lips, as you know, O LORD.
> I have not hidden your saving help within my heart,
> I have spoken of your faithfulness and your salvation;
> I have not concealed your steadfast love and your faithfulness
> from the great congregation.

(Ps. 40:9-10)

Writing stories is a good way of doing that, but how to avoid homiletics, the shoehorning in of religious belief, the sabotage of the fictional dream by forcing one's characters to perform the role of mouthpieces? So-called Christian fiction is often in fact pallid allegory, or a form of sermonizing, or is a reduction into formula, providing first-century, Pauline solutions to oversimplified problems, sometimes yielding to a Manichean dualism wherein good and evil are plainly at war, or offering as Christianity conservative politics. We cannot call a fiction Christian just because there is no irreligion in it, no skepticism, nothing to cause offense, for such a fiction, in its evasions, may have also evaded, in Karl Rahner's words, "that blessed peril that consists in encountering God."

A faith-inspired fiction squarely faces the imponderables of life, and in the fiction writer's radical self-confrontation may even confess to desolation and doubt. Such fiction is instinctive rather than conformist, intuitive rather than calculated; it features vital characters rather than comforting types, offers freedom and anomaly rather than foregone conclusions, invites thoughtfulness not through rational argument, but through asking the right questions. A faith-inspired fiction is, as Anthony DeMello has said of story, the shortest distance between human understanding and truth.

While it may be hard to believe now, in the late nineteenth century Cardinal John Henry Newman was forced to defend having literature courses at all in a Catholic university. His argument was "if Literature is to be made a study of human nature, you cannot have a Christian Literature. It is a contradiction in terms to attempt a sinless Literature of sinful man. You may gather together something very great and high, something higher than Literature ever was; and when you have done so, you will find that it is not Literature at all."

Writing with faith is a form of praying. Evelyn Waugh maintained prayer ought to consist of adoration, contrition, thanksgiving, and supplication. And so it is in the writing of fiction, in which authors can adore God through their alertness to creation and to the Spirit that dwells in their talent; confess their own faults by faithfully recording the sins, failings, and tendencies of their characters; offer thanksgiving through the beauty of form, language, and thought in their creations; and beseech by obeying the rule of Saint Benedict which states: "Whatever good work you begin to do, beg of God with most earnest prayer to perfect it."

PAUL SCHRADER

An Interview by Garry Wills

GARRY WILLS: When I had dinner with you about a year ago, almost the first question you asked me was "Do you still go to church?" When I replied, "Yes, do you?" you said you also went, but that your father wouldn't count it because it's Episcopalian. Since we're here at Calvin College where it all began, and since so much of what you encountered here has stayed with you throughout your work, perhaps the best way to start is for you to give a brief spiritual autobiography of how you got from Calvin to where you are now religiously.

PAUL SCHRADER: Well, I'm an Episcopalian now. I was raised in the Christian Reformed Church in religion that was all guilt and no doctrine and no ritual, and now I go to a church that is all ritual and no guilt. It's hard, and very strange, for me to be saying this to this crowd because usually I say these sorts of things to people who can't call me on it. Here I have to choose my words a little more carefully. That old environment never goes away. It doesn't matter how far or fast you run, you don't outrun that childhood. Those spiritual issues continue to nag until you find different ways to deal with them or *not* deal with them. And you just keep circling around it. John Wayne once said, "I don't like God much once I get him under a roof." I've really been very, very wary of institutionalized religion because I feel it has often been the enemy of spirituality. I do know, though, how I got out of here: the same way a bullet gets out of a gun. How I circled back around I'm not quite sure.

Also, in the business I'm in, you really do have to cover your tracks if you want to do anything that has any religious or spiritual quotient. The lure of movies, the lure of kineticism, is probably inherently anti-spiritual. If you are going to fool around with spiritual issues, not propaganda — then you have to be really tricky. Often, to quote Goddard, no good film is successful for the right reason, and that's true in many ways. You have to figure out how to make the film successful for the wrong reasons, if that makes sense.

GW: I am interested in your comment about doctrine and ceremony. A friend of mine who's Episcopalian said to me one time, "We Episcopalians can believe anything, but we rarely do." I'm intrigued by your comment that you think cinema is intrinsically anti-spiritual, because your great book, *Transcendental Style in Film,* was written precisely about spirituality in the cinema of Bresson, Ozu, and Dreyer.

PS: A lot of what those directors do is anti-cinematic, particularly Bresson, who slows everything down. He gets rid of psychological realism, which is the ground stone of filmmaking. Bresson slows the whole process down, not using movie stars and working totally against what people find appealing about movies. In so doing, he was able to find a spiritual path. This is a very heavy and tricky subject, but I don't really see film as a very useful tool for someone who wants to create religious, transcendental, or spiritual art.

GW: You talked about transcendence in those films. It seems — to me at least — that you achieve a kind of transcendence in *Mishima,* and he does string himself out of the mundane world. Is there not transcendence there?

PS: I won't deny that if that's what you're after. *Light Sleeper* is the film of mine most directly aiming at transcendence. The film has a cycle of songs written by Michael Bean of a Christian group called The Call. I use those lyrics to show where I'm going. The last line of that movie is: "standing at the door/the door is open wide/now I seal my fate/now I walk inside." That's about as close as you can get before they start throwing things at you.

GW: In that film, La Tour [Willem Dafoe] seems to have escaped his own addiction, but he seems to pull his ex-wife down. Is that a necessary cost that his journey exacts?

PS: No, I would say that's expeditious plotting. When I write character studies, I'm really not that interested in who did what to whom. You have to put enough plot in so viewers don't get distracted, but you can't put so much plot in that they think it's about plot. You have to let them know that you really don't care who killed the senator in there; otherwise they lose interest. So it's a tricky little balance on when to interject plot, when audiences get interested in the plot, and when to start pulling back on plot.

GW: Do you find you need to have someone who understands your spiritual concerns to act in your movies?

PS: No, and I think it's better to back them away from it because you can't play it. You have to *be* it. Scorsese and I had dinner with Nick Cage before shooting *Bringing Out the Dead* and said, "All this religious stuff, just ignore it. It's on your tool belt, but the moment you call attention to it, it is no longer effective." You can't let actors try to play that stuff. You cannot make the characters move; you have to make the audience move. That's the trick to any kind of spiritual art. That was Bresson's whole gimmick, holding back so long that all of a sudden when he made his jump you moved — and you filled up the hole. Art fails when I have to do the work for the audience. There is no art in *Erin Brockovich*. You watch it, and you see it happen. Art comes into play when something is withheld from you, and you supply it and become part of the process. As a film-maker I can walk up to the door, and I can talk about the door, but I can't walk through. The artist has to be Moses at this point, staying behind so the viewer can walk through the door. That's why actors can't do it.

GW: My students found all kinds of theological themes in your work, maybe more than you intended to put there. They're especially taken with your filming of Pinter's *The Comfort of Strangers*. In that film, the tempter, as he's written, is a kind of swinging guy, with bare chest and chains, and all that kind of thing. And you changed him and put him in white clothes. Why?

PS: This film is a really nasty little bit of goods. The story is from a novel by Ian McEwan and adapted by Harold Pinter about one couple that gets waylaid by another couple in Venice. It's a nasty little story and distasteful in its notions of men and women, and it's quite sexual. I had to make the film look so beautiful and so appealing that viewers wouldn't realize how deeply corrupt and rotten it was until they were involved. Everything looked as glamorous as possible: the sets, the wardrobe, the hair, and everything. Dante Spinotti shot it, who's one of the top beauty cinematographers in the world. That's a trick of identification if you're trying to get an audience to identify with something that they don't want to identify with. That's how you do something of art: get people to go where they don't want to go.

Take a character like Travis Bickle [Robert De Niro] from *Taxi Driver* who is beyond the pale of normal identification, a psychopath, full of anger. How do you get people to identify with that guy? One way is narration. Give him enough thoughts that the audience shares so they *think* he's sort of like them. Hold back on his more unpleasant sides until later. Also, very importantly, show no other reality but only the world as he sees it. Finally, after watching Bickle's world for an hour, viewers start getting interested and see the world as he sees it. Then more interesting things can happen. The narration starts to fall away because it isn't needed anymore because the audience is there. And Travis can do more unpleasant things, and the audience will follow him. That's one of those tricks that pulls viewers into identifications with what they do not think proper. The main character in *Light Sleeper* is a drug dealer, a very perverse idea on my part. Take the most vilified character in our culture and make him the protagonist — the midlife crisis of a drug dealer. If somebody identified with a character they think is beneath identification, then they have opened themselves up a crack. The door is slightly open, who knows what goes in and out? The strangest things happen once the door has opened even a little.

GW: How much is the director — and a screenwriter — conscious of everything he puts into a work?

PS: Oh, you're conscious of a lot of it because everything is decision. Whether to expose a little bit of leg is a decision. Nothing on screen just happens — nothing. The door is a color for a reason. If a character puts his hand there instead of there, there was a thought behind that. In making a film, the director makes maybe two to three thousand decisions a day, and those very quickly: to do another take, yes or no, or maybe to move that light a little bit. And you're making them at Gatling-gun speed. That's why it's so much fun and there's so much adrenaline. When it's all over and you sit in the editing room trying to put it together you realize that this is really you. It's the culmination of all those decisions, many of which were made with such speed that you didn't have time to consider the alternative. You just say, "Okay, do that." That's where the personality, the upbringing, the education, all of those secret attributes — sexual, psychological, and so on — seep into the work.

GW: Is your freedom inhibited by the fact that you're sometimes using intractable materials — actors, writers, cameramen, and so on?

PS: Well, primarily budget.

GW: Is it sometimes difficult to shape the religious dimension of a film?

PS: *Bringing Out the Dead* recently came out. There's a lot of religious stuff in it, even though I thought I had gotten most of it out. Then I started reading the reviews, and, boy, I realized there's still a lot of it left. The book was written by a paramedic who was Roman Catholic so there was a lot of religious stuff in it before I walked in the room. I was trying to pull stuff out. I have to admit it does bother me when audiences constantly look for Christ figures. I don't care for Christ figures much, and I don't like this notion that a character is somehow more resonant if he's standing under a crucifix than if he's standing under an arc. We are all Christ figures. We are all resonant, and all that gimmickry about symbolism is only an obstruction to true revelation. It is harder to see the Christness in the average person when he is standing under a crucifix because you see a symbol and not the man anymore.

GW: Do you find it's harder to get money and backing because you have the reputation of being a religiously concerned artist?

PS: Yes. And it's harder as you get older, and it's harder as our times become more trivial. So all these events conspire against you. I've been raising money for about six months now, and it is harder. Yet somehow the films do get made. I don't make a living directing films. Right now I'm writing a script for Brad Pitt so that I can have enough money to direct a film for Steve Martin because I have to throw my salary into the pot in order to get the film made. So it is a struggle, but considering the alternative, which is becoming a director-for-hire or having a job, it's easier to fight. It's so invigorating to wake up in the morning knowing that nobody wants you to do what you want to do. It's like a big blast of coffee that gets everything going.

GW: You have had a job in a sense. You've taught, and I know that you take that very seriously. Do you find your students, would-be screen writers, willing to undertake the same kinds of struggle?

PS: No, there has been a sea-change. In the quality of filmmakers, filmgoers, and there's a new sensibility afoot. One of the reasons *Bringing Out the Dead* feels a little old is because it is driven by an older sensibility. Scorsese and I are both products of the 50s and the 60s. In one way, the style is extremely liberating. In another way it's very, very empty. It's the ironic hero. All my life has been dedicated to the existential hero, and the existential hero seems to have come to the end of his path, replaced by the ironic hero. The ironic hero is a very, very interesting cat, but he doesn't have much resonance.

GW: Who are examples of the ironic hero in modern novels?

PS: It's the deconstructed hero, the self-referential hero, the hero who has quotation marks around him and lets you in on the joke. David Letterman is ironic, Johnny Carson is existential. Painting, drama, and architecture have all dealt with deconstruction. Movies are just now, finally, in the last ten years, dealing with deconstruction. That's because movies are the most retrograde of all the arts. Whatever happens in the arts always happens last in the movies because it has the most populist base. By the time it happens in the movies it has happened in the whole culture.

GW: Do you find that the commercial structure of Hollywood is progressively stifling creativity so that a real crisis is at hand.

PS: If you believe that, then you sort of believe in the "good old days." I don't, although it is surprising to look at films from the 70s. Imagine living through a period where people made films like that on a regular basis. But no, it's always hard to do different or good work, and every year some extraordinary films do come through. All of a sudden there's a Paul Thomas Anderson, an original powerful voice. And a lot of it now, with the younger kids, is driven by MTV and commercials. It's not grad-school driven anymore. I was talking recently to Francis Coppola, whose nephew is Spike Jones, the director of *Being John Malkovich* and only a high school graduate. Francis is the epitome of the film school mentality, but he thought it amazing that all these young kids skip film school and jump right into MTV, commercials, or video games.

GW: Your God's lonely man is the existentialist hero. Some people like Graham Greene have been criticized for creating a world in which it seems like the only way to God is to become a total corrupt sinner, at least for awhile. What do you answer to that objection?

PS: There are as many paths as there are people. Anne Lamott is going to read tonight. Her book *Traveling Mercies* suggests that you have to hit bottom before you can stand up. I don't think that's necessarily true. It's a little easier when you hit bottom, especially if you hit hard, because then you know exactly where you are and there's only one way out. But no, I think that subscribes to a melodramatic notion of faith.

JAN KARON

The Miracle and the Myth

In America, we have been busy turning our little towns into big cities and our country lanes into four lanes. That's okay — we're a young nation and that is what young nations do. But more and more, we like to dream about the small town, the village where everybody knows everybody and where the old values still work. Still, that the Mitford novels — about small-town life — have become bestsellers is, to this author, an absolute miracle. A miracle. Who would want to read books with no cussing, no murder, no mayhem, and no sex?

I was doing a book event in the Midwest when a woman and her husband came up to me, and she said, "Miss Karon, I just love your books, but I can't get my husband, Harold, to read a single one because, you know, I mean, like, well, they don't have any sex in them." I just looked at Harold, and I said, "Harold, honey, I'm going to tell you something. There's plenty of sex in my books. You just don't know where to find it." I'm going to quote to you verbatim the lines of the sex scene that I most enjoyed writing. It was in *These High, Green Hills*. Here it is: "She turned to him, smiling, in the dark." That's about as good as it gets, isn't it?

Now how can something so innocuous as these Mitford books sell ten million copies? I think there was a wide vein of readers out there who were just waiting for someone to write a book about them. About *their* dreams and *their* lives and *their* values. Aaron Copland composed a most wonderful piece of music, *Fanfare for the Common Man.* My Mitford books are the fanfare for the common American man, woman, and child because they look at ordinary lives and see something extraordinary and dramatic and full of feeling and worthy to be observed. Worthy, in fact, of honor.

As for the language in the Mitford books, the writer Jean-Henri Fabre said, "My conviction is that we can say marvelous things without using a barbarous vocabulary."

People ask if Mitford is real. It's real in the very same way that *To Kill a Mockingbird* is real. Or that *Peyton Place* is real. Or *Uncle Tom's Cabin* or *Gone with the Wind* or *Pride and Prejudice* or *Lorna Doone.* Mitford, of course, does not actually exist on a map. With one exception. There is a Mitford in America. It's an unincorporated town, fifteen miles north of Columbia, South Carolina. Because it's unincorporated, you probably don't often see it on a map. The town consists of the following: a Baptist church and a barbeque restaurant. What more do you need, if you really think about it?

I also want to assure you that Mitford is real because I not only have lived and still have a home in a Mitford — which is Blowing Rock, North Carolina — but I have visited Mitfords all over the country. Time and time again, I've ended up in Mitford. For example, in Connecticut, I was speaking in the town hall, and the people came with cookies still warm from their ovens. This is the truth. With baskets of flowers with dew still on the roses in their arms. That was wonderful. I've been to a church where a twelve-year-old boy stood in for Dooley Barlowe and sang Miss Sadie's favorite hymn, "I Know That My Redeemer Liveth," with all the sweetness of an angel.

But I think people love my books because when they open a Mitford book they find themselves. You find your aunt and uncle. Your brothers and sisters. Your neighbors, the people you grew up with and go to church with — or don't go to church with. You find that you know these people. In this way, Mitford is about familiarity. And familiarity is about comfort. And comfort is about being able to relax. You never have to wonder in a Mitford book about some mayhem that might happen around the next corner. You can just relax. People have said to me, "I read your books at night and just fall right asleep." I bet there's not another author who wants to be told such a thing as that. I'm proud to hear it.

Maybe, just maybe, there's a Peyton Place somewhere in a tiny corner of Mitford. But if indeed there is, let another author go there. The moon after all has two sides: a dark side and a bright side. Even though there are nuances of darkness in my books — alcoholism and child abuse, depression, diabetes — I lean toward the bright side because the bright is just as real as the dark. I write about reality in the same way that Stephen King or Henry Miller writes about reality. I like how André Gide put it, "Know that joy is rarer, more difficult, and more beautiful than sadness. Once you make this all-important discovery, you must embrace joy as a moral obligation."

I also write to let readers know something I learned for myself in a very personal way, nearly twenty-five years ago. And that is simply this: God really does love us. That's the kernel around which all my stories are wrapped. It's the single greatest truth I know and so, I share it in book after book. C. S. Lewis observed, "I believe in Christianity as I believe that the sun has risen, not only because I see it but because by it, I see everything else." There isn't any way I can't write about Christianity in my books because by it, I see everything else. Consider that a cup of coffee is the human individual and the shot of brandy is the Christian faith. One pours the brandy into the coffee, and voila! they can't be separated again. They *can't* be separated. My faith can't be separated from my work. Even if I never mention the name of Jesus Christ, I can't hide from you who I am and what I'm about as an author. In truth, the work that has no faith is, for me, not a whole work. It may be an amusing or credible or clever work, but not a whole work.

Faith is a critical and urgent and necessary component of human wholeness. For those of you who have not made a commitment — and it *is* a commitment — to know Jesus Christ as your Lord and Savior, your all-in-all, I would acknowledge two important truths that Blaise Pascal, a young Frenchman and a very brilliant mathematician, once wrote: "There is God-shaped vacuum in the heart of every person which can only be filled by God, made known through Jesus Christ." Higher education can't fill it. The love of our wives or husbands or sweethearts or children can't fill it. Writing a book or delivering a brilliant paper can't fill it.

Nothing can fill a God-shaped vacuum, except God. This gifted and eloquent young man also said, "Let us weigh the gain and the loss in wagering that God is. Consider these alternatives: If you win, you win all. If you lose, you lose nothing. Do not hesitate, then, to wager that He is."

I'm going to read to you from my new book, *In This Mountain.* Father Tim and Cynthia are back in Mitford, back to the Grill, back to Percy and J. C. and all the people. I loved writing this book, but it was very hard because Father Tim has some darkness in this book. This is not all smiles and roses. He has a tough time in this book. He suffers. After a time of darkness, he has written this sermon. This is how he — and I — tried to figure it out:

"In the name of the Father, and of the Son, and of the Holy Spirit, amen," he said, crossing himself.

"I wrestled with this morning's message as Jacob wrestled with the angel, until at last I said to God, 'I will not let You go until You bless me.'

"I had prayed and labored over a sermon, the title of which is listed in your bulletin and which no longer has anything to do with what I have to say to you this morning, nor does it delve the meaning of today's Propers.

"What I'd hoped to say was something we all need to know and ponder in our lives, but the message would not come together, it would not profess the deeper truth I felt God wanted me to convey.

"And the reason it would not is simple:

"I was writing the wrong sermon.

"Then . . . at the final hour, when hope was dim and my heart was bruised with the sense of failure, God blessed me with a completely different message — a sermon expressly for this service, this day, this people."

Father Tim smiled, "The trouble is, he gave me only four words.

"I was reminded, then, of Winston Churchill, how he was called to deliver the convocation address at his old school — where, by the way, he had not done well, his head master had predicted nothing but failure for Churchill. He was called to give the address and he stood to the podium and there was an enormous swell of excitement among the pupils and faculty that here was a great man of history, a great man of letters and discourse, about to tell them how to go forward in their lives.

"Mr. Churchill leaned over the podium, looked his audience in the eye, and here, according to legend, is what he said; this is the entire text of his message that day:

"'Young men, nevah, nevah, nevah give up.'

"Then he sat down. That was his message. Seven words. In truth, if he had said more, those seven words might not have had the power to penetrate so deeply, nor counsel so wisely.

"Last night, alone in my study, God gave me four words that Saint Paul wrote in his second letter to the church at Thessalonica. Four words that can help us enter into obedience, trust, and closer communion with God Himself, made known through Jesus Christ.

"Here are the four words. I pray you will inscribe them on your heart."

Hope Winchester sat forward in the pew.

"In everything . . . give thanks."

Father Tim paused and looked at those gathered before him. At Emma Newland . . . Gene Bolick . . . Dooley Barlowe . . . Pauline Leeper . . . Hope Winchester . . . Hélène Pringle. Around the nave his eyes gazed, drawing them close.

"In *everything* give thanks. That's all. That's this morning's message.

"If you believe as I do that Scripture is the inspired Word of God, then we see this not as a random thought or an oddly clever idea of His servant, Paul, but as a loving command issued through the great apostle.

"Generally, Christians understand that giving thanks is good and right.

"Though we don't do it often enough, it's easy to have a grateful heart for food and shelter, love and hope, health and peace. But what about the hard stuff, the stuff that darkens your world and wounds you to the quick? Just what is this *everything* business?

"It's the hook. It's the key. *Everything* is the word on which this whole powerful command stands and has its being.

"Please don't misunderstand: the word *thanks* is crucial. But a deeper spiritual truth, I believe, lies in giving thanks in . . . everything.

"In loss of all kinds. In illness. In depression. In grief. In failure. And, of course, in health and peace, success and happiness. In everything.

"There'll be times when you wonder how you can possibly thank Him for something that turns your life upside down; certainly there will be such times for me. Let us, then, at times like these, *give thanks on faith alone* . . . obedient, trusting, hoping, believing.

"Perhaps you remember the young boy who was kidnapped and beaten and thrown into prison, yet rose up as Joseph the King, ruler of nations, able to say to his brothers, with a spirit of forgiveness, 'You thought evil against me, but God meant it for good, that many lives might be spared.' Better still, remember our Lord and Savior Jesus Christ, who suffered agonies we can't begin to imagine, fulfilling God's will that you and I might have everlasting life.

"Some of us have been in trying circumstances these last months. Unsettling. Unremitting. Even, we sometimes think, unbearable. Dear God, we pray, stop this! Fix that! Bless us — and step on it!

"I admit to you that although I often thank God for my blessings, even the smallest, I haven't thanked Him for my afflictions.

"I know the fifth chapter of First Thessalonians pretty well, yet it just hadn't occurred to me to actually take Him up on this notion. I've been too busy begging Him to lead me out of the valley and onto the mountaintop. After all, I have work to do, I have things to accomplish . . . alas, I am the White Rabbit everlastingly running down the hole like the rest of the common horde.

"I want to tell you that I started thanking Him last night —

this morning at two o'clock, to be precise — for something that grieves me deeply. And I'm committed to continue thanking Him in this hard thing, no matter how desperate it might become, and I'm going to begin looking for the good in it. Whether God caused it or permitted it, we can rest assured — there is great good in it.

"Why have I decided to take these four words as a personal commission? Here's the entire eighteenth verse:

"'In everything, give thanks . . . for this is the will of God in Christ Jesus concerning you.'

"His will concerning you. His will concerning me.

"The thing which I've taken as a commission intrigues me. I want to see where it goes, where it leads. I pray you'll be called to do the same. And please, tell me where it leads you. Let me hear what happens when you respond to what I believe is a powerful and challenging, though deceptively simple, command of God.

"Let's look once more at the four words God is saying to us . . . by looking at what our obedience to them will say to God.

"Our obedience will say, 'Father, I don't know why You're causing, or allowing, this hard thing to happen, but I'm going to give thanks in it because You ask me to. I'm going to trust You to have a purpose for it that I can't know and may never know. Bottom line, You're God — and that's good enough for me.'

"What if you had to allow one of your teenagers to experience a hard thing, and she said, 'Mom, I don't really understand why you're letting this happen, but you're my mom and I trust you and that's good enough for me'?"

He looked around the congregation. "Ah, well," he said, "probably not the best example."

Laughter.

"But you get the idea.

"There are, of course, many more words in the first letter to the Thessalonians. Here are just a few:

"'Pray without ceasing.'

"'Abstain from all appearance of evil.'

"'Quench not the Spirit.'

"These words, too, contain holy counsel and absolute truth.

"But the words which God chose for this day, this service, this pastor, and this people, were just four. Yes, do the other things I command you to do, He says, but mark these."

He gazed upon his former flock with great tenderness.

"Mark these."

I want to write until I absolutely drop over in the grave. God made me a writer. It wasn't like I said, "Oh, Lord, I want to be a writer. That's what I want to be." Instead, the Lord spoke to my heart when I was ten years old. I remember the day: I was standing looking out of the screen door into the yard. It was summertime — and I knew that I was going to be a writer. Or an "author" as I liked to call it because of Mr. Wordsworth and Miss Jane Austen and all those lovely people on that pack of author cards. Remember those? That's who I wanted to be like.

God did speak to my heart when I was ten years old, and I knew that I would one day write books. I can't tell you what a treacherous path it was to get there, though. I was too afraid to write books because how do you know how to write a book until you've done it, right? I went into advertising because I had a daughter to raise, and you can make money in advertising. It's a brutal business. It really is. There are deadlines all the time, and every day you have to be better than you were yesterday. In any case, I was in advertising for nearly four decades.

Finally, I said, "Lord, I can't do it any more — and yet I'm scared. I'm scared to step out on faith. I'm scared to really trust you to let me write books. What are we going to do about it?" I prayed for two years. I kept a journal. I prayed and prayed, and I just worried God to death. You know it's the squeaking wheel that gets the grease.

One day, two years later, God spoke to my heart. I got a green light. I left advertising, and I never looked back. I sold my house and I sold my car. I had a Mercedes, but it didn't matter. I moved to the mountains in North Carolina, where I had some family, and cut my lifestyle in half. I was scared to death the whole time. Even though I knew God had given me the green light, I was still afraid. What was I going to do? What was I going to live on while I wrote this book that I'd never written before?

I drove around in a car with rust on the fenders (and that's really hard after you've driven a Mercedes — but very good for my character). I bought a used computer, and I taught myself to use it. I want to tell you one thing right now: that nearly drove me crazy! To teach myself to use a computer? I've never turned on a microwave. But I did it.

I got all ready, and I sat down to write that book for which I'd given up everything to write. And I found that I had absolutely nothing to say! This is the truth — nothing to say. "Woman's dream turns to nightmare." That brought me to my knees, and I implored God, "God, you've brought me this far. Now please don't drop me. If there are books in me to be written, if this is what you want me to do, you're going to have to mastermind this thing because I don't know what to do here."

One night, lying in bed, the image — a very simple image — of a village priest, walking down a village street, came into my mind. I knew he was a priest because he was wearing a collar. That's all it was. Nothing exciting at all, but I began to follow that in my mind. He went to a dog named Barnabas, and they went to a boy named Dooley, and the first thing you know, the story was telling itself to me. It began to get wheels, and the wheels started to turn, and I started to go with the story, though I didn't know where it was going.

Nothing exciting was happening. Indeed, the biggest thing that happened was that Emma Newland dyed her hair red, and I thought, "Who would want to read this?" I took it to *The Blowing Rocket,* our local newspaper in Blowing Rock, North Carolina, and said to the newspaper editor, "Jerry, I don't know what I've got here." After he read it, he decided, "I like it. Let's run it in the paper every week." Which just goes to show how desperate small-town newspaper editors are! Every week for two years, then, I was on deadline writing that Mitford column for *The Blowing Rocket.* One day, I looked and here was this big stack of manuscript paper — and I realized, "By jig! I do know how to write a book. I just wrote one!"

Then came the agony of trying to sell it. People ask, "How do you sell your book? How do you find an agent?" I have to tell you: I really don't know. There's no formula. In my case, a bookseller who loved my work sent an agent to me. I just followed Mr. Churchill's advice: never give up. I would not stop until somebody bought my first book. I negotiated the contract: $7,500 for that book. I thought that was really big. Well, it *was* big.

And I kept praying because when you've got this first book and you have a publisher — for me, it was a very small press who bought it — you realize there's still the work of distribution. Now you've published a book, but there's no way to get it out for people to read it. So I loaded up my trunk of that old car with the rust on the fenders, and I drove it around to booksellers and introduced myself.

That's my treacherous path. But it's been wonderful — a great joy. In fact, I count it a privilege to write these books. Let me add that when I was six years old, I felt called to be a preacher. Half a century later, I'm an author writing about a preacher — which is a pretty good deal. I got to have both dreams in one.

I would say to any of you here who have some great dream still burning, some coal still burning in your heart about what you want to do or maybe even what God called you to do years ago and you've been too scared to do it, I want to encourage you to pray about it and step out on faith and take a chance and do it. In doing so in my own life, I cannot begin to tell you what a wonderful and consoling and marvelous thing it is. Can you imagine? What if you were me standing up here, and you had written books that all of these lovely people would come just to hear you talk about? You would be thrilled. You would be blessed just like I am.

Do something that's been on your heart for a long time.

JAMES CALVIN SCHAAP

. . . .

Writing and Knowing

It had been a hard couple of months for our preacher. He'd buried the father of three children, a young husband killed in a bicycle accident. Then, an African-American activist, his long-time friend, a strong Christian, was felled suddenly by a heart attack. And finally, after six long weeks of torturous suffering, a member of our church, a high school girl, 17 years old, had just that Sunday morning succumbed to a mysterious virus, despite thousands of fervent prayers from friends, community and church members. A pall fell over his face, and his voice, already troubled with a cold, broke frequently during his sermon.

He preached that morning on the sufficiency of Christ's suffering and sacrifice. He reassured us — and himself — that we can hold hope high through the deepest valley of the shadows because Christ himself had already suffered the appalling worst our human minds can imagine, once and for all — for our sakes.

And then he approached the communion table, fortified, I think, by his own exposition of the text. Rather than read through the liturgical form, he took his place behind the bread and wine and returned us once more to the promise offered in the sacrament — that in taking this body and blood we would not only be sharing in Christ's suffering, but glorying in that once-for-all-time sacrifice. His suffering — so many times worse than ours — makes us totally free. But all of that came haltingly, the bread broken with more care than usual, his face down, the wine poured soberly from the chalice.

I sat on a metal chair far in the back of the church. This was not worship-as-usual — for him or for us. The morning's sadness hovered over the congregation like dank fog, but created rapt attention more characteristic of a funeral than a worship celebration. The startling death of a young girl dried the thirsty souls of an entire congregation.

Maybe that's why I couldn't help thinking what I did. As the preacher walked to the table of our Lord, I kept repeating a single line in my mind: "Read the story. Read the story — I wish you'd read the story."

With an urgency as arrogant as it was distasteful and impossible to stanch, I kept wishing the suffering preacher would read a story I wrote long ago, a story I thought — no, I knew — would make this celebration of the sacrament as fully real as it could be. Through the long distribution of the elements, the prompting wouldn't stop. "If you'd only read the story . . ."

As a Calvinist, when it comes to guilt, I am accomplished. As I left church that morning, despite having partaken of the sacrament, I scolded myself for an insufferable ego. "*My* story, *my* story — read *my* story," the voice in me had urged. What was more dispelling than its urgent volume was the fact that the voice had pleaded for something of my own creation — *my* piece of fiction. A young girl had died at six that morning, the celebration of the Lord's Supper was being offered, and I couldn't stop arguing that the whole church should hear a story I had written long ago.

The arrogance of my reaction verifies my need for the cleansing in Christ's blood; I'm not proud of my pride. But the more I thought about my own inappropriate response, the clearer I began to understand that what my conscious mind was begging for was nothing less than the truth of the sacrament — that all our sadness and sin were shouldered once and forever in a death and resurrection which occurred thousands of years ago. What I wanted to do was tell the old, old story *my way,* the way in which I myself learned the truth of the gospel most memorably — in a story which I wrote, and — here's where the arrogance sets in — in a way that I simply assumed every one else would understand and appreciate with the same vehemence.

That realization prompted me to think again about another old question frequently asked about writing in general both by those who do write and those who study writing — what is it exactly that writers do when they write a story? That day in church some voice in me wanted to offer my own firmly struck apprehension of the gospel truth, not something I'd learned by having the gospel read or by listening to a dozen thoughtful homilies — although I have learned important things in those ways. I began to wonder whether it was possible for me to say that I'd learned the truth about the efficacy of God's sacrifice — not only intellectually, but as viscerally as it was possible for me to learn that truth — by writing a story. That morning in church, I wanted everyone to experience what I had come to know via the medium by which I'd come to know and believe it, via a story whose infrastructure of character, plot, setting, theme had come together, picture-puzzle like, in the process of writing, a story which had thereby become, to me at least, the whole truth. I knew what I believed *because* I'd written a story — that's what I'm saying.

The process of writing — specifically fiction — is very much the process of discovery writers and teachers of writing talk about when they define the task. Writing *is* discovery — and I'm certainly not the first to say it is. What I would like to assert is that writing fiction is a means by which I've come to know what it is I actually believe.

Somewhere far back in my undergraduate education, I remember someone saying, "Believe the tale and not the teller." I've no idea how deconstructionists would toy with that old saw, but the notion still seems to me to hold the truth. When there is a discrepancy between the writer's talk and work — what she says she believes and what the work appears to suggest — I really believe the verification is the work because the work is, in fact, the incarnation of belief — idea made flesh. The work incarnates what the writer truly believes — his or her testimonies or denials to the contrary.

If children order the chaos of their lives, as Bruno Bettelheim says, by the fairy tales they hear, then why shouldn't a similar structuring occur as the story is created in the mind of the writer? A story does not argue principles, but it does proffer understanding of ideas and their consequences in behavior when such things are embodied in the lives of fully realized characters. Through story, we learn by becoming — both as readers and writers.

What sets me to thinking these things is a letter in a recent *Poets and Writers,* a trade magazine for North American writers, a letter which appeared in response to a feature article I had written about writing and the Christian life. There is nothing new or startling in the letter writer's response, but it forced me to consider once again the complaint perennially leveled against all of those who, like me, try to be serious about their faith and their writing. What my article had suggested and their publication of it had implied is that Christians can do serious literary work and, in fact, are doing it. Here is the substance of the letter that took issue with what I wanted to say: "A working/writing life grounded (literally) in myths about gods and souls and spirits and such may be Schaap's idea of an anti-vacuum, but to lots of us it has the look of just the opposite: a life circumscribed by authoritarian non-ideas." Christians, circumscribed by their mythologies, are incapable of writing anything but apologetics, he says.

Perhaps I could end the speech right now and quote from O'Connor, who knew well the very same criticism. Here's what she says in "The Fiction Writer and His Country":

> I have heard it said that belief in Christian dogma is a hindrance to the writer, but I myself have found nothing further from the truth. Actually, it frees the story-teller to observe. It is not a set of rules which fixes what he sees in the world. It affects his writing primarily by guaranteeing his respect for mystery.

That's O'Connor's answer. G. K. Chesterton is helpful here, as well. In his *Orthodoxy,* he slips the noose over the head of the modernist, when speaking of the same species of criticism.

> In one sense, of course, all intelligent ideas are narrow. They cannot be broader than themselves. A Christian is only restricted in the same sense that an atheist is restricted. He cannot think Christianity false and continue to be a Christian; and the atheist cannot think atheism false and continue to be an atheist.

Theoretically, I've now answered the criticism, lining up a pair of superpowers to take out the enemy position. Let's just throw in Eugene Peterson, who claims that, to him, writing is not simply a literary act, but a spiritual act as well.

But as all of us know, however, wonderfully imaginative writers do a whole lot more than create a battle of ideas. Defining writing, like writing itself, begins in full retreat from abstraction and theory. Writing begins in substance and sense; it begins in manners, O'Connor says, not mystery, though it well might end there.

So I still face a certain existential problem here. Just as it is possible to hear the gospel and not *know* its truth internally, it's just as easy to listen to O'Connor or Chesterton and not *know* the truth of their rejoinders. I'm talking here about *knowing*, about the conviction of my own faith. And the more I think about it, the more I'm sure of what it was that prompted my emphatic, but fortunately silent appeals to the preacher as he stood at the table of our Lord. What I was begging for was not, simply, an intellectual acceptance of the truth of Christ's sacrifice, but a holistic and tenacious avowal of what I have come to know deeply and sincerely about the truth of the gospel. My testimony, internally given, my full-fledged belief in the efficacy of Christ's sacrifice, while undoubtedly shaped by a lifetime spent within the body of believers, was made most complete by my writing the story. That's what I want to explore here — how writing stories teaches me what it is I believe.

Listen to O'Connor: "I have to write to discover what I'm doing. Like the old lady," she said, "I don't know so well what I think until I see what I say; then I have to say it over again." The act of writing clarified her thinking. In creating stories, she investigated what she believed. That's what I'm saying happens in writing, and obviously I'm certainly not the first. "People ask me what my novel means," said Jon Hassler at a recent writers conference. "If I could tell you what it means, I wouldn't have to write it."

The story that haunted me that morning in church was one that I had written years before, an unusually autobiographical story about a time when I worked at a Wisconsin state park. One day I was at the registration booth at the park entrance, where it was my job to sell park stickers and register campers, when a truck pulled in lugging a rack of canoes. I knew very well that canoeing on Lake Michigan was, at best, a dangerous undertaking, but I didn't dare to say that to the young social worker driving the truck, nor the pack of kids in the back. I remember thinking that their taking those Alumicrafts out into the Lake Michigan surf was risky, at best.

But they did, some capsized, and some of those kids drowned. I saw nothing of the events myself because I continued to work in the registration booth at the entrance to the park. But I remember very well the tongue-lashing I took from the boss, who marched down to the registration booth from the park office hours later and told me in no uncertain terms that by failing to warn the park's visitors *not* to go canoeing, I was myself responsible for what had happened. I was eighteen years old. I don't remember his exact words, but I know that he told me I should have known better, having been born and reared on Lake Michigan. And he was right.

That night I remember telling my parents about what had happened at the park. It was a headline news story, of course — television news crews were all over the park — so they would likely have heard anyway. But I remember *not* telling them about my part in the story. I was a rather typical late adolescent, chafing — as many kids do — under parental rule. I didn't tell my parents the whole story because, in part, I didn't tell my parents much at all about my life, about what I was thinking and doing. I didn't tell them the whole story because, well, they were my parents. Some of you will understand.

It's important to note that this incident did not somehow haunt me throughout the years — nor does it today. I remember the fiction writer Lawrence Dorr once saying, years ago, that some nightmarish horrors of his own holocaust experience in Hungary during World War II were somehow put to rest by his "use" of them in stories. As many of us know, writing out one's memories and ideas carries a certain therapeutic quality; that's why therapists frequently suggest their patients keep notebooks and diaries. But I want to make clear that my selling those kids a sticker and thereby granting them admission to the park and the lake was not something that haunted me. In fact, I remember remembering the incident. I was teaching a class of college freshmen, attempting to explain what had happened in a story or poem I've long ago forgotten. I was standing at the blackboard when suddenly that story came into my mind as a means of explaining something else. I even remember saying to the class that the story of the drownings in Lake Michigan would create a great story. But it hadn't haunted me. I'm not talking here about writing as therapy.

Whatever the reason, this story, "The Voice of the Body," is what resulted. It's not a long story, and it hasn't been read by thousands of people, nor is it included in any edition of *Best American Short Stories*. I'll leave it to others to judge its literary merit. But the story is important to me for two reasons: first, it is, like few stories I've written, especially autobiographical; and second, it is *my* proof of what I have discovered in the process of writing.

The Voice of the Body

Once our Brad hit high school, he took one look at his older sister, a senior honor student, and opted for a whole different course of study. Mary is bookish, tall and thin, and given to wearing plaid skirts of perfectly medium length. Every day of her high school career, she walked by herself to the bus stop or drove alone to school, and loved the quiet company of solitary mornings. Not once did we yell her out of bed or shoo her out the door. But from the first day of ninth grade, our Brad decided he'd have none of his sister's world. He set out on his own course, and if Ann and I would count the hours we spent wringing our hands about the boy we once wanted so badly, we'd tally enough time for a two year leave-of-absence. But you don't take leaves from your kids.

He sat beside me this morning in church in much the same pose he always takes, slouching with his leg up against a hymnal, face down while he pushes back his cuticles with the edge of a dime. But I knew it was a pose designed to hide — maybe from me, or from himself, maybe even from God. This morning he was in church — I mean really there — even though we'd tugged him along for all the Sundays of his life.

Maybe it's a wonder it's taken this long. At eighteen, he's already a man.

Most anywhere south of here people would say most of the weather we've had this week is still winter. Early June isn't summer at all on the lakeshore. People wear jackets and keep their sweatshirt hoods up around their ears at the state park where Brad works. Damp gray haze lies so heavy along the shore that in the morning water beads on picnic tables all over the park, even though there may have been no rain. Sometimes a whole week of workdays can pass and you can't paint a thing with that kind of moisture. By calendar and climate, early June around here is really late spring. When the sun comes, it's a joy.

Brad was working in the booth at the park entrance Friday morning, maybe the first sunny day in two weeks of gloom. I know the job. Lots of things have changed around that park in the last twenty years — there's nature tours now, a new visitor center with wildlife displays, and the beach is finally coming back after too many years of high water. But some things haven't changed from when I worked my way through college down at the park twenty years ago. Somebody has to sell entrance stickers and register the campers. It was Brad's turn in the booth.

He told me he was outside when that Chevy van came through, an old wreck tugging a rack of Alumicraft canoes. He'd just grabbed a handful of camper receipts from the little box at the exit. There hadn't been much traffic into the park that morning, even though the blessed sun burned through the haze and likely pulled the soft blue-green from the long row of cedars I helped plant years ago down the road to the campground.

Brad let that conversion van into the park and the beach, sold them a daily sticker — two bucks. That was his part. All of it.

Ten kids from that van went out with two social workers, and four of them, delinquent kids from the city, went down, drowned in heavy surf not more than fifty feet off the beach. They made it out quite a ways, I guess, but two of them swamped and dumped, and four kids died. Two of those bodies were recovered that afternoon, and two stayed out, like ghosts floating in the swells.

I didn't know exactly what it was that Cecil told Brad until Brad himself told me last night on the beach. We live on the lake. Friday night I heard the front door slap shut, and when his cycle never popped, I assumed he went out to the water by himself.

Last night he took off again in silence, so I gave him fifteen minutes, and then went out myself and walked north towards the park because I realized he was probably looking for that last body. The moon raised a sparkling triangle over whatever little waves hadn't yet bedded down for the night, and lights from the cottages down the beach stood in perfect order like a line of troops.

I found him about a quarter-mile down on the Sprigsbys' dock, staring out toward the moon, his arm wound around a guy wire holding the runabout up above the water. The thin chill in the breeze off the lake kept your face cool and wet. "It's cold as April," I said, coming up from behind him.

"You out here?" he said, as if he hoped it might be someone else.

I walked past him over the planks and stood at the end looking out toward a necklace of lights from some ship. "I used to dream of someday standing here and seeing Michigan," I told him. "Just once in my life, I'd like to see land way beyond the blue." I turned towards him because I wanted to hear him say something, anything at all. "I think maybe if we'd get up on the roof of our place some night when things are really clear — maybe in a tree or something. Take some binocs along. Maybe we could pick something out."

He shrugged his shoulders. "Ninety miles. Too much curve in the earth," he said. "You couldn't see over there even if it was crystal clear."

"Top of the power plant maybe?" I said.

He pulled the zipper of his jacket all the way up beneath his chin. "You could figure it out — how high you'd have to be."

"When I was a kid I used to think you could see it when you'd see these long lines on the horizon, like sand dunes — "

"Probably fog banks," he said.

I turned back to the horizon. The barge lights hadn't moved. "It's only a dream," I told him.

Somewhere down the beach a heavy bass from a party beat through the stillness of Saturday night.

"One of them's out there yet," I said. "It could turn up miles from here."

We hadn't really talked much about what happened. Brad doesn't really talk much at all to us anymore. Ann says since he's turned sixteen his only mode is silence, interrupted by an occasional grunt.

"Guess so," he said.

"Where'd the one come up today?"

"Fifteen miles down," he said, pointing down the shoreline towards the lights from Port Jefferson. "It gets battered up, I guess. You wouldn't think it would, not rolling in the water. Besides, it's so cold this time of year. You'd think a body wouldn't look that bad at all."

I didn't know then what exactly what was going on. I didn't know what Cecil had told him. He's young. Eighteen is too young for all of that, but I guess you think that way when it's your own you're worried about. "You blaming yourself somehow, Brad?" I said.

"Somebody's got to take it," he said. "Four of them dead. It's somebody's fault. I sold them a sticker. I let them in."

I tried to laugh just to lighten things. "You're taking the whole weight of the world on your shoulders," I told him. "You'll strain something if you try to do that."

"Cecil told me it was my fault."

I couldn't believe it. "What do you mean?"

"He said I should have known better. I was born here, he told me. I should have known you can't take a canoe out into those waves — that's what he said."

I know Cecil's a fine man, an old war horse from Korea who worked himself up to Park Director by sweat and loyalty and a powerful love for the lakeshore. He gave me a job years ago, and when I asked him about Brad last summer, he never hesitated.

"Cecil said that?" I said.

He twanged the guy wires as if they were the strings of a bass viola. "He's full of crap," Brad said. "It's not my job to be a lifeguard. I only sold them a sticker. He can't blame me."

Sprigsbys have a canopy on that deck, so they don't keep a tarp over the boat. We know them well. For some reason, Brad swung himself inside and sat down behind the driver's seat.

"We all need to blame somebody," I told him.

"It wasn't my fault."

139

"He doesn't blame you either."

"You should have seen his eyes," Brad said. "You ever see Cecil mad?"

"I used to work for him myself."

"He was mad. He reamed me out down at the booth, comes limping down from the office like he does, and just about tears my throat out."

"He didn't mean it," I said.

"The heck he didn't."

I know why Cecil did it. I know Cecil. He comes into the bank two or three times a week, deposits the take from the stickers and registrations. He's a fine man, but a dozen TV cameras all over the beach and all those reporters poking mikes at him, asking him how on earth four kids could drown in a well-maintained state park, and I can see him standing there speechless, a man who works with his hands but never was a talker. Besides that, right there at his feet are the bodies of two boys drowned in his park.

"It wasn't my fault at all, and he had no right to chew my butt the way he did," Brad said.

I turned around and walked to the side of the boat. "Then why do you think it is?" I said.

"I don't," he said. "I ain't a lifeguard."

"You said that already," I told him.

"That jerk social worker shouldn't have let them put those canoes in. You can't canoe in waves that high, not in Lake Michigan. What kind of stupidity is that anyway? — geez."

"He didn't know."

"He should've."

"You talk to him at all?"

"I sold him the sticker is all. Don't even remember him. Long hair, I think. A beard. He said the guys kept their rooms clean. 'Which way is the beach?' he says. 'These guys got a day off for keeping their rooms clean.' He says it for them, looking around toward the back seat, you know — not for me."

"That's all you remember?"

"Shoot, and I'm going, 'I don't even keep my room clean.'"

"So he didn't know anything?" I said.

"Guy with half a brain could see you can't canoe when the water's up. That don't take any smarts."

"So it's his fault?" I said.

"Guy like that doesn't know the lake. They shouldn't send anybody down here who doesn't know the lake."

"Who's *they?*" I said.

"The guy's boss. I don't know. Whoever sent him down to the park. How am I supposed to know? It's just not my fault."

He sat with his elbows on his legs, toying with a ski rope, his broad shoulders — like his mother's family — squared, his thick arms packed into the jacket. At fourteen he stopped wearing my shirts because his chest didn't get into them anymore, but big as he is, he's not strong enough to carry those dead boys.

"You been looking for that body, haven't you?" I told him. "You were out last night and you're out again tonight because you want to find it."

"Can't a guy take a walk on the lake?" he said.

"No law against it," I told him. It was early. It couldn't have been much past eight. I figured I could help him somehow, maybe I had to. "Do the lights work on the Farmall?" I said. "You used it when you were seining smelt, didn't you?"

"They work," he said.

"Maybe we ought to take a ride," I told him.

He turned around on his seat, looked right at me.

"You never know," I said.

He shook his head. "I looked half the morning. Cecil put me on the tractor and sent me up and down the beach, one end of the park to the other. He says we just as soon not have people bumping into that thing by surprise."

"You had enough?" I asked.

He looked down at his watch. "It's Saturday night," I told him. "You haven't been home this early in years."

*   *

I let him drive. I sat up on the fender, and the lights gave us enough illumination for us to spot a body up on shore or still rolling in shallow water. The air was cool and damp, of course, so I grabbed a couple stocking caps while Brad was getting the tractor out of the shed. I pulled on another sweater and told Ann what we were up to. She'd been reading.

"What are you going to do if you find it?" she said, taking off her glasses.

"I don't think we will," I told her, grabbing Brad's heavy jacket.

"Then why are you looking?"

"I'm going along for the ride," I told her. "He's the one that's looking."

We rode on the slant of the beach edge, six miles down to the mouth of the river, as far as we could go. Some places where the beach is gone, he'd slow down and take the water, the lights bouncing off the surface in a way that made me afraid we'd feel some clunk, then turn and watch a face or an arm or a leg emerge from the track of the big wheel beneath me.

When we got to the Sauk, he stood at the edge of the river, the lights disappearing into the water and the wispy fog. He pushed the gas back to an idle, and stared for a moment, and I knew he was thinking about the river currents out into the lake, about what they might do to that last body, how they might fan its drift miles down the beach, far beyond us, south even to Chicago. I know he was thinking that. I know it.

"That's it," I told him, over the engine noise.

He reached for the gear shift between his legs and swiveled around to back up over the dry sand, and he never said a thing. We went faster back up the beach towards home, our tracks, where they were visible, like a reminder that we'd covered all this ground already and no real goal could be found anyway. I didn't think the Lord would wash him up like that — just for us.

He pulled off the hat I'd given him and stuck it in his pocket, then stood up, keeping both hands on the wheel, his eyes moving back and forth over the beach — going too fast, I thought.

When I used to fish out there with Brad, Ann said she could hear us talk no matter how far out we went, our voices carrying through the open stillness as if there could be no secrets on the lake. That night I wondered what the people thought up and down the beach when they heard us go by, not once but twice, and saw a huddled figure in a stocking cap leaning on the fender of a tractor driven by a boy standing up and staring at the water as if he might find some monumental treasure tossed up by the wash of an evening's gentle waves.

We never spoke during that long ride. But I knew that if I tried to yell over the engine's heavy popping, I'd be heard by the whole world. Every word. So I kept quiet because it seemed to me then that I had something to say that wasn't meant for a crowd.

Brad needed that body, needed to pull it himself from the maw of the killer lake, as if he were in fact the lifeguard he swore he never was, as if he still could rescue someone already dead for two days. But it wasn't that boy he needed to rescue. I think it was himself.

✳   ✳

Sunday morning came as perfect as a storybook Easter. Ann stayed in bed and I brought her coffee, along with the front page of the *Journal*. I read all of the sports before Jeremy got up to grab the funnies and Sarah came down asking about Brad.

"He isn't in his room?" I said.

Ann must have heard Sarah's announcement.

"Maybe he stayed overnight someplace," Sarah said. Ann came up behind her and shrugged her shoulders.

When I went out back to the boat shed, I saw the Farmall was gone and I wondered how on earth he could start that thing without either of us hearing it. I saw the tracks through the pine needles out back, and watched the gouges run west down the lake road instead of east past the side of the house. He didn't want me along.

I walked out to the water and looked both ways along the shore. A single track ran north up the beach towards the park. A man in a brown hunting coat walked his collie my way, maybe fifty yards up, just past Vandivers', so I waited.

"You didn't see a tractor, did you," I said, "Farmall, an old orange one?"

"Nobody out here but me and Pepper," he said.

A blue-green choppy mask broke into rippling waves just off shore, little waves, as if the hand of God were somewhere just beneath the whole lake rocking it gently.

"He's still looking?" Ann said when I got back to the house.

"Where is he?" Sarah said. "Is he fishing or what?"

In a way, I guess, he was.

*　　*

Church starts at ten, and he goes with us every Sunday whether or not he wants to. It's a rule we have. As long as he lives with us, he lives by our rules — and our rules include church. I'm a believer, always have been. Not that I don't have doubts, but so did King David sometimes.

We were all dressed up and ready by the time I heard the Farmall roll up the beach. I didn't say a thing when he came in the front door and left the tractor stand out front.

His face — his eyes — seemed vacant, and there was a hollowness in his voice. "I found it," he said. "It was only about a mile up from the park. Can you believe that?"

Ann looked at me from across the table as if he'd just said something really profane.

"You leave it there?" I said. It was a stupid question, but I didn't know what to say.

"I called from a cottage. It's already picked up — "

"What'd you find?" Sarah said out of nowhere.

I waited for him to answer that question because I wanted to know what he'd say. But he looked at me as if I were the only one with the voice.

"He found the body of the boy who drowned Friday," I told her, gently pushing the company tag down into the back of the neck of her summer dress.

"Wow," she said, and she pulled a hand up to her face.

It was Jeremy who said it, even though I wondered myself at that very moment, and I'm sure Ann did too.

"What'd it look like?" he said.

I've seen Brad speechless for the last four years, but I never saw him so robbed of words. He ripped open the clasps of his jacket and stripped it off his shoulders, all the while looking down at the want ads on the table.

"Was it all blue or what?" Jeremy said.

He's ten, and he's seen his share of TV death.

"Sometimes sand rubs off all the hair," Jeremy said to all of us, as if we really wanted to know.

I kept waiting for Brad.

He threw the coat over the love seat and looked right into his little

144

brother's eyes. "He was dead," he said. "Nothing spectacular or nothing. He was just plain dead."

And then he looked at me, as if I had a sermon.

*   *

We've never had a day's worry with our Mary. This summer she's working in a student ministry in Sequoia National Park. During the week, she scoops ice cream in a fancy concession in a tourist trap, and on Sundays she helps out in a little park ministry that meets in the forest, logs for pews.

But Brad has always been another story. Mary professed her faith and took communion when she was fourteen, stood up in front of the church all alone and answered the questions. I remember how the preacher gave her this little hug up front once it was over, and neither Ann nor I will ever forget her smile.

Brad is already four years older than Mary was when she told the whole church that she loved Jesus. Some Sunday mornings we almost have to dress him to get him there. I'd rather not know, sometimes, how he spends his Saturday nights. When he goes to college next year, I'm sure Ann and I will spend more time praying for that boy than we have for Mary in all of her years.

Brad's never said a thing about faith to me, not one thing. We haven't forced him. He's never professed his faith. I don't think he's any kind of agnostic; he just lets it go somehow because it's part of the baggage of his parents' values — it's what he's rebelling from, I suppose, part of the world he thinks he has to leave in order to become who he will be.

I've asked the Lord to make this sullenness of his, this rebellion, this dark kind of brooding, strengthen him someday, so that in some future time his sneering, like Paul's, would make him a saint. But I haven't seen a thing yet to assure me I've been heard.

We had communion this morning. Sometimes I wish I were a Catholic so that I could say that this bread and wine is more than just a symbol, more than just grape juice and a dry cube of bread that points at a higher reality. In our church, that's all it is — a token remembrance of Christ's shed blood and broken body. You eat it and drink it to prompt a memory some don't have. At times, I wish it were the real flesh and blood.

✳   ✳

So I'm sitting there this morning waiting for the bread and the wine, Brad right there beside me, chewing his fingernails, his knee up against the pew in front of us. But I knew it was different for him this time, because I knew that the blue face of a boy drowned for almost three days hung in his mind, a face he claimed he really hadn't seen that Friday morning in the back of the van, a face he'd seen for the first startling time that very Sunday dawn.

When the sun rises over the lake, it gilds everything with a sheen that's heavenly gold. But I knew that morning that nothing the sun could do could wipe away death from the face of a boy who could have known that taking out a canoe in surf swept up by a rough east wind was dangerous — if only he'd known, if someone who knew had told him as much. No gold lay over that face in the lakeshore dawn.

So I grabbed Brad's hand once the bread had been passed. I grabbed it and I opened those fingers stained with state park green paint. I opened it to calluses and a width that long ago surpassed my pink banker's hands, and I shoved that bread there in his palm, even though he's not supposed to partake, not having professed. I force-fed my son the body of Christ.

"Take, eat, remember and believe," the preacher said, and an entire church — all except me — raised the body to lips waiting for the relief of our own guilt, sin washed forever out to sea in the blood of Christ's death.

And Brad looked at me as a child might have, as he might have himself before he'd become the problem we'd prayed about for so long. With my thumb I pointed at my mouth.

His eyes glazed almost, not in tears but in fear.

"Take it," I said. "Go on — you know what it is."

And I grabbed his hand again and raised it, held it up to his face until he took the bread into his mouth, held it there until it turned, as the Catholic in me prayed it would — just today — into the body I know he needed so badly to find.

146

"Remember and believe that the body of our Lord was broken for all our sins," the preacher said.

And I pulled his hand back down from his lips and held it the way I used to, the way, years ago, he once wanted me to.

And I'm the one who cried.

———————————

That story is close to ten years old, and when I look at it again I remember some of the impulses I felt to write it the way I did. For instance, I remember a Sunday morning when someone called our house and told my 12-year-old daughter that a friend of hers was in the hospital, being treated for burns. Her house had burned down. This happened just before worship on a Sunday morning, and I remember sitting beside my daughter that morning and knowing — on the basis of her deep attention — that that Sunday may well have been the first Sunday of her life that she was really "in church." That realization found a way into this story.

But what I remember best about the whole process of writing that entire story is the sheer joy I felt at the moment when it came to me in its fullness — notice the word choice, deliberate passive sense — "came to me" — or even "when I discovered" — or "when I stumbled on" — or "when I finally *knew*" after hours of writing, how the story would end. I remember the delight I felt when suddenly it suddenly it seemed so right that the father, sitting there beside his son in church, would force-feed his boy the bread — the body — he needed to find. I remember standing up from my chair and knowing, at least from my angle, that there was something exceptionally fine in that single gesture — the odd juxtaposition of masculine power and loving intimacy, a gesture, to me at least, so believable and breathtaking that it stunned me when — and let me once again use the passive language — "when it came to me" in the deliberative process of creating that story.

Many of my friends who do imaginative work know the exhilaration which comes with that kind of discovery, when the confluence of character, plot, and setting leads us to something that seems, to us at least, to appear as the perfectly concluding gesture, meticulously engineered by the givens of the story, yet surprising too, even — and perhaps most importantly — surprising to the writer. Once more, O'Connor: "The writer," she says, "penetrates the concrete world in order to find at its depths the image of its source, the image of ultimate reality." That's what happened when I wrote that story.

What is fiction here? My father worked in a bank, but my family never lived on the lake. My father and I never had a long discussion about the drownings. I didn't take the tractor up and down the shoreline, looking for bodies — but my co-workers did. The Lord's Supper never brought me any particular solace for what I assumed to be my culpability in what happened that day.

What happens in writing is that certain elements of real truth mysteriously mix with imagined scenes and characters — Brad is not me, my own father is not the narrator; but there are prototypes. The process of writing blanches and distills what the memory offers to the fictional process, shapes and identifies anew both characters and the settings, then weaves everything together into something which is both old and new, both unreal and yet very real, both false to history and true to our experience of life. Everything I've created in this story, from its various sources, leads to this final, single gesture, this new artifact — that's the process undertaken and accomplished in the creative fictional mode, methinks. "The fictional process," says John Gardner, "is the writer's way of thinking, a special case of the symbolic process by means of which we do all our thinking." As Calvin Miller says, "We who tell stories find out who we are and why we are born."

It is undeniable that the emotional truth which attracted me to the story of the drownings was the guilt of the sticker-seller, a guilt I knew fully. What pulled me into the story was an exploration of a conscience heavy-laden with the deaths of kids, deaths which could — but not within a court of law — be placed at the feet of a teenage boy who sold the stickers. I remember *that* guilt, and I remember carrying it alone. Once my parents were off to bed that night, I remember taking out a piece of paper and writing down my thoughts, denying my guilt. I wish I had that piece of paper, but I don't. At that point in my life, when I was still light years away from ever thinking of myself as a writer, I must have somehow understood that talking to someone — even a piece of paper — might be helpful. So I did.

That personal dialogue — me and the paper — may well be, however, the basis of what drew me back to the story. For the nature of the conflict here is obvious: vivid and real guilt for the deaths of four boys, deaths for which I couldn't be legally charged, but which occurred because of sins of omission I knew very well, having been born on Lake Michigan. As I began to write that story I did not have that emotional truth in mind. What brought me into the story was an event, an action, an anecdote — the story of a father and son moving up and down the shoreline of Lake Michigan, at night on a tractor, looking for a dead body. That event — writing a story that would include a late-night flood-lit search for a dead body — was what I was after when I started composing. That scene is what drew me into putting the pencil to paper. But it took the writing of the story itself for me to identify the true nature of the emotional conflict which had drawn me to it. The process of writing identified that problem and defined it as sin and guilt. By the laborious process of creating a world of realizable truth, of "felt life," by the process of creating the necessary material reality of the story — the look of the lake at night, the sound of an old Farmall, the furtive conversations between a father and his alienated son, the words the preacher traditionally repeats — through those specifics I came to discover not only what had brought me to the story, but even more importantly what action or gesture would get me out or get me home. That's why I say, from my point of view, the writing itself proved to me the efficacy of the sacrament.

This process yields, or so it seems to me, what Gardner calls "concrete philosophy," which is not to say that it is philosophy at all, because it isn't. What it is, is idea made flesh. One of the toughest jobs of teaching introductory literature classes is explaining what we mean by theme; and the reason it is such an exacting job has less to do with poor students or ineffective teaching than the difficulty we will always have of distilling a major idea from the text. Story doesn't *mean* anything, really. Story is story. What MacLeish said of poetry is equally true of story: "a poem should not mean/But be." Story is, as were Christ's parables, concrete philosophy — it is not the same as, but it is akin to "the word made flesh."

What I am saying is that for me at least, writing the story is a process whereby I discovered what it was — and is — I believe. I believed in the efficacy of the sacrament before I read the story — I'd taken communion in varied states of attention hundreds of times. But the process of composition, the "art of fiction," as John Gardner would call it, the marriage of experience and imagination which is so much a part of the fictional process affirmed viscerally, fundamentally, and definitively what it is I believe. That's why, in that difficult worship some weeks ago my imagination kept arrogantly insisting that the reality of Christ's glorious substitution for our sin would be more vividly manifest in the minds and hearts and souls of all the parishioners — if someone would only read aloud my story of guilt and redemption on Lake Michigan.

It is time to return to the unsettling letter. Once more, here's the line I'm toying with: "A working/writing life grounded (literally) in myths about gods and souls and spirits and such may be Schaap's idea of an anti-vacuum, but to lots of us it has the look of just the opposite: a life circumscribed by authoritarian non-ideas." What I would offer in response is that the process of composing that story led me to a discovery of what I truly do believe. There can be no question about the fact that it enhanced my faith, but I really do believe that writing the story was itself a faith journey, a tour of discovery.

The letter-writer, I'm sure, would respond to my comments by saying that the closure of the story was not something I learned, but instead something generously supplied by a system of belief which remained aloof from whatever discovery I considered myself up to, that very system of belief which defiantly circumscribes my freedom. If I were the letter-writer, I'd consider this entire explanation a highly suitable demonstration of the delusion Christian writers must maintain in order to ply their craft. Christian writers have to believe they are free to discover, but as anyone outside the circle of faith can readily see, we're not and I'm not. After all, my own joy at the discovery of the appropriateness of the story's climactic gesture is undoubtedly constructed upon my own already existing "belief" in the efficacy of sacrament.

The issue which lies beneath all of this is, finally, free will or determinism: to what extent am I really free to discover anything, through the process of writing or the scientific method or any other process for that matter; and, an equally valid question Chesterton says we might ask of the letter-writer: does his rejection of God really free his mind to discover anything not already deeply planted in the value system which his criticism of my story affirms he has? To what extent is he really free, am I really free, are any of us really as free as he would assert real writers must be? That's the question which lies unanswerably at the deep reaches of his criticism.

In April's *Atlantic Monthly* (1998), Edward O. Wilson argues for "the biological basis of morality" in an essay taken from his new book *Consilience,* a book, by the way, I've not read. But he says he believes that what we commonly call the religious experience will "eventually be explained as functions of brain circuitry and deep genetic history," in other words, our mythologies, our faith systems, and the sources for what we consider to be our moral imagination will all be discovered to be hidden somewhere in the labyrinth functions of human biology.

That such discoveries will occur is, of course, Wilson's faith, as it is the faith of the person who won't believe in my own autonomy as a Christian. But, for better or for worse, my faith is elsewhere. Mine exists in the reality of an omniscient God whose divine authority is very real, but whose nature both defines and demonstrates the perfect manifestation of what we humanly consider to be divine love.

And that very truth is exactly what it was I learned by writing a story.

SILAS HOUSE

No Bible-Beating Allowed

I've always seen writing as my way of testimony. One of the main things I want to do in my writing is to let people know that I believe that we live in a world that involves a God — that he really does exist and that we ought to pay him some attention.

This doesn't seem like a major statement to make, but if you look at modern media, I believe it is. We live in a culture that doesn't even want to acknowledge God's existence. Despite what you think about Mel Gibson's film, *The Passion* (and I'm not sure what I think about the film, actually), one thing I appreciate is that it forced the media to talk about Christ. Sure, they did it in as negative a way as possible for the most part, but for the first time in recent memory, people actually ignored everything the media said and went out to see the movie. People didn't flock to see *The Passion* because of coverage in *Entertainment Weekly* or *People* or *Entertainment Tonight;* they went in spite of that coverage, to see for themselves. We live in a time where the media rules our lives. They tell us what kind of music to listen to — which is the only possible explanation for the popularity of Britney Spears. They tell us what kind of books to read and what kind of movies to watch. But *The Passion* put God and Christ back into the daily conversation of Americans. And I can't think of anything more positive than that.

What I do in my books is not so much try to preach a sermon — I don't try to save anyone or convince them of my beliefs. Instead, I do something very simple: I try to remind my readers, first, that we live in a God-created world and, second, that there are people out there who believe and worship. Even if the media wants to act as if these people don't exist and even if the majority of literary or mainstream books never acknowledge God.

One of my favorite quotes is by Leon Bloy: "Any Christian who is not a hero is a pig." What I love about this quote is that I'm not sure I have it completely figured out. What I *think* Bloy means is that Christians have to take heroic measures every day, the way Christ did. One of the most heroic acts in history is when Christ happened upon Mary Magdalene being stoned to death for prostitution and intervened. He stepped forward and took a stand for her. This, then, is the one thing I keep reminding myself: if I'm going to be a Christian, I have to constantly take an unpopular stance.

It's easy to be a hero in today's culture because we have so many opportunities to speak up — mostly because a lot of people feel free to bash Christianity. When I'm out on book tour, what I encounter over and over is Christian-bashing. Let's face it: it's not cool to be a Christian. When a lot of people hear the word "Christian," they automatically also think fundamentalist. In the writing world particularly, many people think that all Christians are racist, homophobic, close-minded, Bible-beating freaks. In fact, if you're gathered with a bunch of so-called intellectuals, you can announce that you once committed all kinds of acts of depravity, and they won't bat an eye. But if you announce that you follow the teachings of Christ, they will gasp aloud.

Let me give you a couple of examples. Recently, I was at a conference where I was giving a reading with several other writers. One of them was a poet who stood up to read a poem entitled, "Easter Sunday." Before she read it, she looked at the audience very nervously and said, "This poem is about church, but I assure you I don't go. I don't even believe in God." She said this in a very defensive manner, as if she thought she would be mocked if she didn't clear this fact up before reading.

While in Florida recently, I was at a very posh reception at a wealthy couple's home with the director of the festival where I was appearing. The reception was held around the pool, which was surrounded by a

Mediterranean garden. On nearly every tree, there hung beautiful Japanese lanterns of various sizes. Within each, a candle burned throughout the night. At the end of the night, we were among the last people there, and we helped the host unlatch the lanterns and blow out the candles. The director opened a particularly big one and, standing on her tiptoes, peered through the metal door to see the candle inside.

"My God," she said to everyone, "this lantern is huge. Does Jesus live in there?" She fell into fits of drunken laughter.

The hostess quickly stepped forth with a straight face and said, "No, I assure you, Christ is not alive anywhere on this earth or in heaven."

Everyone else there laughed, as if this were the funniest thing they had ever heard in their lives. I was dumbfounded by her remark, mostly because of the tone of hate that overtook her voice when she said "Christ" as if it were a dirty word. I was so puzzled by their amusement that I remained silent. I had the opportunity to be a hero, and I let it slide by me. I have regretted not saying something ever since, but I knew if I spoke up and said I believed that Christ was very much alive and watching over every one of us, I would have been considered a freak, a fundamentalist, a Bible-beater, a conservative. They would have called me a Republican, a word that today carries the same weight as the word "Communist" carried when I was a child. On the plane ride home, I decided that I would never be in another situation where I wouldn't speak up, where I wouldn't take heroic measures for the God that I know exists.

Since I believe heroic measures have to be doled out in small doses, I use my writing as a way to announce my faith. Throughout my novels, I try to remind people that we live in a God-ruled, God-created world.

I was raised Pentecostal, so that's another factor to add to this prejudice I feel on a daily basis. When people find out you're a Christian that's one thing, but when they find out you're Pentecostal, that's quite another. People always immediately think that I'm a snake handler and that I follow a very old-world, strict doctrine. Yes, growing up, women in my church didn't cut their hair or wear pants. Men never wore short sleeves to church. One image that will remain with me forever is our preacher going to the lake with us one time and waterskiing in full Levis and long-sleeved dress shirt. But no one in the church forced them to do these things. My mother cut her hair, sometimes wore culottes or long shorts. She loved jewelry. Everyone was allowed to plan their own salvation.

So in all three of my books, I try to present Pentecostals as real, live, breathing human beings. They're not religious fanatics. They're not in constant terror about the rapture or about how everyone is going to hell. They're simply normal people with strong beliefs in God.

I also usually have a main character who is struggling with his or her spirituality. I've had Christian writers criticize me about this before, but I believe that one of the best things about being a Christian is that we can explore our faith every day. I myself don't completely understand the Bible or Christianity or my own feelings of faith, so I'm constantly calling these things into question. This sense of doubt that hangs over me all the time used to make me feel like a bad Christian, but now I realize this constant learning process is part of being a Christian. If you read my novels, you'll see that my protagonists tend to go through the same thing, but they always acknowledge God and they always try to live a Christ-inspired life.

I also always try to shoot my books through with light. So much of modern literature is gloom and doom, despair and violence and sex. Although despair and violence and sex do happen in my books, my novels are ultimately about leaving the reader with a sense of joy and hope, the two things God and Christ have given us most fully. If we want to write about a God-ruled world, we have to include these things.

Two short scenes from my second novel, *A Parchment of Leaves*, will illustrate how I try to sprinkle spirituality and religion through my books. I say "sprinkle" because if you give it to people in too large a dose, they feel as if they've been hit over the head with a Bible. In order to open people up to the world of religion and spirituality, I believe we have to do it very subtly, very slowly.

When read out of context, these scenes may not seem very restrained, but remember that they are short passages in a long work. The book is narrated from the perspective of a beautiful Cherokee woman, Vine, in about 1914 or 1915. In this scene, she, her daughter Birdie, Vine's best friend Serena, and Serena's son Luke have gone for a walk up on the mountain.

I watched the trees swaying. They moved as if they were un-
derwater, so slow and graceful that you wouldn't even notice unless you stopped to watch. The leaves felt thick and seemed full of
juice that might taste good if I broke one open. I touched them
lightly, afraid I might harm them, and felt of them the way a blind
person might read beads of braille.

I wondered if the trees were God. They were like God in many
respects: they stood silent, and most people only noticed them
when the need arose. Maybe all the secrets to life were written on
the surface of leaves, waiting to be translated. If I touched them
long enough, I might be given some information that no one else
had.

I let my hands trail against thick tree trunks . . . and felt of
them the same way I might have savored the touch of someone I
loved. Luke and Birdie were like brother and sister, walking in
front of us holding hands. Sometimes Luke would let go of her
hand and begin to run up the trail, and Birdie would scream out
for him to wait. . . .

Luke stopped, waited with his back to us until Birdie caught
up and took his hand once again. Serena went back to singing,
and I reached down to let my fingers brush the tops of ferns that
burst up between rocks lining the path. I thanked God that my
baby could walk and run, that she could holler out with a voice as
high and powerful as her father's, when he used to come over . . .
to court me.

I'm trying to do two things in this passage. First, I want the reader to
be reminded that there is a God in the world and that these are people
who are aware of him on a constant basis. My favorite line is "I wondered
if the trees were God" — I think people only notice trees and God when
they need them. Secondly, I'm trying to present a complex character who
can acknowledge God throughout the book. Here, for example, she
thanks God that her baby can run and play, a reminder of the thankfulness we should practice on a daily basis.

Later, I take the reader to a Pentecostal service with me. In part because it works wonderfully for the book, and in part because I want read-

ers to experience a Pentecostal service and see that it's not as frightening as they might think. Vine was raised a Quaker and has a very naturalistic, firm belief in God. She's attending the Pentecostal church for the first time at the urging of her mother-in-law, Esme:

> There was much hollering and clapping and amens. I couldn't help but to look around. This was all so new to me.
>
> A whole crowd of women went to the front of the church. One of them spoke verses, and the rest joined in. Soon everybody in the church was singing: Men with great booming voices, and women who sung high and lilting. It all blended together perfect, the way a storm has all the right sounds in place at the right time. The windows were opened and sunlight fell through them in bright rectangles. The music was beautiful to my ears — so beautiful, this joining of so many voices, that I felt the urge to cry but didn't. . . .
>
> Now a lanky man stood beside the women and strummed along on his guitar, and a woman took a tambourine from the front pew. The song got much faster. The women patted their feet or slapped a hand against their thighs. Many of them started to clap along to the beat, and their arms moved out quick, their elbows bowing out in great big motions. They leaned their heads back and closed their eyes and sung louder.
>
> Birdie stood beside Esme, clapping. She sung along. Esme held on to the back of the pew in front of her tightly. She nodded her head to the music and feebly patted one foot. I looked at her hands. Her skin was chalky and thin. Her veins were cloudy blue. I started to stand with Esme, just as a sign of respect, but I knowed how the Pentecotals would react. A person who had not been baptized and stood in the church was seen as giving a sign that they wanted to repent. I didn't want a crew of them pulling me toward the altar.
>
> The music was stirring, though, and I longed to clap along. Saul sat stiffly beside me. I wondered how many times he had sat in these pews as a child. Is that why he hadn't gone to church more, once he had grown up — because he had been forced to go

so much as a child? As if he knowed I was thinking of him, he reached over and took hold of my hand.

The choir changed songs, and the piano player slipped right into the next. They sang even faster. The music seemed to be taking possession of everybody in the church. Everyone except me and Saul was standing now. Clapping and hollering, raising their hands in praise. . . .

One of the women started running the aisles. I knowed that this was called "shouting," but the woman wasn't saying a word. She trotted up and down the aisles, slinging her arms from the sides of her body. I could see a shiver working its way up her back. She danced in place, taken by the Spirit. She danced so hard that the bobby pins loosened in her hair. Her hat fell to the floor. Other women joined her. Men stepped out into the aisle, too. They shook their arms over their heads like they were pushing at the air, and spoke in tongues. The words were beautiful. I couldn't help but wonder if they were putting on, though. I couldn't understand how a person could be overtook like this, hypnotized in such a way that they started speaking words that were not their own. Great streaks of sweat run down the men's shirts. The women were all shouting, and one of them fell to the floor, where she started shaking like somebody taking a fit. The pastor grabbed a towel from a stack on the front pew and handed it to one of the women, and she spread it out over the trembling woman's legs so her dress wouldn't ride up to shame her.

Now Esme's head seemed to roll about on her neck. One hand jabbed at the air, her fingers held very straight. She started to speak in tongues, and then I knowed this was genuine, for it made chills run up the backs of my arms. The words rolled from her mouth like strange wisdom. I had heard that the Pentecostals sometimes broke out in Hebrew. I didn't know if this was what Esme was speaking, but it was sure enough a foreign language. Birdie kept her eyes on the singers. How did she know the words to this song, too? Maybe Esme had taught them to her.

Energy pumped through the church like something unleashed. I could feel it traveling through the air, running from the pulpit to the back pew. I felt it wash through me and near about knock the breath out of me. Surely the Spirit was here. I had never knowed such a feeling in my life. I held on tight to Saul's hand and he looked over and smiled. He was used to all of this. He had told me that I might be scared by the people shouting and speaking in tongues, but I wasn't. Not one bit. I envied them their joy, even if I didn't understand it.

Then there was a woman leaning over the pew in front of me. Tears run down her face, but she didn't wipe them away. Her brow was fretted together as if she was bewildered. She bent over the back of the pew, and her breath was hot in my ear. "The Lord is dealing with you," she said, her words quick and breathless. "Come pray with me."

I couldn't just come right out and say no.

"This world is a short-timer, honey," the woman said, her face so close to mine that I thought I could smell the salt on her cheeks. "But eternity lasts forever. Come give your heart over, let the Lord take away your problems."

"I'm not ready," I managed to say, and I realized that my lip was trembling.

The woman put a hand on my shoulder and bent on her knees in the pew in front of us. She had a kind face and the prettiest red hair, which was pulled into a tight knot atop her head. "You just think about it," she said, but the music was so loud that I had to read her lips. I nodded. The preacher stood on the altar before a line of people who seemed to sway before him. He had a bottle of oil in one hand. He turned the bottle up to let a drop fall onto his thumb, then pressed his thumb onto the foreheads of all the people in line. One woman fell back as if pushed, but two men caught her by the arms. Esme had slipped out of the other end of the pew and was making her way to the prayer line. Birdie walked beside her, holding on to her hand. Seeing this, I finally did cry. I hoped that no one could see me.

Pastor put his whole palm flat against Esme's head, leaning his head back to pray, and people gathered around her, touching her back and praying together. I thought, *These are good people.*

The crowd parted, and Birdie led Esme back to the pew.

And then Esme was falling. Her body seemed to fold up and she fell right on top of Birdie. No one seemed to notice for a moment, and the music went on. Birdie laid there with her legs under Esme, shaking her. Saul sprang to his feet and gathered Esme up in his arms.

She was limp as a rag doll. He held her for a long moment, the way he might have held Birdie. Slowly the people began to notice what had happened, and the music faded — first the singers, and the piano, and then the guitar. Some people were so caught up in the Spirit that they continued to speak in tongues, and their voices seemed to echo on the gathering silence.

The pastor rushed over. He anointed her forehead with oil again and prayed aloud. The congregation joined in, their voices gathered in one single prayer of a hundred different words. I felt like I could hear each prayer on its own, all at the same time.

"O God, touch our sister, right now, and make her whole. Take this affliction from her body so that she may stay with us awhile longer — "

"Touch her, Jesus. Heal her body. You have the power if it be your will, sweet God — "

"We know that all things are possible by your grace. . . ."

Saul had closed his eyes. He pulled her up closer to his face like he was breathing in her smell. I noticed her small feet, dangling alongside Saul's leg. Her hands, palm up. *I have killed her,* I thought. *With grief.*

After a long time of thundering prayer, they all seemed to know when to stop at the same time and moved back a bit to give her air. America Spurlock pushed through and broke a smelling salt beneath Esme's nose, and Esme come out with a jerk. She looked up at Saul like she was waking up from a dream. She put one hand to his face but then let it fall to her side again. It seemed she could not bear the weight of it.

I pulled Birdie up onto my hip and we walked out of the church. Everyone looked after us without a word, not knowing what to say. Pastor followed, saying things that I paid no attention to. Saul said, "She just needs to rest a bit. Go on with your meeting," in a polite manner, and Pastor stood in the door as we walked away.

Saul carried her up the road, and Birdie cried into the nape of my neck. All around us, birds were singing, as if they knowed it was Easter and their praise needed to be heard.

Here, I'm not trying to recruit readers, but to allow them to see a Pentecostal service in a way they might not have been shown it before, but they see it in a way that they themselves might first experience it: as an outsider in the church. I hope that readers can experience the beauty of the service.

Ultimately, what I'm trying to do in my fiction is make my voice heard about my faith in a very subtle way. I think when people read my books they don't come away feeling as if they'd read necessarily a Christian book, but I think that they know that the author is probably Christian. That's the great thing about fiction — that I'm able to testify through my characters and make my faith known through my characters in an understated way. It may not be a hugely heroic measure, but it's my way of sharing my faith and testifying.

We have the opportunity to be heroes every day, and I am going to try harder to do that. I'll never let another lantern comment go by the way like I did before. I hope that you won't either.

JOY KOGAWA

An Interview by Henry Baron

HENRY BARON: We all listened to Elie Wiesel last night, and we know from reading his works that what he experienced as an adolescent in World War II had a life-lasting impact on him as a person and as a writer. You also had a World War II experience, though you are younger than Wiesel. Something happened to you and your family that I think had a profound influence on you and your writing as well, as is clear in works like *Obasan* and *Itsuka*. Would you tell us a bit about those experiences?

JOY KOGAWA: Let me begin by saying that I don't think we can make any kind of comparison between the events in Europe and those in North America. It's a great mystery, isn't it, that particular holocaust. I think the world has been completely changed by that sense of helplessness that follows when there is an evil that is unimaginable.

In *Obasan,* there is a reference to what others have called the "other Holocaust," the atomic holocaust in Japan. In its own way, unthinkable — not the numbers who died, but the idea of a power that is so great. We cannot see the atom, and yet it unleashes that kind of immense power.

I've wondered if there isn't a corollary: an unseen good that would be even more powerful than all of that evil. It seems to me that there is. It resides within the infinitesimal moral choices that we each make from moment to moment. Things that seem so tiny, so insignificant, so fleet-

162

ing that they're hardly worth noting. Indeed, they could be just a thought that goes through us.

It seems to me that, in the human condition, we have a power that is not yet unleashed because it is not yet recognized: the power for good; the power of love that resides within us, moment by moment; the power of prayer. If we just knew this moment by moment power, we would turn over whatever it is that we're anxious about and entrust it to that overwhelming power of love and good.

At any rate, there were questions I wanted to ask Elie Wiesel if I could have. In my latest book, *The Rain Ascends,* the narrator is a middle-aged woman, another one of the many insignificant people in our world. There's nothing particular about her that would make her stand out, but she wars within her being over the problem of good and evil. And over the fact that her clergyman father — whom she worshipped as a child and loves more than anybody in the entire world, the person who taught her about love and about the love of God — is a child molester. Though she learns about this during her adolescence, she goes into a vast denial of it. For her to finally come through that denial, she identifies herself by adopting the metaphor of "Hitler's cat." As such, she feels she was born to stand with her father through his hell — and her own. In that stance, she feels like Abraham at the altar, sacrificing Isaac. She believes that she has been commanded to tell the truth, but it is a daunting task. The book begins with a dream that she has: that the goddess of mercy is the goddess of abundance. Before I wrote this book, I really didn't understand how those two things went together. But when the book was finished, I understood.

What I wanted to ask Elie Wiesel is related. I've heard that for Wiesel there is no mercy for those who committed the crime. No mercy. I don't understand that. To me, that is a problem. If we are defined by the "other" and that's who the other is, a criminal, how do we embrace that definition of who we are? That would make us completely evil, if we are mirrored back by that much otherness.

What I understand now, having gone through the journey with Millicent in *The Rain Ascends,* is that the victim is not ever called to forgive the criminal. That's an obscenity. They cannot — it's inhuman. It is divine, but as humans to forgive is impossible.

What the victim is called to do is to become strong, to enter the abundance. The strong are called to be merciful, not the weak. In the story that Jesus told about the king who was asked to forgive the debts of his subjects, the king was asked to forgive the debt, not the debtor asked to forgive the king. The person who finally becomes strong may then be in a position of being capable of forgiveness.

Having understood that, I then understood how mercy and abundance belong together. Because if you find the abundant way — through actions of mercy performed in your life towards you — then, you are granted the grace of being able to forgive. Not before.

Certainly, people are in different places in their journeys. People who have been victims do have a job — and their jobs are to cry for justice, to name the criminal, to stand up, to be heard. All of these things. But I think in North America we have a cacophony of voices crying out that they are the victims. Through this cacophony, we have lost the sound of our own power, lost the responsibility that comes with being privileged citizens of privileged nations. What I've found is that it is much, much harder to assume the identity of the powerful, to assume the identity of the victimizer in the world, than it is to assume the morally superior identity of the victim. When I had to leap over from my former position [as a victim of WW2 internment] and practice that other identity — and I think what we have in the identity of the Christian today is the identity of the victimizer in so many ways — it was very difficult. This is why I think that, ever since the Holocaust, the place of militancy in Christianity is very misplaced. Triumphal Christianity and militant Christianity are not appropriate identities for Christianity today.

HB: In *The Rain Ascends,* you have the main character, Millicent, take her moral anguish when she discovers that the person she loves more than anything else has betrayed her again and again to the church, and the church does not respond the way she needs to have the church respond. What is behind that for you? That has been a common experience, of course, for many people. There's a commentary here. Explain.

JK: Philip Yancey was talking this morning about point of view. All Millicent is talking about in *The Rain Ascends* is her point of view, though her point of view is not one that is very commonly talked about, I think. When we hear stories about child molesters, we hear the point of view of the victims. And, although we find it difficult to understand, we hear the point of view of the victimizer. Indeed, the victimizer is often a person who experiences himself or herself as a victim — because that's the identity that we most readily cling to.

Millicent's point of view, then, is that of a family member of the victimizer. Millicent's sister-in-law, Eleanor, is uncomfortable with Millicent's take on the situation:

> "God knows how many victims there were," Eleanor said. "Just stop, for once in your life, and think about them. The families. Consider the victims, for heaven's sake."
>
> She was asking me to hear the wailing in the night, to consider the suffering I did not see, to consider another point of view. My reply was that these considerations were not my province. I was his child. His well-fed cat, if you will, and I was witness to the defense. I was retained before I was born to be his advocate.

We live in a very complex world where there are many points of view and many different needs. Interestingly, the viewpoint of church — here the Roman Catholic church — has undergone a shift. There was a great scandal in Newfoundland involving Roman Catholic brothers. For too many years before this broke, the Canadian church had sheltered the brothers because they identified with the institution — they had not identified with the victims. Now there's been a turnabout where the church says it will identify with the victim. But what of the family of the victimizer? Millicent, in going and speaking to the church, recognized that she was being completely not seen. Her point of view was not the point of view of the church, and her needs were completely ignored. One other thing Elie Wiesel said last night was that we need to tell the story that nobody else can tell. We have a responsibility to tell those stories. Our point of view, whatever it is, is what it is. So the church has a point of view which it can tell. And so on.

HB: Presumably, it's God's point of view.

JK: The church's point of view? Has it been, in the past? We look through history and we ask, "has the church unerringly been where God is?" An institution, once it is created, assumes its own power and its own story and becomes as flawed as every other human thing is.

HB: So the church becomes a betrayer too?

JK: I think betrayal is part of the human story. It lies within us. The person who says "I have never committed a betrayal" does not know himself.

HB: Now, as a child, you and your family were uprooted. I'm still trying to get you to talk a little bit about your own personal experiences of victimization.

JK: I don't know how many people know the story of Japanese-Americans, but there is a parallel story about what happened to Japanese-Canadians. This capacity we have to take a person or a group of people, demonize them and make them the enemy in our minds, even when they are our neighbors, is a very human trait. We do it today — we are continually creating demons. When we get together with a friend and gossip about somebody else because we feel hurt by that person, what we are doing is manufacturing a demon.

Anyway, we were the demonized people of the day. The fury of that demonization was that the entire community was uprooted and relegated to the cesspools.

The racism that I imbibed as a child was profound. For years, I was proud to be, as we put it, "the only Jap in town."

We were "concentrated" in the sense that we were gathered together and then put away. Afterwards, each person, concentrated in that way, had a unique story to tell in the community. All I did was give one small point of view from the age that I was when it happened — 5, 6, 7, 8, and 9. There were other points of view, particularly of adults, who had a broader conception about what was going on and had a political point of view.

The kind of racism that got into me was the invisible kind. It got into my self-perception: a sense of unworthiness, of ugliness, of inferiority, of all of those things which made me experience myself as a person who could not speak, who would not lift her hand up to ask a question, who did not expect to be heard. It's all in here.

HB: How did that find its way into *Obasan?* As I read *Obasan,* I found myself having to fight the temptation to identify the main character with the author. But the more you get inside of Naomi, the more you feel that this is the story of not only Naomi, a fictional character, but to a larger extent of the author.

JK: I think that this book is very strongly autobiographical. When I began writing *Obasan,* I thought "how am I going to write about all of that?" I organized it around three places: Vancouver, where I was born and raised until the time that we were shunted inland; Slocan; and Alberta. All I had in terms of structure for the book was prairies at the beginning and the prairies at the end.

Initially, I didn't have the point of view of an adult in the book, but I came across her eventually. I found myself in the archives in Ottawa where I found the letters which form a big chunk of the middle portion of this book. They were material from a young woman whose materials had been donated to the archives. So, though I never actually met her, she became a character in the novel. She is fiction, and yet she is a counterbalance in voice to the child's voice.

What I can say about every book that I've written is that each one of them has changed me. I know there are writers here and people who want to be writers. The journey of the pen is a transforming one. It's worth going on because when you use the pen as a pick-axe to delve as deeply as you can go, it will bring up the most amazing jewels — not just of memory, but of insight, of understanding.

There is a saying which is attributed to Jesus in the Gnostic Gospels, I think: "If you bring forth that which is within you, that which you bring forth will save you. If you do not bring forth that which is within you, that which you do not bring forth will destroy you." I think that there is a calling to bring forth that which is within you. That is, to participate in the act of creativity, in the act of creation, in making known what is not yet known to yourself.

Not only do you tell it for the reader, revealing what the reader already knows but doesn't know that he knows, but I think that that's what you do for yourself when you write. You uncover. The closer you get to what is most deeply true to your conscious search, the closer you get to what is most deeply true in the search of others. The most wondrous thing is to discover that we're on this journey together.

HB: Was *Obasan* a book that *had* to be written? In *Obasan,* you talk a lot about silence, and you mentioned a moment ago that this displacement and shame which fell upon the Japanese-Canadian community reduced you, in a sense, to silence, to a sense of insignificance. Was the book a way of trying to recover a sense of significance, of finding the words?

JK: Did the experience reduce me?

HB: Yes. Was the book something that had to be written in order to recover yourself?

JK: I never did know why I wrote this book. I started out in 1964, struggling with the problem of good and evil. Out of that struggle came ten years of poetry. When I started writing *Obasan,* I was still in the mode of writing poetry. I'm not a terribly conscious person. I don't ever pretend to understand a lot of things that others do, or read things that others read, or have that kind of scholastic, intellectual discipline. When I was writing poetry, I was trying to be true to my own puzzlement. Writing *Obasan* wasn't a political effort nor was it any conscious therapeutic effort — or any of that. It was just a search — the pen's search. And the book is what happened. It just amazes me that the book keeps marching on.

HB: You started out as a poet, you were a poet before you became a novelist, and I trust you're a poet still. Would you share one or two poems with us?

JK: It's funny, you know. Sometimes I face an audience, and I realize I am going to read something. I look through my books, and I puzzle, and it all turns to ashes. I find myself sometimes thinking, "how could anybody come to a reading when it's so boring?"

Anyway, this is called "Fish Poem":

Moving into the slow
Pool beneath the voices
to the quiet garden where
airtime songs are
cloud shadow and
sun games — what
matters here in this cool
inverted sky are small
darting fish
colored cues shimmering
past the hooks, beneath

the nets, succulent, safe
and swift as prayer

Here's another one, "Water Song":

that once
on singing water walked
on water still
walks he
in atmosphere
so dense in miracle
we here find fins
for flying

I'm reminded of the last poem I wrote. It was for a friend of mine who died named Wilber Sutherland. He was a Christian leader in Canada, and I was asked to write a poem for his funeral:

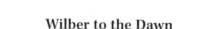

Wilber to the Dawn
(for Wilber Sutherland 1924–1997)

and so, dear friend,
still bound as we are here
by tides of human bonding
we have gathered to applaud
the journeying

and you
who, so far as i can tell
from heaven came
and to heaven have gone

and while on earth's plane
made heaven home

from living room to living
room you go
while we in this garden
or that, as mary sat
in various states of unbelief
wait for the great
surprise

how happily you have lived
without disguise
in all your many book filled speaking days
in boat or beach or tent
or auditorium, in church
and synagogue and meeting room
and deeply in the words and
ready arms, wilber
with your eagerness to
serve

you did that
hour by faithful hour
and with such willingness of heart
in service of your truths
and of the god we both call
love

within this universe, i pray
you still move, you live
and have your being in this same
element of love where we
this side of eden
toil

until like you, to the tomb
we come, that
busiest place of the
holiest one
in a journey to death
that is wholly
undone

this is no memory, this
now the moving of the
wind here in this room god's
dear presence and an involuntary
thankfulness

wilber of the onward way
wilber to the dawn
i celebrate with these
your many loves
a well sung song
for you drank freely,
again, so far as I can tell
from the sweetest well

BETTY SMARTT CARTER

....

Tired of Victory, Bored by Defeat:
Restoring Proper Sadness to Christian Art

⎯⎯⎯⎯⎯⎯

S ome writers hate research, but I love the way it allows me to put off
the actual act of writing. I've adopted the approach that the big net-
works used to take towards children's programming: if you think hard
enough, just about everything qualifies as educational. As preparation
for this talk, for instance, I began with an article on Leonardo DiCaprio
in *Time* and worked my way steadily toward a stack of *Entertainment
Weekly* in the library reading room. A couple of novels under my bed
seemed relevant — as did an online slipcover catalog and a slew of old
email messages. Leave no literary stone unturned. That's my motto. Not
even if the stone in question is the warranty agreement that came with
your toaster. You never know where you might find answers.

About a week ago, though, I realized I'd better do some serious work,
so I put aside the trash I was reading, skimmed through an online volume of the U.S. legal code, and there, by some grace dispensed especially
to the distracted and disorganized, I came across an interesting law:

Any party who states, footnotes, acknowledges or any other way
makes reference to the term "Christian Art" in the title, text or footnotes of any lecture, talk, sermon or public announcement shall immediately, and without unreasonable delay, provide duly necessary
explanation of said terms to any party or parties listening or read-

ing transcript of such lecture, talk, sermon or public announcement, whether body present or remote, by or before the time of commencement of such lecture, talk, sermon or public announcement, except in Puerto Rico and where local statutes apply.

Which, if you boil it down, means that it is your right to hear my explanation today on the ambiguous term "Christian Art," and my sworn duty to give it. If, in fact, I don't explain to you exactly what I intend by those words, then according to law, you cannot be held accountable for any nasty things you say about me at dinner.

Unfortunately, it would be easier to get a very large Christian artist through the eye of a very small needle than for me to define what exactly a Christian artist is or what he does — at least in a way that would please all relevant parties. However, for the purpose of this talk, let me define Christian art very broadly as "any work that assumes the existence of an omnipotent, yet personal god, and acknowledges the call of the gospel." For example, if Shusaku Endo writes a novel about a priest choosing to deny Christ in order to save persecuted Christians, that is Christian art. If Tim Robbins directs Sean Penn in a movie about sin and redemption, that is Christian art. If James McBride writes a memoir of his white, single mother — daughter of a rabbi, co-founder of a Baptist church — struggling to raise ten black children, that is Christian art. If Bruce Cockburn writes songs about Latin American politics which are grounded in his Christian view of justice, that is Christian art. If Jerry Jenkins produces a series of novels about the biblical antichrist, that is Christian art. If Pat Robertson choreographs and performs his own modern dance piece illustrating in movement how the wrath of God shall be visited on a certain Republican presidential candidate, that is Christian art. And if my five-year-old daughter draws a picture of Jesus floating in clouds, that, too, is Christian art.

Can only confessing Christians practice Christian art? Does it always deal with religious themes? Is it always grounded in orthodoxy? I don't think so.

I do believe, though, that all Christian art must acknowledge the God we know from the Christian story — whether to applaud him, wrangle with him, or just take his presence for granted, like a backdrop on a stage. Sometimes, as when we examine the poetry of George Herbert, Christian work can affirm, teach, and even evangelize. Elsewhere, as in the novels of James Baldwin, the work can teach us how to grieve, how to rejoice, how to long for justice. Some art, like the films of Ingmar Bergman, who claimed not to believe in God at all, will seem only God-haunted, an angry cry in the dark — yet a cry all the same.

Even with such a broad definition, though, we all have to agree about one thing: because of cultural shifts, most artists outside the church no longer feel the pull or authority of Christianity. Because so few are lapsed Christians, I doubt many of them anguish nowadays about the existence or goodness of God. No embryonic Bergmans out there, for instance, unless they're being raised Southern Baptist. If artists think at all about God's silence, they're probably glad for it since they'd rather live in a world without authority.

In fact, most contemporary artists who speak openly about Christian ideas are actually Christians. They come from many traditions: Catholic, Anglo-Catholic, Orthodox, mainline Protestant, evangelical, and fundamentalist. The quality of their work varies as does the content, but most, I think, hope to represent the world as they see it, a world with a design and a purpose.

They also seek to find an audience that won't shut them out. There, of course, is the rub. Because art is not so much a product as a conversation, artists must always speak to and within their culture. Yet, who's listening to the Christian artist? The art world at large is in the middle of another conversation — many conversations, actually. To them, the Christian artist is like an old woman tugging on your sleeve when you're trying to catch a really juicy piece of gossip. "Shut up!" you think. "I'm trying to hear what's going on!"

This helps explain why Christians, whether Catholic or Protestant, so often speak only to their own kind. It helps explain the boom of evangelical fiction and the rise of a parallel universe: Christian contemporary music. In a different way, it explains why Robert Duvall could not find a financial backer for his film, *The Apostle*. No one believed there'd be an audience for it. We who speak about Christian things must speak mostly to each other because others will not let us speak. While regrettable, this is not our fault.

We do have much to be ashamed of, however. Because of our isolation, we've failed to develop well as artists. We're inbred, and we've developed some really serious theological mutations. Imagine a teeter totter upon which sit two very stubborn and rather ugly children. The teeter totter represents the culture of Christianity, and the children represent two extremes on the cultural continuum. On the one side, we find the culture of victory: where happiness is the Lord's, and joy is the litmus test for true belief. On the other side, we have the culture of defeat: where hope is gone, and no one really misses it. The labels "conservative" and "liberal" don't work for these extremes, though it would be easy and even fun to divide the world along denominational or political lines. No matter where we look, we find religious people clustering on different sides of the very same teeter totter.

And yet, it's not impossible to make generalizations either. Those of us who grew up in evangelical churches know exactly where many of our people exist on the joy/ struggle continuum. Let me offer you the lyrics of two songs which I often sang as a teenager at conservative Grace Presbyterian Church in Georgia. The first song comes from the hymnbook:

Oh, what a wonderful, wonderful day, day I will never forget.
After I'd wandered in darkness away, Jesus my Savior I met.
Oh, what a tender, compassionate friend, he met the need
of my heart,
Shadows dispelling, with joy I am telling, he made all the
darkness depart.
Oh, heaven came down and glory filled my soul,
When at the cross my Savior made me whole.
My sins were washed away and my night was turned to day —
Oh, heaven came down and glory filled my soul.

The other song borrows its meter from "We're Off to See the Wizard" from *The Wonderful Wizard of Oz* and was made up by my brother, in tribute to one of our church officers (whose name has been changed):

Ben Barker is a lecher.
The very worst lecher at Grace

If ever a lecher there was he is, and I'd say it right to his face.
Of all the lechers that are letching at Grace,
Ben Barker is worse and what a disgrace.
Disgrace, disgrace, disgrace, disgrace, disgrace, disgrace!
So why was he elected the chair of board of deacons at Grace?

Of course, the discrepancy between these two songs may be as shallow as teenage cynicism and hardly worth mentioning — I'm old enough now to realize that heaven probably does not quake at the thought of a lusty deacon. But at the age of fifteen, when I believed that every dark thing was truer than everything light and that no one could be both innocent and wise, I thought that the second song somehow bleakly cancelled out the first. Sin, death, and despair trumped the richest eternal blessing, any day.

I had learned this from experience because I existed in an overtly pious, but covertly swinging, evangelical church of the 1970s and early 1980s where my own teetotaling, WW2-era parents seemed incredibly naïve and out of context with the happy hour crowd around them. Imagine D. L. Moody and Susanna Wesley guest-starring on *The Love Boat*. Scandal followed upon scandal, not only in our church, but in the denominational mission board my father helped establish and where I worked part time. Leaders rose and fell, individuals struggled with temptation and private pain. Two women at the board had affairs, a friend of mine there had an abortion. One of the top executives had a bad habit of staring down my shirt, and yet we all made a joyful noise: "I've got the joy, joy, joy, joy down in my heart."

In the evangelical world, victory has long been obligatory. Like a Disney happy ending. If you sing in a choir at an evangelical church, think how many times you've wrecked your voice on a victorious ending. The gigantic crescendo, accompanied by great flourishes at the piano, the conductor waving his arms so violently you're afraid he'll pull his shoulder out of socket. Or, if you're unlucky enough to attend a church where you have to sing to taped accompaniment, think of the truckloads of trumpets, trombones, and tympanis that those music production companies must haul in to make your victory sound joyful, sure, and immediate. Now to be fair, I haven't quoted any of the darker, richer hymns which I grew up singing and which I still enjoy the most. Most of them speak of the suffering Christ, "Man of Sorrows" or "O Sacred Head." Consider the very fact, though, that so many people for so long felt uncomfortable singing sad songs in church. Evangelicals have often thought that to admit grief and failure is to question God's omnipotence — and possibly turn away converts too. Never mind that Paul longed to be delivered from his life — and even called himself the worst of sinners. They figured he was just showing polite humility, like a housewife apologizing for her dirty house, knowing full well she just spent the last three hours cleaning it. Never mind that Jesus sorrowed unto death in the Garden of Gethsemane. They work up a lot of sympathy for his past sorrows, but they don't want to admit their own in the present. Sure, the suffering Jesus is a popular presence at revivals and crusades, but once they've walked the aisle and prayed the sinner's prayers, it is the risen Christ that they choose for their role model. He offers them victory for the Christian life, victory now. And victory now is the measure of true belief. No victory equals no faith. Is it any surprise that so many people have faked it?

When it comes to the arts, I guess it's no surprise that the evangelical audience seems content only with work that entertains, evangelizes, advertises, or educates. Take a look at your average Christian bookstore. Apparently many Christian readers don't want to enter too long the experience of real human pain, suffering, death. Fiction, above all, should not be too much like life. It must not contain too many evil people or have too much suffering in it. And if it has to show some suffering, the suffering should be distant and unfamiliar. Evil people should be Nazis or Antichrists. Good people should, for the most part, be white and middle-class. Victory must appear in the last ten pages of every book. Non-Christians must either be converted or run sniveling in misery. Christians must repent of sin, usually unbelief and lust, though rarely greed. And everybody who's repented should seem changed and happy. Because that's the way it is, isn't it?

It's easy to say disparaging things about so-called evangelical art. In *The Scandal of the Evangelical Mind,* Mark Noll concluded that evangelicals have mostly succeeded at intellectual pursuits when they have left behind evangelical ways of thinking and borrowed from other Christian traditions. "The scandal of the evangelical mind," he writes, "is that there is not much of an evangelical mind." I suppose you could say the same thing about evangelical art. In fact, critiquing it is so easy it seems mean.

But who is to blame for evangelical mediocrity in the arts? I often hear the blame placed on the artist. Sort of the "we lack a good talent pool," or put another way, the "how come the devil has all the good writers and painters?" argument. I have a hard time believing this, though, since evangelicals have succeeded at just about everything else.

When it comes to fiction, at least, a lot of blame certainly lies with publishers — secular publishers, who view anything openly religious with illogical suspicion, and religious publishers, who for business reasons, promote famous names and sensational subject matter over truth and excellence.

I believe, however, that a great problem with the evangelical audience and perhaps with artists themselves, has not to do with evangelical beliefs, but actually a lack of them. If, for instance, evangelical writers feel that they must manipulate their story in order to make God look good, and if the readers feel that they must be comfortable with every ending, then their faith must be even smaller than they fear it is. They've entirely missed the message of Job, Ecclesiastes, and many of the psalms. Is God more patient with our pretense at success than with our doubts and questions?

Now let's pull down our end of the teeter totter, and take a look at ourselves, because I expect many of us long ago joined the culture of defeat. Most of us grew up in church, and we are Christian cynics. We easily criticize those who make things too simple. Complexity is our religion, though we like to call it "mystery." Sorrow is our friend. If you're like me, it happened to you in high school or early in college — maybe even earlier than that if you came from a family in ministry. I turned cynical in the eighth grade, the year I stopped liking my parents. It was reverse metamorphosis, the butterfly turning into an ugly wormy thing. All the beautiful parts got sort of sucked inside, and I spent the rest of my teenage years nurturing my unhappiness. At least, though, I never changed my wardrobe. I hate to shop so much that I kept wearing frilly blouses all through the era of my despair, even as an ultra-cynical student at Wheaton. Yet there particularly, I saw so many feathery pastel beings, mysteriously mogrified into scowling, solitary creatures. The same nice girls who had led cheerleading squads and taught vacation Bible school just two years before, now suddenly dressed in long black coats, dyed their hair, talked about Nietzsche.

Why do so many of us do it? We who want to be Christians and also want to be artists — why do we so often become angry and cynical. I guess the most cynical answer is that it's fashionable among the people we want to impress. People run in tribes: they adopt the dress, manner, speech of the culture they've chosen for their own. They tend to cluster around leaders who may or may not be truly gifted, but who manage to convince everyone else they're indispensable. Artistic people, although they like to think themselves original, are really no exception. A lot of self-expression is just group expression. A lot of hero worship passes for non-conformism.

But even if all that is true, it says nothing about why we choose the culture of cynicism to begin with. We do it partly, I guess, because it seems more honest. We're like kids traveling across Tennessee: over and over, they pass barn signs and bird houses that say "See Rock City!" So they barrage their parents to take them, but the trip seems too long and the ride up Lookout Mountain takes hours, rather than minutes. Still, all the way they're thinking, "It's going to be great. It's going to be so cool!" Then they finally arrive, and they take a look around — this is it? Just rocks?

When we reach adulthood, we look back and justly recognize that life stinks. The journey was bad enough. Parents were not perfect, friends were not faithful, but the arrival is even worse. Since childhood, we secretly hoped that we'd mature into lovable, fascinating, and talented people, adored by all. Instead we turned out selfish, unhappy, and disappointed. Mutant Christians. Monsters of religious inbreeding. Given that we've begun to live in permanent disappointment, cynicism seems more adult, more mature than the artificial cheerfulness we grew up with.

Cynicism may be more honest, but just like forced cheerfulness it arises from a lack of faith which is also a lack of hope. We're afraid to hope in God because hope can be painful and dangerous. Hope requires us to remain on the road, even after breakdowns, bad restaurants, tacky over-priced theme parks, and highway construction. Hope requires us to believe in advertising which we cynics have taught ourselves never to do. Yes, you will win a diamond ring, just for dialing this number. Yes, you really are one of ten finalists in the Publishers Clearinghouse sweepstakes. Yes, you will have a free steam cleaning with no purchase necessary. And yes, God is as good as his word. He will heal us, and he will bring us joy. Hope requires us to envision a day when we might be able to sing, "I've got the joy, joy, joy, joy down in my heart" and really mean it. We who scorn the joy-mongers and victory-lovers have forgotten that victory really is assured. Joy really is possible.

We artists who belong to the culture of cynicism have one foot in the book of Ecclesiastes and the other searching for a place to stand. We cannot deal with innocence and faith in others. If I tried to write the book of Daniel, for instance, the hero might pray in his window, but curse God in his heart. If I tried to write about Timothy, I would probably give the poor boy a secret obsession with Ephesian girls. He'd take a little wine for his stomach, get carried away, and chase after his own sister. Yet, I know that my problem is not cynicism about people — which is actually very well placed. My problem is cynicism about God himself. I do not believe that God is good. I do long for him and that is why I pray to him and write about him. But I often despise my own longings because I feel so little return.

How do we restore proper sadness? Here's my easy answer to all of the problems I just raised. One writer who has taught me much about art and about faith is Alan Paton, best known for his book *Cry, the Beloved Country.* In *Too Late the Phalarope,* Paton tells the story of a deeply religious, white South African man, Pieter van Vlaanderen, who lusts after a black girl, sleeps with her, and lands in prison for disobeying the Immorality Act. The book is not mainly about race, though, except insofar as the incredible bigotry of Alfred Connors belies his Christianity. It is a story about law and grace, a story which could happen among people of any color. Paton's hero is a good man, a leader in his community, a loving father and husband, a famous sports hero, known as the Lion of the North. Yet he comes to a bad end because he cannot live by the law, and no one will offer him mercy. As Pieter's aunt relates his sad history, she remembers a day some years before when a new preacher arrived at their little church and delivered a sermon about back-sliding Christians:

No, he had not come to preach only about backsliding and back-sliders, but about repentance and mercy, that a man might turn again, taking his part again in God's plan for the world, so that through a man, himself healed and refreshed, might flow a stream of living water to refresh us all, his home, his church, his town, his people, and the world. . . .

"That's the sickness of our times, "he said," that we are afraid to believe it anymore. We think of ourselves as men in chains, in the prison of our natures and the world, able to do nothing, but having to suffer everything. God's plan? Ah, that's another thing that's done to us, history, and war, and narrow parents, and pov-erty, and sickness, and sickness of soul, there's nothing we can do but to suffer them.

"It's a lie," he said, and again he struck the wood with his hand. "It's the lie we tell to ourselves to hide the truth of our weak-ness and lack of faith. Is there not a gospel of God's love, that God's love can transform us, making us creators, not sufferers?"

Yet after the service, the young preacher meets Pieter van Vlaanderen:

I saw that my nephew was watching the young dominee, with some strange look in his eyes, and I guessed that the preaching had struck him in the heart, though I could not have told you why. Then the young dominee looked at him, and with the look in his eyes that so many young men had when they looked at Pieter van Vlaanderen, and in a moment he was with us, with his hand out-stretched, and his eyes shining.

"You're Pieter van Vlaanderen," he said.

And at the sight of the boy, with his eyes shining and his face all eager, I saw what I had seen before and could not understand, that the lights went out suddenly in the house of the soul, and its doors and windows were shut and its curtains were drawn, and the man stood there outside it in the dark, with cold and formal welcome.

Then Pieter's thoughts emerge for a moment:

And I thought, I could tell this man. And I was moved to the depths when he said this mercy was beyond all computation for no lesser mercy could have healed me of my sin. . . .

And then when he hit the wood with his hand and cried out that it was a lie that we were in chains, when I saw that he believed, I said to myself again, I could speak to this man.

Then when he came to me outside the church, as a boy comes to a man, calling me the Lion of the North, I knew I could not tell him. . . .

The Lion of the North! How little do men see, that a man so fresh and clean as he, should call me the Lion of the North!

Alan Paton would never have sailed to the top of the Christian fiction charts. He wrote about South Africa as a wounded country and the Christian community there, though outwardly moral, as a place of silence, hypocrisy, and racism. This is why he's still read in public schools. Yet he could not have written so well about fallenness and suffering if he hadn't understood, too, the promise of mercy. Paton knew that God is great and good. Who today could write a novel this powerful, this universal, and this Christian? Would anyone publish it? Would anyone sell it? Would anyone read it?

If you were an artist or an aspiring artist, I would call you to a proper sadness in your creative work. Neither a rejection of sorrow, which has produced some well-intentioned but horrible art, nor an idolatry of sorrow, which has produced some great art but may do more harm than good. If you're a member of the audience rather than of the art community, I ask you to allow artists to picture the world as it really is, full of muck and grime. We should not only be able to speak or hear the truth about ourselves, but let us all preach to one another that God is good, joy is possible, the Holy Spirit does sanctify believers. Let our art reflect the righteousness of Christ, while it demonstrates that the bread of life is ultimately more satisfying than the candy of cynicism.

DAVID JAMES DUNCAN

··

The Collision of Faith and Fiction: Cleaning Up the Wreckage

T hat indefatigable lover of Christ and equally indefatigable lover of books C. S. Lewis gives us a wonderful definition of the way that faith and writing intersect. He observes,

> Literature is a series of windows, even of doors, and good reading can be described as either an enlargement or a temporary annihi- lation of the self. This is an old paradox: "he that loseth his life shall save it." We therefore delight to enter into other men's beliefs, even though we think them untrue, and into their passions, though we think them depraved. Literary experience heals the wound without undermining the privilege of individuality. In reading great literature, I become a thousand men, and yet re- main myself. Here, as in worship, in love, in moral action, and in knowing, I transcend myself and am never more myself than when I do.

My title today is really less a title and more a job description. When I step out my door in Montana, my home is as tranquil as anything the beautiful, biblical word "wilderness" might lead you to imagine. But I don't spend my work life outside. Instead, I spend it in the intersection between faith and writing. A place which contains, as we writers know, neither traffic signals nor stop signs nor speed limits — and thus, endless wrecks. In a nutshell, what I do is check out the wreckage from the near constant collisions between imagination and reality, ink and paper, skepticism and belief, inner and outer worlds. These dichotomies side-swipe each other, crash head on, run each other off the road, then stand there name-calling and recriminating and screaming at each other. My job is to ignore the noise, clean up after the crashes, bury the mangled bodies, salvage the usable scrap, and sell the best of that scrap to maga-zine and book publishers. Still, I do try to recoup my sanity and rest my imagination toward the end of the day by stepping out into that wilder-ness I mentioned and casting flies at the local trout.

I first encountered the intersection between faith and writing when I was seven years old. It happened in a second grade classroom in Decem-ber. My classmates and I were told by the teacher, Miss Hansen, to write a story about Christmas, and since none of us had written anything be-fore, Miss Hansen left things pretty open. We were welcome to babble about reindeer, elves, Christmas trees, snowmen, Santa, Mrs. Santa. At seven, though, I didn't mess around: I set out on a bona fide Christmas fiction and made my hero Jesus Christ himself. My main attraction to Je-sus at that age was that his father was God, and God had made the world and trees and rivers and stars and mountains and birds and clouds and sunlight and raspberries and wilderness. I loved the world God had made so much that I hoped one day I might love God a little, too. To be honest, this hadn't happened yet. Loving God's world made sense to me the way loving peanut M & Ms made sense. Loving God himself, on the other hand, was like loving the unknown and invisible people who work in the peanut M & M factory.

The second thing that attracted me, at seven, to Jesus was that even though he started out as a plain old little boy like me, he had grown up to become someone so mysterious and great that my grandmother and mother were teaching me to pray to him. Talk about a success! I tried to imagine me or any kid I knew growing up into someone people would pray to — it was unthinkable. But Jesus had pulled it off. I also liked it that when I felt like praying, which again, to be honest, wasn't often — I could pray to a guy who'd once been a little boy like myself. It was almost like knowing somebody who worked at the peanut M & M factory.

When I sat down in that intersection between faith and writing to pen my Christmas story, there were a few things I didn't know: on the writing side, for instance, I didn't know what a quotation mark or paragraph or comma was. I'd never heard of things like scene, plot, dialogue, irony, symbolism, metaphor. I'd been literate a year, damn it, and that was good enough.

On the faith side of the project, there was Christian doctrine I hadn't yet mastered, though I felt I knew the basics. I knew, for instance, that Jesus was born the year they started counting, December 25th o. I knew he was the son of a good Christian couple, named Joseph and Mary with the last name.... Well, Joseph and Mary Christ was my guess. I knew that Joseph was a carpenter, and I knew that Mary was the only virgin in the whole wide world — which was a miracle. But she had lots of kids anyway — which was another miracle. Their son, Jesus, was the biggest miracle of all because he was God's son, too.

This multiple dad thing was what fired my story. First off, it caught my imagination because all three of my brothers were adopted, and I wasn't. This really bugged me as a kid: picture your parents ordering you and your siblings to go weed the garden or muck out the chicken house. When this would happen, my big brother John would sit beside me, grumbling, "My real parents would never make me do this. My real parents are trapeze artists in the circus." By contrast, *my* real parents were the two grouches who just put our noses to the grindstone. I figured Jesus could have worked this "God is my real father" thing on his siblings the same way John worked the trapeze artists on me.

My other fascination with Christ's multiple dads was that Jesus was a good boy, the best boy ever if the Bible has it right. Good boys deserve birthday presents from all their fathers, I'd say. But Jesus' heavy-duty father was either invisible or up in heaven, so how would presents get from an invisible or heavenly father down to a deserving, yet earthbound son?

This was my literary mission. My general sense of the situation was that Jesus was going to need some faith to make the birthday gift from the invisible dad work out. What if he sat at home on his birthday, grumbling like some modern child of divorce, "God is my real father. Big whoop. When is invisible, all-powerful Dad going to visibly remember my birthday?" If this is the tone Christ took, I figured he was out of birth-day luck. But what if on his birthday morning, he got up and went out alone into the part of the world that God actually made and people hadn't yet messed up, namely the wilderness, and walked around out there with an alert eye and a hopeful heart. Maybe cool things could hap-pen, if Jesus simply believed they would.

Since I didn't know what paragraphs were, my first story was one paragraph long. Its title was spelled D-e-b-o-r-h-a. I'd only seen the name in a book and didn't have a clue how to pronounce it, so I said it "DEE-Boar-HA." It went like this:

> It was the day before Christmas. Jesus was going to be seven years old. He had fed all the animals but the sheep. When he got to the fold, one of sheep was gone. Its name was Deborha. Jesus ran to his house and ate his breakfast.

(For some reason that's my favorite line in the story. It's one of those de-tails that other writers about Christ haven't dared to imagine. Not Nikos Kazantzakis. Certainly not Norman Mailer. Not even the gospel writers. I captured something fresh there, I think. I might pen a whole novel some day called, "Jesus ran to his house and ate his breakfast.") But on with the story:

> Jesus ran to his house and ate his breakfast. Then he went up in the mountains and looked for his lost sheep, calling Deborha! Deborha! He looked and looked, and at last he saw some wool on a bush. He walked and walked and a little later said a prayer, Dear God please help me to find Deborha. Amen. Then Jesus thought he knew where to look. It was over in a pasture in another place where a spring of water was. When he got there he saw Deborha! Oh Deborha, I've been so worried about you. But just then he saw something moving. Deborha, you have a baby lamb. Last year God gave me a sparrow with a broken wing, and this year he gave me a lamb, said Jesus. When he got home, he remembered Mary his mother had promised to tell Jesus the story of when he was born. Mary said, one day I was cleaning house. Our angel came to me

and said go to Bethlehem there you will have a baby his name is to be Jesus. So we went to Bethlehem. When we got there that night we were very tired. The inn was full but the innkeeper was nice so he let us go to the stable for the night and there Jesus was born. Angels sang and told shepherds to go to the stable where Jesus was born. There was a big star in the sky and a wise man gave Jesus something made of gold. Then the angels came again and here we are. That night Jesus and Mary saw a star almost as big as the one in Bethlehem for the first Christmas. The End.

When Miss Hansen read this fiasco, she nearly ended my literary career on the spot by kissing me on the cheek, right in front of God and everybody. Later though, she got "Deborha" published in a PTA anthology of kids' writing called "From These Roots." I had to admit, kiss and all, that I kind of liked seeing my stuff in print.

My first grown-up fiction appeared in a 1976 *North American Review*. It was called "Her Idiots" and again featured both sheep and this Jesus-on-his-birthday-like need for faith in the unseen. My sense is that you've got to really trust that gifts are secretly coming to you in order to find what's silently being given. I also love Simone Weil's argument that God is truth and that a life spent simply telling the truth, however religious or sacrilegious your truth may sometimes appear to be, cannot help but lead you to a God who is truth. I'm not sure she's right, but I hope she is.

In the name of that God, I'd better admit that there was a big difference between "Deborha" and my second story about sheep and shepherds. The difference was that by 1976, I'd caretaken a farm and tended a flock of actual sheep. I found them very different from biblical sheep. Here's a look at the protagonist of "Her Idiots" telling the unbiblical truth about her first actual flock:

Leaving the cabin, she strolled toward them, seeking, as with any new acquaintance, the eyes. And she expected to see stupidity. She'd been warned. She expected loveable ignorance, perennial victimhood and a vacuous yet genuine innocence worth the costs of feed and endless vigilance. But as she strode in past the mist, squatted beside an ancient ewe and met for the first time that direct, all-uncomprehending gaze, she was astounded: nothing had prepared her for such unspeakable nonintelligence. The eyes were hideous. Two piss-colored ice cubes. They understood nothing, never had nor would. Their seeing was not perception, it was radar — a cold, bloodless means of determining locations of meaningless objects. The eyes didn't disappoint her: they appalled her. She rose to escape them and had gone a little distance when for no reason, the entire flock started and bolted madly away. . . . Dried balls of dung clattered on their hind legs and tails as they ran, and she laughed at the sound. That was the first day. At first it seemed funny.

How difficult it is to imagine, once you actually know some living sheep, that good shepherds like David and Jesus could actually love the damn things. For me, trying to love and care for sheep felt like some kind of boot camp, designed to prepare me for the real life-and-death combat of trying to love and care for my fellow humans. Maybe the good-shepherd-state I was trying to reach is best described in a James Herriot story from *All Thing Bright and Beautiful:* a Yorkshire farmer comes into Herriot's veterinary office beside himself with grief because he's just lost his favorite pet pig. Herriot listens in astonishment as the Yorkshireman keeps blubbering, "He was just like a Christian was that pig. Just like a Christian." To see both sheep and humans, all humans, the way that farmer saw his pig — that's my spiritual goal.

When I was nine years old, the wilderness gave me a tangible gift which resulted in feelings of wonder and gratitude far greater than the gift itself seemed to warrant. Feelings so great that only a creator, and not just the created object, seemed to me to account for the intensity of my feelings. In other words, when I was nine, my love for the peanut M & M spontaneously began to include the M & M manufacturer.

It was a kind of grail object that bestowed my first faith feelings. It turned out it was nothing but a fish — my first large, self-caught rainbow trout. There was not a question about the name of the feeling that this mere fish gave me: it was love, love so vivid it spread from the trout to the entire river to the mountains and slopes and snows that formed the river. In "First Native," I wrote about it this way:

One of the signs of a true artist, according to the Asian epic *Mahabharata,* is a willingness to work patiently and lovingly with even the most inferior materials. I mention this bit of lore in conjunction with the story of my first large native trout, because the fly rod with which I caught that trout was, essentially, a nine-foot-long opportunity to seek this sign of the artist in myself. The rod wasn't mine. Neither was I at that time. We both belonged to my dad, actually. But one day when I was about half the rod's length, the dad we both belonged to placed the rod in my hands, stood me on the banks of Oregon's Deschutes River, showed me the salmon flies crawling along the sedge grass and alder leaves, said "Good luck," then thrashed out through a current too swift and deep for me to wade, out to an island, where he'd begin to work the far riffle — leaving me utterly alone and utterly stunned, with this double-David-lengthened rod in my hand, this gigantic green river in front of me, and this gigantic opportunity, the first in my life, to find out whether there was, according to the *Mahabharata,* any sign of the artist in me.

I didn't know, that day, that my fly rod was inferior. With nothing but a stumpy green glass spinning rod to compare it with, I'd have been equally delighted with a Leonard, a Powell, or a pool cue. Which is lucky. Because a pool cue was, basically, what my father had given me. It consisted of three yard-long luminous, hexagonal lengths of Tonkin bamboo, the world's finest. The same bamboo, after American B-52's turned the Tonkin Gulf into a moonscape, was worth its weight in gold. My rod, however, was a pre-war effort: priceless raw material converted into a fishing instrument by Yankee craftsmen who'd taken the same degree of care, and produced the same weight of implement, as the makers of some of our finest garden hoes. . . .

Its action brought to mind things like spaghetti, wilted lettuce and impotence. The scrinchy, out-of-round wheel and antique braided fly line upped the weight total from hoe to shovel. But what did I know? And, not knowing, what did I care? It is faith, not knowledge, that leads us into paradise, and at age nine, I had perfect faith that my reject rod, reel and line were the most magnificent tools and the Deschutes the most magnificent river that any sort of Dad & God combo could have possibly bequeathed me.

My paradise, though, had its raunchy edges. To pursue what needed pursuing, I had to step through a bunch of waxy-leaved vegetation that only retroactively identified itself as poison oak. Then, like some nine-year-old prefiguration of a contemporary fundamentalist homophobe, I had to catch the small, helpless, male homosexual salmon fly — or I assume it was male and homosexual, since it was riding around on the back of its dead ringer, who in turn was riding the slightly more voluptuous-looking back of what I took to be the female, since the probe thing coming off the middle male, the straight one, I guess you'd say, terminated in her fuselage, I guess you could call it, and she seemed perfectly serene about this. Anyhow, I nabbed the little humper up top, he seeming, in terms of the future of his race, the least gainfully employed. Drafted him, you might say, which makes me think: why would anyone *want* to join the military? Because the instant I drafted this guy I impaled him. No boot camp or nuthin'. Just impaled him, from one end clear out the other, on a #10 barbed steel bait hook. No apology, no prayer: that's where I was, in terms of the spirit world. But the little trooper I just skewered — think what you like about his sexual orientation — was about to enact a Passion Play that I would never forget.

That he remained alive with my whole hook running through him didn't affect me at first. That his little legs kept kicking, and that the legs, or maybe they were arms, that weren't kicking started hugging my finger — even that didn't affect me much. But when I pulled his little arms off my finger, swung him out over the river, and he, seeing the wild waters below, suddenly opened multiple golden wings in the sunlight and tried, hook and all, to fly, he finally hit me where I live . And homophobe, hell, it was *way* worse than that: I felt like this nine-year-old Roman asshole who'd just crucified a little winged Christian. When he hit the water and, still fluttering, sank, a cold stone filled my throat. I have tried, however awkwardly, to pray for every creature I've knowingly killed since.

And yet — when I drifted my little winged Christian into a foam-flecked seam in the lee of my father's island, things happened that would very soon lead to me to martyr many, many more such Christians. What can I say? We all live by sacrifice. As Tom McGuane once put it, "God created an impossible situation." But then salvaged it, I would add — or at least made the impossible loveable — by creating native trout.

For the first long instant of contact with my first great native, I saw nothing — just felt the sudden live pulsing, punching, shouting clean into the marrow of my know-nothing nine-year-old hands. For those little white hands, to keep feeling that wild electric pulse, suddenly forgot all about the things they did or didn't know and began to work the ginked reel, dorked line and impossible rod with the passion and patience of some ancient craftsman straight out of the *Mahabharata.* Neither my hands, nor I, have been quite the same since. And when the fish, still invisible, turned from the quiet seam and shot into the white-watered heart of the river, my fly rod was never the same either: it was five inches shorter.

That native's first long run turned the whole hollow canyon and me into I don't know what — a oneness, music, a single-stringed guitar, maybe; and the way that blazing blue river played us, the sizzling song the line sang in the water, this alone would have indentured me to the Deschutes for life. But then my native revealed itself — the rainbow, the whole shining body flying up out of the water, filling me for the first time, then again and again, with so much yearning and shock and recognition and joy that I can no longer swear that I remained in my body.

Every fisherman knows the basic alchemy: you place an offering on a steel point; you throw it in a river; your offering sinks despite the beating of its wings; you feel terrible, yet dare to hope a miracle will take place; then one does: the river converts your meager offering into an unseen power that enters your whole body through your hands. An old metal reel you mistook for tackle starts to shriek like a wounded animal. Your old rod breaks, but keeps lunging. Your heart does the same. Then, with no wings at all, native life comes flying out of the river — and that's when that hook's point pierces *you*. A barbed point, you realize later, because even when the day ends, the change in you does not. By the time you hold the native in your hands, it is you who has been caught; you who shines, and feels like silver; you who came, long ago, from water; you who suddenly can't live without this beautiful river.

When I was a young man I wanted to completely escape all religious zealots, rigidity, dogmatism — and instead enjoy, as constantly as possible, the love of the God of wilderness and rivers. In my late teens and twenties, I gave wilderness living and the hermit's life a couple of pretty solid tries. What a surprise to discover that some of the most sociopathic zealots and dogmatists in the world are living out in the pristine wild. What a double surprise to discover that, if I stayed too long and too Jeremiah-ically alone out there with them, I was in danger of joining them. I very slowly came to realize that one of the mixed, yet inarguable, blessings that God has given humanity is humanity. As I said before, I had been taught by rivers and wilderness that if you trust that gifts are coming to you, you become more sensitive to what's being given. I still use rivers and wilderness this way, in order to restore trust. At the end of what we can call my "Walden Phase," however, I found myself yearning to expand that same trust to include humans. In this spirit, it came to me that a total escape from zealotry and dogmatism was impossible and wrong for me.

As an Adventist kid, my Calvin, so to speak, was a prophetess called Helen G. White. Like Brother Calvin, Sister White was long gone by the time the pain and confusion she bequeathed my family came into full bloom. Isn't this almost always the way it is in family dogma wars? Aren't they head-on faith collisions that ex- or current fundamentalists or Catholics suffer as young men and women — not with defunct prophetesses or popes or patriarchs, but with the mothers, fathers, grandfathers who raised us as best they knew how?

My experience is that out of faith, fear, and zealousness, some people, who sincerely loved me, took my siblings and me by the hand as children and nailed those hands to a psychological cross that's been almost as impossible for us to escape as the New Testament original. My experience is, even if you manage to tear loose from such indoctrination, it leaves you scarred for life. I know ex-fundamentalists and ex-Catholics who disagree — who think they've escaped the childhood cross, the parents, the punitive nuns, the pews, the guilt, the scar and are now scot-free. This is not my experience. My experience is that the scars of a vehement religious indoctrination remain with us for life. We can escape the "us versus them" dogmas, the patriarchal rage, the judgmentalism, the institutional rote-think, the repressive and suffocating sorts of "Christian fold," but we can't escape that childhood scar. For those of us who have had a non-refusable, non-negotiable religious heritage pounded into us as kids, I feel the pounding must not be run from, but must be answered. That's what I've tried to do in my own writing, most notably in *The Brothers K*. We've got to steal back the ritual wounds from childhood, and find the least dogmatic, least self-destructive, least parent- or patriarch-hating, most open and profound and loving and forgiving meanings we can for those wounds.

Only then can we find, in that collision between faith and writing, ways to clean up the wreckage.

ANNE LAMOTT

An Interview by Linda Buturian

LINDA BUTURIAN: Which fiction writers do you like to read?

ANNE LAMOTT: John Grisham's a perfect travel fiction writer. He's a Baptist. And the new book is much less law, much more dark night of the soul for the main character. I love *A Map of the World* by Jane Hamilton. I love Alice Munro and Alice Adams, but she's my friend, so I don't know if that counts. I like the novel *Midwives* by Chris Bohjalian. I read a lot of poetry. People send me poems. Mary Oliver, Jane Kenyon, Rumi, Cavafy the Greek poet.

LB: What books do you like to read with Sam?

AL: I really love all the E. B. White books, although I find them almost unbearably poignant, and we both sob at the end of *Charlotte's Web*. We love Roald Dahl, though I hate his politics, of course.

LB: Regarding funny Christian writers. Know any others?

AL: C. S. Lewis is great. He's not goofy-funny, but he's so droll and interesting. Frederick Buechner is a wonderful Christian writer who has a terrific sense of humor. Most Christian writing is not classically funny, although sometimes on the Christian station, especially the AM Christian station, which is much looser than the FM, they have speakers who are really hilarious. They'll have women on in the afternoon who give a half hour pitch, and it will be like Erma Bombeck, but overtly Christian and self-deprecating.

194

It's such a joy to laugh, and I think a lot of us feel if God doesn't have a sense of humor, we are just so doomed. Christians that aren't really hardcore fundamentalist must feel that if they're going to get a whole segment of the population, they better start having some sense of humor because it's such a turn-off to hear this earnest, judgmental line.

LB: I've found it hard to write about my faith in fiction. It's easier in my non-fiction. I like the characters you've given belief to in your novels: Rae in *Crooked Little Heart* and Marie in *All New People*. They are human, susceptible to disbelief by others, vulnerable to ridicule, but true in their childlike faith. How do you do it?

AL: Well, I do it like I do everything — with a lot of false starts and really awful first drafts. With both of those two characters, Marie and Rae, there was a lot more originally about their Christianity. I took so much of it out because it sounded pontificating and flat-footed. It is hard to write about faith without coming across as proselytizing and as too earnest or self-satisfied, which I just can't stand. So I go out of my way not to lay that trip on people, not because I care that they know I'm a Christian, which everybody who reads me knows now, but because it's just such bad writing mostly. So anything that has stayed in has stayed in only because it wasn't as bad as the stuff that got taken out. Rae has such a nice sense of humor, and the people in the Ferguson family tease her so much. Marie just doesn't care. Rae and Marie's families and best friends tease them, and my family and best friends tease me, but it's pretty gentle. I'm not ever really attacked.

It's just like real life where you do your walk, you let people know what you're doing. When people ask what I'm going to do about something, I don't *not* say that I'm going to pray and meditate — meditate, in the sense of probably looking up scripture and thinking about stuff and talking to the pastor and then thinking some more. I don't *not* mention that that's what I'm going to do. In fact, I do mention that that's what I'm going to do, but partly just to annoy everyone. But at the same time, when I write, it tends to sound like that's what I hate most in the world: people that seem to have all the answers who then make everybody else feel like they're not doing as well. So I write a lot; then, I take out all but the stuff that I really love.

LB: I am somewhat of an insomniac. The other night I was lying awake obsessing about some inane thing, and all of a sudden I imagined myself as a child in God's family, and I saw myself as a six-year-old, worrying with her blanket and afraid of everything, especially the dark. When you lie awake at night, what kind of child are you in the family of God? How old do you feel?

AL: I've had a bad time sleeping since I was four or five. I've always been somebody who's had pretty tough nights to get through. I don't really feel like a child of a particular age when I can't sleep. I feel like a person in such need, and I feel stricken and so lousy. A lot of us were raised thinking that we were bringing stuff on ourselves. So if I was having a hard time sleeping, someone was apt to tell me just to relax. You know, I've been sober for a long time and a Christian for even longer — I have a lot of tools and skills, a lot of self-hypnosis and relaxation skills — and I often still can't sleep. So I don't feel like a two-year-old or a four-year-old or a 45-year-old (which I will be next month), but I feel like a child of God, like somebody who is really, really challenged in this one area. It's awful.

One of the reasons I'm so raggedy today is that I was awake and not in my own bed last night, wherever I was — I can't even remember — St. Louis. I had to get up really early to come here, and of course I'm on California time, so I'm already way off kilter, and literally for the life of me, I couldn't sleep. Then, of course, the panic was kicking in and the trying to self-will myself into falling asleep, and the effort to control something that is like a force of nature. Through it all, on top of it, there was a voice that was like the feminine side of God, the mother side, the very, very gentle stroking side. I also feel Jesus lying in bed with me quite a lot, stroking my shoulders very gently. I reminded myself that if I couldn't fall asleep at all that I would get through today, no matter what. That nothing, not principalities or insomnia, could separate me from the love and the strength of God.

I guess a lot of times I feel about eleven. Sort of pre-pubescent. I don't feel like a snappy kid who's trying to experiment with her image and sexuality, but rather someone who's right on the cusp of that who doesn't feel like an anything yet, who doesn't feel like a kid anymore and certainly doesn't feel like a young woman or young teenager. I feel kind of in that limbo-land of not having any identity particularly. But that's not always a bad thing. It means that I can be a little bit formless and a little bit outside of that need to have an image or a definition to hang it all on.

LB: A friend of mine says, gently, that I'm a narcissist at night. He's right. There's no God outside of my mind.

AL: I've had a lifetime of people projecting their shit on me because they sleep well. I'm very active in recovery, and people that have 25 and 30 years [of recovery] will say, "Well, no one ever died from lack of sleep." I have had it with people's opinion about this thing I have. I feel like I have been spiritually given a gift that they don't have, one that they won't get, because they put their head down at eleven and they fall asleep. I also refuse to lay a creepy trip on people if they're real fat or they can't get their food life together or if they have a hard time with depression. I don't feel like "Wow, you know, you're not working your program. Why don't you turn to God?" It's so sick, so mean. And it's why I love Jesus so much: I don't think Jesus would ever say that no one ever died from lack of sleep. Jesus doesn't see that I'm being a pain in the ass or that I'm trapped in my overactive mind. Jesus just sees my pain.

It's like when Jesus is on the cross with the crooks on either side of him, and one of them is saying what a joke he is and what a sorry-ass excuse for a savior he is, if he can't even save himself. The other thief really gets it and he says, "This guy didn't do anything wrong. He just deserves compassion because he's in this awful situation." So one of them is very moved. It's so nurturing to Jesus for somebody to have that compassionate response to him, instead of that derision.

I've had many men in my life, and they were all good sleepers. I've never been with a man who slept like I did, and most of my girlfriends are good sleepers. Most of the people I'm close to have other stuff: they're anorexic or they're fat or they can't get their careers jumpstarted and I don't say, "Well, for God's sake — why don't you just do this or do that." I just say, "It's really hard and we do it imperfectly. I know what that feels like. It's lonely and God loves you exactly the same when you're in what somebody else might call a narcissistic trance." It's all the same to God. God just sees the need.

It's like that hymn, not the famous "Amazing Grace," but that hymn that goes "Amazing grace will always be the song I sing, for it was grace that bought my liberty." The chorus says, "He looked beyond my wants and saw my needs." God looks beyond our craving or our rage at not falling asleep or whatever the mental turmoil or the agitation is, and he doesn't see that you're blowing it or that you're not doing a good job being you. It's part of what makes you you. He's not here to take it away. I don't even think he's here to get you to sleep. He's here to fill it with his love, his tenderness, his company, his presence. That's why we're Christians.

LB: Let's talk about the evil man and the dog in *Traveling Mercies*. I made the mistake of reading that story before I went to sleep, so I lay awake worrying about the retriever. I like how you pursued God's love to its radical end. That's what's amazing about Jesus; he loves that sick man as much as he loves me. But, like T. S. Eliot says, "All time is eternally present." And I'm frozen in that bad moment on the beach with the man hurting the dog, and I really wanted to go with you when you told your son that the dog wouldn't always be with that man. I want to know where that hope comes from because I think all of us, on some level, are frozen in a moment of terror, and we're waiting for the heat and light of grace to release us.

AL: I'm not sure that what I meant was that the dog would ever get away from that man. What I meant was that the dog's life with that man was a drop in the bucket, and that the dog had such a dignity and presence about him. I don't overthink things like whether pets go to heaven, but I assume that if there are no pets in heaven, I'm hardly interested. I mean just barely.

I feel that all souls are eternally present too. There's God's love and there's stuff that appears to not be a part of God's love. I don't have the eyes to see and the breadth of understanding to perceive.

This man who had the dog is also a child of God. The mystery is that God loves that man who was abusing the dog. I don't think the man is satanic and not worthy of God's love. I don't think John King, the guy who did that horrible racist crime, is not one of God's children. It's our condition taken to the nth degree, our condition without having had as much love as we managed to find. It's who we are — with a biochemistry that is so vulnerable to acting out stuff so violently.

I might yank Sam's arm but that's about the worst I do, though I'm not proud of it. Still, it's a pretty big distance between what I do and what

John King did. But at the same time I have to believe that God loves John King and holds him in his heart and that when John King dies, he will have a soul with a spark of divinity in it, and it will be reunited with the source of that. The part that was his personality — or the wound that made him be a person capable of atrocity — will be behind him. Whatever happened in his family or in his blood chemistry that made this way of being on the earth his reality is not who he is eternally. It's who he is personality and character-wise. He wasn't born that way: he was born like your baby or mine. I believe he came here just fine. He may have had a predisposition to craziness and violence that was treatable by drugs and therapy, but he wasn't living in a household and culture that got him the help he needed.

I believe that Jesus doesn't say you should love everybody unless they kill somebody or unless they're really cruel to a pet. Jesus doesn't say that. He just says, I'm really sorry — there are no loopholes. You can hate what these people do. But you have to love them or you're delusional and you're thinking you are better than they are. The truth is that we've all sinned and fallen short. You love this guy anyway and you pray for him and hold space for him to find his way home too. Because he seems to have gotten very badly lost along the way.

I don't know that that dog will ever get away from that man. I think it's possible that that dog will get killed by the man, and the man is going to aggravate the wrong person and get killed himself. I don't think sadism means you're not worthy of God's love because we have sadism inside of our beings. Cruelty is part of what it means to be human.

LB: What do you want to convey to Sam about God?

AL: I want to convey that we get to be human. We get to make awful mistakes and fall short of who we hope we're going to turn out to be.

That we don't have to be what anybody else tries to get us to be, so they could feel better about who they were. We get to screw up right and left. We get to keep finding our way back home to goodness and kindness and compassion.

That there is actually an even deeper stream that runs through us, and it's the stream that flows home to God and that flows from God through us daily, bringing with it the living water of life and of hydration and of tears and of that which waters the garden.

You get to screw up and if you're lucky, you feel the pain of that. It's like the line I quoted in a book, "that we're not punished for the sin but by the sin." If you're lucky, you can stay open enough to life and present enough to feel awful when you really screw up. When you do, the solution is not to try to pump yourself out of it by trying to amass some more power, but instead to get very surrendered and humbled like it talks about in the last lines of the chapter of Micah, "To walk humbly with your God and to love justice and mercy." To be a part of *that,* instead of the power and the domination and the ego.

I want him to know that no matter what happens, he's never going to have to walk alone. That God, as I understand God, does not talk loudly, in audible or profoundly mysterious ways, but that God speaks through the love of our friends and the love of the people who write — who wrote the Bible and who write the most brilliant stuff that we're going to come upon that resonates with truth. It's like that wonderful line, "the spirit rejoices in hearing what it already knows." There is love and intelligence beyond all understanding that animates wonderful writing and art and music. And we hear God there and we see God in the faces of the people we love whether we ever see them again or not. That's what I'm trying to convey to Sam.

LUCI SHAW

- -

Reversing Entropy

I love to tell the story
of unseen things above,
Of Jesus and his glory,
of Jesus and his love . . .

This Sunday School song, echoing from my earliest childhood memories, suggests a question — just how do we tell the story of *the unseen?*

So, it's about Jesus and his glory — but how and when have we witnessed heavenly glory? We can perhaps speak of Jesus' love with great personal authenticity, but without viewing Jesus in the flesh, without seeing him at the Father's right hand, words fail us again. Without the visuals, how do we know enough to form a narrative? Is imagination useful here, or may it lead us into dangerous waters?

Narrative is a word originally derived from the Latin *noscere* — to know, and a related word *gnarus* — knowing. Perhaps that is another way of saying that story is how we come to know the world.

As most poets and writers acknowledge, we *do* live in a world susceptible to narrative and imagery. We all find ourselves, without ever asking for it, to be part of a cosmic epic that continually unfolds as future becomes present becomes past.

We try, in the moment, to make sense out of what may often seem surreal, horrifying, incongruous, paradoxical, irrelevant, absurd, while retaining a kind of eschatological hope that God's order, peace, design, glory, and joy will fill all the spaces in our widely scattered personal and cosmic jig-saw puzzles. We look forward to a time when, like Moses, after his Sinai encounter with Yahweh, our faces will shine in a way that no earthly description could illuminate. We watch and wait for the fulfillment of the prophecy of Isaiah 11:9 that assures us, "The earth will be full of the knowledge of the Lord as the waters cover the sea!"

Manna

They asked, and he brought quails,
And gave them food from heaven. Ps. 105:40

I'm not asking for quails for dinner
and if they flew in my window at mealtime,
in a torrent of wind, I would think
panic, not miracle.

Time is so multiple and fluid. I gain a day
flying east, and lose it again returning.
I am ravenous to know where I am today.
And who. And how am I to be fed? And if
the prayer I offered this morning at first light
was known and answered last week
am I in some horizontal pleat of time,
some rock crevice in the mountain's shoulder
with a Great Hand shielding me from
the tempest of too much knowledge?

You never know what a simple request
will get you. So, no expectation of birds
from heaven. Rather, I will commit myself
to this quotidian wilderness, watching for what
the wind may bring me next —
perhaps a small wafer tasting like honey
that I can pick up with my fingers

and lay on my tongue
to ease, for this day, my hunger to know.

(Unpublished poem)

Meanwhile, here we are, caught in time and rooted in space. Time, multiple and fluid as it is, is an essential part of our writing. And, as we might guess, the word *story* is linked with the word *history* (from the Greek word *historia,* the learning that comes by narrative telling), and *poem* comes from *poema,* a word that reflects the idea of something being made. Without a sense of time, the forward movement of living and growing, or purpose and events and progress and change, the shape of history and living would be without meaning. And as a Christian I do believe that life has meaning, that we are heading somewhere, and that growth is happening and wisdom increasing.

The epic poem of the world is imprinted everywhere — the growth rings widening in the boles of trees, the wind- and water-carved art of coastal sandstone rocks, sharp "young" mountains contrasted with the older range formations of the Himalayas and the Andes, the up-ended strata of geological shift, inscribed parchments and tablets, the artifacts discovered in archeological digs, the fossil evidence, and the eroding edges of continents that cannot be reclaimed any more than lost innocence.

We may be trapped in time, but God is not. It is a dictum of physics that at the speed of light (and the timelessness of God who is not, as we are, bound by time, but is outside of time), the *now* of the on-going present *includes* the pivotal moments in history of Creation, the Exodus, the Incarnation, Crucifixion and Resurrection, and the arrival of the Holy Spirit to be our pathfinder into truth.

Present

At light-speed, God-speed,
time collapses into now so that
we may see Christ's wounds as
still bleeding, his torso,
that ready sponge, still
absorbing our vice, our toxic shame.

He is still being pierced
by every hateful nail
we hammer home. In this
Golgotha moment his body —
chalice for the dark tears
of the whole world — brims,

spilling over as his life blood
drains. His dying into the earth
begins the great reversal —
as blood from a vein leaps
into the needle, so with his rising,
we surge into light.

(Unpublished poem)

Story and poetry have the power to grasp bits of the past and carry them into the imaginative present, rescuing us from the pitfalls of abstraction. It is not insignificant that much of the Bible, including the deutero-canonical books, is narrative or poetic in form, and that the characters and plots and images revealed on the sacred pages are not so different from those that surround and involve us today. As North American theologian Eugene Peterson has said,

> Somewhere along the way, most of us pick up bad habits of extracting from the Bible what we pretentiously call "spiritual principles" or "moral guidelines," or "theological truths" and then corseting ourselves in them in order to force a godly shape on our lives. . . . Mighty uncomfortable. . . . [But] it's not the Gospel way. . . . As we enter and imaginatively participate, we find ourselves in a more spacious, freer, and more coherent world. We didn't know all this was going on! We had never noticed all this significance! . . . Story brings us into more reality, not less, expands horizons, sharpens both sight and insight. Story is the primary means we have for learning what the world is, and what it means to be a human being in it. No wonder that from the time we acquire the rudiments of language, we demand stories.

And we feast on poems, connecting with their emotional highs and lows.

Peterson continues: ". . . God isn't a doctrine David talks about but a person by whom he's led and cared for. God isn't a remote abstraction that distances him from the conditions of his actual life but an intimate presence who confirms his daily life as the very stuff of salvation." There we have it — the God who is Other but in whom we live and have being. The God who is both transcendent as well as immanent, both *there* and *here*. The Lion and the Lamb. The Spirit and the Word. Story and poetry continually attempts to fill the unsearchable spaces left by mystery and paradox. Mrs. Blake said of her husband William, "I miss the company of my husband; he is so often in Paradise." Unlike Blake most of us are not mystics. We are earthbound, but with the longing for and an occasional glimpse of a wider, more profound understanding of our existence.

Story and poetry are the most familiar and accessible ways for human beings to understand the world. Despite the tenets of post-modernism, itself a meta-narrative, a "horizon-less landscape," again and again, through writing, this world relaxes into coherence, in the process becoming less inchoate or disjunctive. Every time we tell a story or write a poem or compose an essay we give chaos a way of re-integrating back into order; we reverse entropy; pattern and meaning begin to overcome randomness and decay. We find satisfaction in juxtaposition and linkage and succession and resolution as things split and differentiate and flow together again.

Not that it's all pre-packed and programmed. I like to think that the uncertainty principle allows for surprises. Imaginative writing often veers off in unexpected directions, to the astonishment of the writer. Freshness and new insights happen in a continuous stream as we learn from our own stories, our poems, our imaginations. How many of us writers — novelists, poets, essayists — are taught by the words and images that come to us (like unanticipated gifts, without our even trying) from quite literally, God knows where? A poem fragment:

> . . . My imagination has always been a window for you
> to open. Sometimes it's like this: a drab day, and then
> a little dance begins in the brain — bubbles rising like yeast,

a quickening spirit hovering over the waters. Dreams begin
to come in three or more dimensions, rhythms pulse in waves,

phrases nudge me like little fists, sounds begin to click
together, green turns real enough to be written as a word
on paper. Skeptic, and no scientist, I am being tuned to
the narrative of heaven. My own poems persuade me the way
an available womb, and labor, persuade a baby to be born.

("Holy Ghost")

This element of the transcendent, what British author C. S. Lewis
called "patches of God-light," what many of us have experienced as epiphany, hints to us that this is not just our story (we realize, perhaps ruefully,
that we are only a minuscule part of it). Just as a bicyclist riding along a
country road through the woods may be dappled from time to time with
the bright light of the sun, so we, in the course of everyday living, may be
made aware of a brightness and a vision of what is above, beyond us, and
so find ourselves, along with other travelers, linked into that larger universe. Described variously as "cosmic consciousness," or by Aldous
Huxley as "mystic experience," examples are everywhere. A recent poem
in the *New Yorker* by Maurice Manning said it like this, in the final lines of
a poem titled "Analogue": ". . . Oh, revelation only ever comes/at sudden
crossings — the heart hopping like a happy frog." And Sylvia Plath argued:

. . . Miracles occur,
If you care to call those spasmodic
Tricks of radiance miracles. The wait's begun again,
For that rare, random descent.

In an imaginative sense we are invaded by mystery and transported
into a place of even greater and more persistent reality than the "real"
world we know. Jesus welcomes us, in his parabolic stories, into a realm
of truth that would be otherwise impenetrable to us. What Jesus had to
say about transcendent truths may be literally unspeakable but meta-
phorically suggestive and rich with insight. Metaphor bridges the gap between unknown and known. The stories Jesus told are, to varying de-

grees, metaphorical. Annie Dillard comments, in *Living by Fiction,* that the parables are "a hermeneutic of the world."

In the Gospel of Matthew, chapter 13, Jesus' friends ask him, "Why do you tell stories?" It's a good question. Often a Gospel parable will start out with the words, "The kingdom of God is like . . ." and then proceeds to sketch a story that may be hard for us to comprehend in terms of that kingdom. Have you ever wondered why some of the Jesus stories seem to complicate or even obscure rather than clarifying and simplifying truth? Perhaps it's that God, who knows us better than we know ourselves, is not content to speak simply to the rational intelligence, but informs us instead through imagination, intuition, wonder, epiphany, in moments of crystal insight and lifetimes of pondering.

Though theologians draw principles out of these narratives that seem logical, the principles themselves remain abstract. The Bible wasn't written as systematic theology. We can talk in broad terms about "soteriology" or "atonement," but until such ideas are fleshed out to us in story and imagery, say in the life of Christ who "purchased" our salvation (another metaphor), or the blood-letting of sacrifice to achieve atonement, such considerations do not touch us deeply. But images and stories print themselves on our minds (and even our senses) in such brilliant color and three-dimensional texture that time and distraction cannot obliterate them.

The parables were never meant to be dissected analytically; they were designed to be absorbed by the senses and the imagination and *felt,* the sub-text of ideal, principle, and truth absorbed almost unconsciously as the mental image and the quickening power of poetic narrative suffuse the understanding over a period of time, a kind of divine soft-sell salesmanship. And this, in our time, is the Spirit's work:

> . . . the third
> Person is a ghost. Sometimes
> he silvers for a moment, a moon sliver
> between moving leaves. We aren't sure.
>
> What to make of this . . . How
> to see breath? . . .

... This for sure — he finds
enough masks to keep us guessing:
Is it really you? Is this you also?

It's a cracked, crossover world, waiting
for bridges. He escapes our categories,
choosing his shapes — fire, dove,
wind, water, oil — closing the breach
in figures that flicker within
the closed eye, tongue the brain, sting
and tutor the soul. Once incarnate
in Judaea, now he is present
(in us, in the present tense),
occupying our bodies — shells to be
reshaped — houses for this holy ghost.
In our special flesh he thrives into something
too frequent to deny, too real to see.

("Holy Ghost")

God does not always speak openly, plainly, directly, as he did to and through Noah and Moses and Jonah. While figurative language often leaves us with vivid impressions, or teaches by analogy, it may also cause puzzlement about what is being meant. Metaphor not only enlivens and suggests, but it furnishes a kind of screen between the object and what it is being compared with. Can we ask *why?*

First, there is the difficulty of myopic, fragile human beings facing the reality of the God of glory. Emily Dickinson's succinct dictum goes like this: "The truth must dazzle gradually/or every man be blind." In C. S. Lewis's words: "God is the only comfort; he is also the supreme terror; the thing we most need and the thing we most want to hide from. He is our only ally and we have made ourselves his enemies." And so a full frontal view of the Almighty, swift as light, sharper and more intense than a laser, with the energy of the universe flashing out of him, would paralyze, flatten, and annihilate us.

Perhaps that is why the Creator gives us imagery, instilling his ideas and truths, his grace and love, into our minds through story and psalm, through poetry, prophetic vision, and dynamic illustration, so that the truth dazzles us gradually.

Scripture is full of such imagery. "All right," you may be thinking, "we can all accept that poetry is implicit in metaphor, and analogy can bring truth closer and render it more memorable. But what are we to make of prophetic writings, vivid and forceful, replete with brilliant visions as they were, but also laden with enigmatic or oblique messages?" One sometimes wonders why the divine directives were transmitted at all if they were so cryptic. The surreal visions of Ezekiel and the revelations to St. John in particular may seem like hallucinatory ravings. Why lamp-stands and burning swords? Why the tantalizing riddles about vials and scrolls and bowls and seals and pale horses and scarlet women and lightnings and crystal seas in the Revelation? Why the bizarre "wheels within wheels full of eyes" of Ezekiel? Why all those unearthly beasts with their hybrid wings and horns and hooves and talons? Commentators interpret such symbolic language with widely divergent results.

Another question. God is Spirit. How, with our limited senses, may we *see and hear* this transcendent deity? And why, if our Creator wants us to trust him, to know him, to be his friends, does he seem deliberately to conceal or disguise himself? John Stott, the venerable and deeply-orthodox Anglican priest and writer, was quoted recently in the Sept. 2003 *Christianity Today* as saying, "The invisibility of God is a great problem." Why is truth so often presented as "mystery"? Isaiah cried out, in seeming frustration, "Verily thou art a God that hidest thyself." The writer of the Proverbs proclaimed a paradox: "It is the glory of God to conceal a matter."

Even in the New Testament, apart from the Revelation consisting mainly of historical narrative and hortatory teaching, mystery abounds. It is defined as something secret, hidden, not known to all. There is the "mystery of iniquity," but also the "mystery of godliness," "the mystery of the Gospel," and "the mystery of the kingdom." There is "the mystery of marriage" — between man and woman and between Christ and the Church, and "the mystery of Jew and Gentile united as one body in Christ." There are others. All mystery feels like fog. It presents hiddenness. It demands strong faith to walk into it believing that one day it will be de-mystified. We know from the Proverbs that people perish where the vision has been dimmed or extinguished. If we had been God, we tell ourselves smugly, we wouldn't have done it like that.

Jesus himself gives us a clue why God does it like that. The Gospel of Mark records that "with many parables he spoke the word [to the people]. . . . He did not speak to them without a parable, but privately to his own disciples he explained everything." Matthew tells us that Jesus' followers asked, "Why do you speak to the people in parables?" Jesus' answer:

> To you it has been given to know the secrets of the kingdom of heaven, but to them it has not been given. . . . This is why I speak to them in parables, because seeing they do not see, and hearing they do not hear, nor do they understand. With them is fulfilled the prophecy of Isaiah that says: You shall indeed hear but never understand, and you shall indeed see but never perceive. For this people's heart has grown dull and their ears heavy of hearing, and their eyes they have closed. . . . But blessed are your eyes, for they see, and your ears, for they hear.

Jesus made a clear distinction between those who *want* to hear and understand, who *yearn* to see and believe, and those who deliberately clap their hands over their ears or shut out any illumination with tightly closed eyes. The inner "sense organs," the spiritual eyes and ears of spiritual "insight," created to receive impulses and signals from beyond, may become atrophied through disuse or disdain, and the result is indifference and dullness to the colorful inner landscape of creative insight and divine revelation.

"Puzzles are to be solved, but mysteries are to be experienced," says Robert McAfee Brown. We, like those followers of Jesus, have glimpses of knowing, of seeing something transcendent that confirms our faith. But because it is *faith* — having to do with things not yet seen — we also must often live with the biblical experience of feeling baffled and puzzled and even skeptical.

And the greatest mystery of all was the Incarnation — Eternal Spirit, Mighty God becoming flesh in Jesus Christ. Like Mary we ask, "How can this be?" And we are compelled to enter imaginative mode as we try to penetrate the Mystery. The dis-junction brought about by the Fall, the rupture in divine-human relations, compels us to ask the narrative queries Who? What? When? Why? How?

The *When* is a complex matter of history and archeology that might be unfolded at length, a task quite beyond me. The *Why* invites us into the arena of the Almighty's continuing desire to bring humanity back into unity and harmony with himself, through what Eugene Peterson calls "passionate patience" as the Creator subjects himself to our human temporality. The *What* is an on-going revelation of the divine. The *How* is quite beyond us — the visitation of the angel, the pregnancy of a virgin, the singing angels, and the traveling star. But the *Who* was God bringing within our human vision a form of himself that human beings like John *could* see and hear and touch. "From the very first day we were there, taking it all in — we heard it with our own ears, saw it with our own eyes, verified it with our own hands. The Word of Life appeared right before our eyes; we saw it happen!"

> . . . how may we,
> *his distant pilgrims,* know him real (whose
> Garden presence still guards the gnarled,
> secret olives)? Faith listens for his story
> in the everyday neigh of a donkey,
> an explosive obscenity, the threat of
> armed soldiers, sweat on any dark skin,
> the clink of coins, thorns pricking, metal
> clanging on metal, a cloth tearing.
>
> ("Slide Photography, Mt. of Olives")

That's the kind of epiphany we need now. Sometimes it comes to us like a gift, out of the blue, and all we can say is *Thank you. Thank you.*

Recently, reading the narrative of Acts chapter 9, I felt a sudden jolt of insight as I reread the account of Saul's riveting experience on the road to Damascus. I felt *I was* Saul. I could feel the immense clarity that engulfed him as "suddenly a light from heaven flashed around him," and gave him a crystalline display of who he was from God's perspective, and the dramatic, life-changing reversal that was being asked of him. Entering that experience was like wine for me, or perfume, or the most warming sunshine. It was lucid, brilliant, vivid, unclouded. With Saul I had glimpsed God, and I understood with Saul that this energy from God was transformative. I could perfectly realize why he was transformed into Paul and was never the same again.

The impression lasted in my imagination for several hours, as I revisited and re-imagined it. In a crowded day I tried to find a quiet place where I could recapture it and live it again — that reality, that sense of Presence. Now all that I have is the memory of a memory. But even the memory remains transformative.

I am most aware of the action of the Holy Spirit in my life when a new image or phrase makes its way so insistently into my imagination that I have no option but to write it into a poem. I learn a lot from the poems themselves, those small presents freely given.

A story from the life of Denise Levertov is worth recounting here. In her essay "A Life That Enfaiths" in *New & Selected Essays,* she recounts:

> As I became, a few years ago, more and more occupied with questions of belief, I began to embark on what I'll call "do-it-yourself theology." Sometimes I was merely trying to clarify my mind and note down my conclusions-in-process by means of the totally undistinguished prose of journal entries. Sometimes, however, *it was in poems that the process took place,* and most notably in the first such poem I wrote, a longish piece called *Mass for the Day of St. Thomas Didymus. . . .* The poem began as an experiment in structure. . . .

Levertov thought to herself that it might be possible to adapt the framework of a choral piece that included parts of Masses from many periods — medieval, renaissance, baroque, classical, and modern — not in chronological order, yet with a striking unity because of its liturgical framework. She writes:

> I thought of my poem as "an agnostic Mass," basing each part on what seemed its primal character: the Kyrie a cry for mercy, the Gloria a praise-song, the Credo an individual assertion, and so on:

each a personal, secular meditation. But a few months later, when I had arrived at the Agnus Dei, I discovered myself to be in a different relationship to the material and to the liturgical form from that in which I had begun. The experience of writing the poem — that long swim through waters of unknown depth — had been a conversion process. . . .

In effect, Levertov had been transformed by her own writing as she experienced unintended changes in her understanding through the poem she herself was working on, and the efficacy of truth and its substance in her own unconscious.

We are all, whether or not we are conscious of it, swimming in waters of unknown depth. St. Paul prayed for his friends that "the eyes of their hearts might be enlightened." The stories, the poems, are there to be attended to, to be absorbed if we are willing to give them our attention, to follow the path of exploration and observation, eyes and ears alert, to follow the word, even giving over our conscious control of where it will lead. Madeleine L'Engle calls this way of life "becoming the servant of the word."

Like Mary, with her available womb, like the ancient prophets, standing in the gap, a foot in two worlds, with souls attuned to both heaven and earth, like the psalmists listening for celestial tunes and translating them into the real poetry of both desolation and exaltation, like the Son of God himself become flesh, we fulfill our destinies by telling and re-telling the story that weaves together divine transcendence and earthy human experience.

Let us go forth together, rejoicing in the power of the Spirit! Alleluia, Alleluia!

MADELEINE L'ENGLE

. . . .

The Cosmic Questions

———————

. . . One day when I was three, I woke up with my right knee hot and swol-
len. My mother took me to a doctor, who sent me to a specialist who put
me in a leather and steel brace — much worse than this Darth Vader
thing I have on tonight. It made me cry. She told me later that it made
her cry too, so she took it off. We never went back to the doctor and that
was probably the best thing she could have possibly done for me.

I went back to being about as normal as I was ever going to be, as far
as my knee was concerned. It was apparent by the time I went to school
that I was not going to win any relay races, that I was not an asset to
team sports. And so, after school instead of going out and playing with
the kids, I went home and read and wrote. I began to find myself as a storyteller. That's one of the advantages of being very bad at one thing and
learning that I could do something else. I wrote my first small story when
I was five, and my mother kept it for a long time. Fortunately, it's been
lost — we don't write immortal prose at five.

But we do start to ask questions. The big questions. The cosmic
questions. The questions I did have sense enough never to ask at school.
The perennial question: why? But it wasn't "why can't I go out and play"
or "why can't I eat candy," it was why, if God is good, do terrible things
happen? Why is there war? Why are people mean to each other? Why is
there a sign on that little girl's front door that says, "Diphtheria"? What is

diphtheria? Is she going to die? What is death? Where do we go when we die? Obviously, I was not a child who went to Sunday School because Sunday School teachers often tend to answer questions that don't have answers, so I feel quite blessed. My father was a drama and music critic and my parents slept late, so I went to eleven o'clock church with them. I loved the music, I loved the liturgy, and without knowing it, I fell in love with the great words of Cranmer and Coverdale and the King James translation of scripture, which, inaccurate though it is, is wonderful, is glorious.

Who goes to heaven? Is anybody left out? As a left-out child, I didn't want anybody left out. My parents taught me that God is love. Total love. And love does not leave anybody out, particularly those who are hurt or unhappy. When Jesus said, "I am not here for those who are well, but for those who are sick, those who know they are broken," I knew that meant *for me.* If I felt left out by my school friends and my school teachers, I did not feel left out by God.

I read and I wrote. I listened to my father, coughing his lungs out. He'd been gassed in the First World War. It took him until I was nearly 18 to finish coughing his lungs out. He had sense enough not to fool me by saying there would never be another war. I would say, "Father, there won't ever be another war, will there?" This was that war which was supposed to end wars. But the nations were already lining up for the next war, and the next, and the next. I read in 2 Samuel, "In the spring of the year is the time when kings go to war. . . ." Not much has changed.

My grandmother died, a favorite uncle died. What happened? Where did they go? Why? We read stories, and we write stories because we ask the big questions to which there are no finite answers. We tell stories about people who give us our best answers, in the way that they live and work out their lives and treat other people and try to find the truth.

We moved to Europe my seventh and eighth grade years, and I learned on the hockey field to ask to play goalie. Goalies don't have to run. All you have to do is be intrepid and not mind if you get knocked down. But my knee cropped up again as a problem. At the Anglican boarding school I was sent to (this Anglican boarding school kept me from Anglicanism for at least another twenty years), I was taken out of study hall one night and taken up to the infirmary, and there was the nurse, the matron, and my homeroom teacher all with smirks on their faces. They had me lie down on a long table. They took out tape measures, and they measured me. I had no idea what was going on, what they were doing, except that they were smirking. Then I was sent back to study hall. About two weeks later, I was called out again. They opened this box, and in it was a big shoe with a huge lift on it. I knew one of my legs was longer than the other — I compensated. I didn't want this thing, but they took away my shoes. So I went down to the cloak room, put on my rubber boots, took these shoes and went up the hillside and dug a hole and buried them. Then I quoted Shakespeare's words, "Blessed be he who saves these bones, but cursed be he who moves them." That's not quite right, but that's the way I felt about it. They could not get out of me what I had done with the shoes, so they finally gave me back my school shoes and let me go on. My parents wrote a letter saying, "leave her alone." (I envy people who can sit back on their heels, and I've always wanted to be able to sit in full lotus position but that's never been a possibility.)

Here again, though, I was filled with the great words, with the great language, which they couldn't avoid because, at an Anglican school, we had morning and evening prayer — badly read by one of the mistresses. But at least there were the words, there was the language.

We came back to the States, and there I went to an amazing school run by a woman who grew up in the day when it was not considered nice for Southern gentlewomen to go to college — because most colleges are hotbeds of atheism. So she waited for her parents to die, and then she took herself off to Smith College as an undergraduate in her forties, came back, and started her school. Every December, we did three plays from the Chester cycle. At Lent too, we did great medieval plays. Wonderful language. And every spring, we did one of Shakespeare's plays. One of my better roles was Sir Andrew Aguecheek. Because I was tall, and it was a girls' school, I got all the good men's roles. One year, the girl playing the most important shepherd in the Christmas play could not react properly. When the star came on, we were supposed to *react*, and she was not reacting properly. The headmistress picked up a chair, ran up on the stage and flung it at Martha. She reacted! So there I was learning good direction — she was a magnificent director. Good language all put together.

I never got on the basketball team, though I was tall. But I was an actress. And I edited the school magazine, and the teachers actually liked what I was writing. Most of us went to the Episcopal church on Sundays, and that's when I began to learn to write poetry — during the sermons. The minister was very dull, and I might not have ever written poetry had it not been for that. Again I was asking the questions, and during holidays, looking to my father. When I was seventeen, he finally died. Why do we die? What happens? What does God do with us?

Religion classes did not give satisfactory answers. I often have trouble with Paul of Tarsus, but he gave the best answer I've ever heard. He was talking about that glorious impossibility that we're going to get after death, a spiritual body, and when he was asked to explain it he said, "Don't be silly." That's the best answer. We don't know. All we do is trust. I believe that what God's up to is going to be good.

So I went to college. The first Sunday I went to church and nobody spoke to me, so I never went back. I grieved for my father, though I didn't realize that my depression and my angst were ways of grief expressing itself. I spent four years absorbing great writers. Living with their works. Absorbing their use of language, their questions, their characters. . . . I fell in and out of love. I finally wept tears of grief for my father and was purged. I read Plato and Aristotle, and because we had to take a science, I took psychology and dabbled in Freud and Jung. And I wrote stories and about half of what was to be my first novel.

We were also required to take a sport, so again I was goalie. One of the seniors got pneumonia and died. Again came the unanswerable question about death. How can we love God if we do not understand that we are going to die and that God is not going to abandon us?

I didn't have a place in my schedule for a music course, but I did get an hour a day in one of the music rooms to play the piano. As I played Bach's themes, I realized that he was asking all of my questions in his themes and answering them with structure. I learned that Beethoven's music deepened as he grew deafer. A friend told me that, in his symphonies, Mahler was expressing his outraged grief at the death of his child. I struggled with the perennial question of God's will and our will. And no, God did not make Beethoven deaf for the glory of the music. God did not want my friend in the senior class to die. Bad things happen largely because of what we have done in the past and in the present. My father died because of war, people fighting other people.

The Second World War did not seem to be ambiguous, but it was still terrible. I graduated from college in 1941, right into that war. I did not understand hate, and again I thought of Samuel, "in the spring of the year when kings go to war." We just keep doing that. I finished my first novel — amazingly, it was published, and it did very well. I had no idea that after several other fairly successful novels, I was going to go into a decade-plus of nothing but rejection slips.

Having my children and trying to raise them and living in a house which we could never heat in the winter was a challenge. Once when we had a washing machine, everything froze in it. I remember being given Anne Morrow Lindberg's beautiful book, *Gift from the Sea,* in which she suggests that every young wife and mother go to the sea for two weeks and walk on the beach, and pick up pebbles and shells and commune with herself. At which point, I flung the book across the room: "Fine for you, Anne Morrow Lindberg! Who's going to come take care of my kids while I go to the sea?"

Two nights a year in January at the time of our anniversary were what I got. They were better than nothing, but there wasn't much time for communing. Communing with God or nature or myself. It was struggle. Nevertheless, grace was given in all kinds of ways. The center of the village and of our lives was the old colonial Congregational church, which had been redecorated in the worst of Victorian excesses. But there was there an incredible sense of Christian fellowship — of Christians loving each other. It was a good meeting place for my husband and for me, he with his Southern Baptist background and me with my Episcopal background. (Believe me, when my mother-in-law learned that her baby boy was going to marry what she called "a bachelor girl," living alone in New York City in Greenwich Village, working in the theater, who had published two novels and was an Episcopalian — that was the worst blow of all.) In that church, we found friends who are still friends for life — who had to teach the city girl how to can and freeze and prepare for winter and to use and treasure the fruits of the earth.

I also learned why I'm not a Congregationalist. At that time, the decade of the 1950s, no symbol of any kind was allowed. Now, there's a nice plain wooden cross by the sanctuary; then, that would have been considered popish. Kneeling was for your bedside at night when you said your prayers; you did not kneel at church. When the minister said, "Let us pray," you bowed your head *very* slightly. I was asked to start a choir. I learned a lot with the choir: I learned a lot about people, a lot about failure, a lot about myself. All of which came out in what I was struggling to write.

In the church, God was approached intellectually, and my minister friends answered my questions. My questions did not have answers — and their answers threw me off. They gave me German theologians to read. Now there is one great use for German theologians: insomnia. Those long, Germanic sentences. Never use two words when you can use twenty-two. Again, they had too many answers. They had no sense of the incredible mystery I felt when I went out at night with the dogs after I'd got the kids to bed and looked at the stars — and there was creation.

Two weeks ago, I was in Lakewood, Texas — which is in the middle of nowhere — and there were no lights of any kind. I went out and looked at the stars. There was the comet. This great big blob, pulsing. Four times bigger than we are. Again, I had the sense of the wonder of creation, that to God a baby or a kitten is just as important as all of that glory.

But, within three years, four of our closest friends died — and that's a lot of death. Again, came the questions: What happens? What in the Congregational church is the theology of resurrection? Once, in an evangelical college, some outsiders were directing some hostile questions to me. One of the most angry ones was, "Do you believe in the literal *fact* of the resurrection?"

"Well," I said, "I stand with Paul in the resurrection of Christianity, but you can't cram the glory of the resurrection into anything as thin as a fact. It's way beyond fact. It's glory. It's what we live by."

That wasn't what they wanted to hear. But I do stand with Paul. All the things I believe in, that make my life worth living, are impossible in ordinary, literal terms. Incarnation — God leaving all that glory and coming to us as an ordinary, human, mortal being — is impossible. Without my absolute belief that God does lovingly make us and then will never abandon or annihilate us, I could not have written through that decade. I could not write now. How can we explain anything that we live by on a literal level? How can we understand the Word that shouted all the galaxies into being, abandoning all power and all glory and coming to us as a servant?

Perhaps if I had been more satisfied with the theology of the Protestant 1950s, I would not have been left probing. My minister friends were sympathetic, but they'd been given the answers in seminary. Their theology was too literal, too explainable. Then, I discovered a book by Berdyaev, the Russian theologian, who opened doors and windows, particularly when he talked about worshipping a "forensic God." That was not the God my parents taught me. The God my parents taught me was a God who was in it with us, in all our griefs, all our pains, all our joys, all our laughter.

But how was I to talk to my children about all of this? A seven-year-old girl came into our family because of the untimely death of her parents. How did I talk to the kids at prayer time about death? . . . Prayer time was the longest and my favorite part of the day because I loved my children's prayers. One night during the 1950s when we thought we were close to war, my son, who was about four, was saying his list of "God blesses" and suddenly he said, "And God, remember to be the Lord!" I thought, I don't have to teach this kid anything.

My writing reflected my questions and my responses, not my answers. I wrote *Meet the Austins* as a Valentine for my husband and had a long struggle to get it published. It's a simple little book about an ordinary family living ordinary lives, which meant that they had to face and live through the ordinary problems of life: the death of a beloved friend, the unexpected, the joyful, the funny and terrible. I'm not sure why it frightened publishers, but it did for two years. Then the publishers who finally took the book were so scared of it that they didn't publish it for a year after it was announced.

I too struggled with the ordinary problems of life. Living in an old farm house that was always cold in winter, working with my actor husband at the village store, raising children for a decade with its fear of communism, fear of nuclear war, fear of thinking anything new. When I got overtired, which was much of the time, my knee hurt, but I paid no attention to it. It was old pain to which I was moderately accustomed.

I was still struggling with my questions, and for some reason I picked up a book of Einstein's. Now, since I'd avoided science as much as possible, I do not know why I picked up that book. But in it, I read that anyone who is not lost in rapturous awe at the power and glory of the mind behind the maker of the universe is good as a burnt-out candle. "I have found my theologian!" I thought. I began to read more Einstein, Planck, and quantum theory.

It was the discovery of particle physics and the wonders of science that led to *A Wrinkle in Time,* which came to me when my kids were seven, ten, and twelve. At that time, my husband was restless; he'd made a success of the village store. What to do? "Go back to the theater," I said, "it's where you belong." So we took our kids out of a small dairy farm village, which we thought was quiet, to the middle of Manhattan and the world of the theater. Ironically, we found it much quieter than the country — with PTA and driving the kids hither, thither, and yon. In the city, they could take the bus. It was wonderful.

It was a big move. We had to rent our house. Since we had three dogs and seven cats, my husband said firmly to the children, "We will take one dog and one cat." Our seven-year-old looked at him with his big blue eyes and said, "And one child, Daddy?" We decided to take all three children.

And to take them on a long tent camping trip to bridge the gap between these two totally disparate lives. I'd been to Europe. I knew the East Coast of the United States, but I knew nothing much about the rest of my own country. It was a beautiful and eye-opening trip. I had a box in the front seat, full of books and magazines on the making of the universe, on the science that I was just discovering. That was theology for me. Who made it all? Why? I would sit outside our tent at night and look up at the stars, at the wild beauty of the night sky, and feel surrounded by the presence of the maker. The great storyteller. The Sunday that we were at the Grand Canyon, we were horrified that church was held in a building, instead of out in the glory of God's own church. Perhaps the canyon itself asked too many questions of why and how and when.

In my mind, I began to write *A Wrinkle in Time* which was, for me, an affirmation of my theology and my love of God, a God who loves us so much that he sent his only begotten son to us to teach us how to be human. Human beings are not ordinary — we are extraordinary. Why did God make us as we are? Why did God give us the terrible and dangerous gift of free will? How do we find out what is our will and what is God's will? I kept wanting to know and asking more questions.

I was happy to return to New York where lots of people were asking questions. It was the city of my birth. It was and is my home. We were given good scholarships for our children in an Episcopal school, and so I also went back to the church of my birth. My Baptist husband responded to the beauty of the liturgy and the symbolism.

A Wrinkle in Time began its long journey from publisher to publisher to publisher. It fascinates me that when the book was finally published, it was hailed as a Christian book. It is now one of the ten most censored books in the United States, along with the *Diary of Anne Frank, The Grapes of Wrath, Huckleberry Finn,* and other wicked books. Not a word of these books has changed. What has changed? What has happened? What is happening? Why have these books suddenly become dangerous?

The question is far larger than a list of books. What are Christians afraid of? I thought perfect love cast out fear. But slowly, I'm learning what some of the fears are and where they come from. An article in the [New York] *Times* tells of some women who wanted middle school textbooks removed from schools because they were afraid they might stimulate the children's imaginations. "How can we believe without all of the God-given imagination we possess?" I thought. Then I realized, long after reading that article, that in the King James translation, "imagination" does not mean what it means now. It's another of those words that has changed. It's a bad word: "Put them down in the imagination of their hearts!" So these women, were taking "imagination" as it was understood back two or three hundred years ago. . . . In reading those good and glorious sentences, then, we have to make sure we know what the words mean, and "imagination" does not mean what it meant back then.

I'm fascinated by words and by how they shift and change and grow and move. The language that comes from the media is appallingly bad. The media makes the terrible mistake, particularly in commercials, of making us believe that normal is nice. Then, if things aren't nice we get upset. Normal is not nice. Normal is like the weather: unexpected, wonderful, terrible, but not nice.

Back in New York, I learned changes in language. The world

changed. I changed too. The sixties exploded. An eminent group of theologians decided that God was dead. I read a couple of their "God is dead" books and decided I didn't have their problem. If they wanted to get rid of the cross that was fine with me. My children grew, left home, gave me grandchildren, my husband died — all of the ordinary things of life and death and being mortal human beings. My knee began to be more and more bothersome, and finally, it was apparent that it was finished with its job, and it needed to be replaced. Two years ago I had a brand new knee put in. And wouldn't you think that would have been the end of it? The new knee had been put in in such a way that the foot couldn't support it, so the foot became more and more deformed and more and more fractured. Two weeks ago, I had my foot taken apart and put back together again. . . .

My writing is always enlarged and changed by what is happening. Before I had the surgery, I was struggling with a cane. We've had a brutal winter of snow and snow and more snow. I'd struggled to get over snow drifts, and always, arms would come around me, and I would be helped across the snow by one of the street people. That awed and humbled me. . . .

I was committed to give the Perkins lectures in Wichita Falls, Texas, and in preparing, I began to look at the life of Jesus in an entirely new way. It came from a question that somebody in my church asked about one of the late parables — which is quite a rough one. I started looking at the parables in their chronological order. They start out gently and humorously. As Jesus gets closer and closer to death and to being misunderstood, the parables get harsher and harsher until we get the parable of the owner of the vineyard who sent his servants to collect his dues. They were stoned; then he sent his son, and they killed his son. Jesus is telling that parable to the people he knows are going to kill him. *Where* the story comes is very important in understanding what Jesus is trying to tell us.

I began to realize that when Christ came into the world as Jesus to be a human being *that* was his promise. Not to do God things as Jesus, but to be a human being. He kept that promise faithfully, all the way through. He could have avoided the cross, but he didn't. He kept his promise, to be human. . . .

Books surprise me. They don't do what I expect, they know more than I do, and my job is to listen, not to control or dominate or manipulate, but to listen. Listen to the story in the same way that, when I pray, I try to listen to God. Get out of the way, and listen. God has ways of making us do what is needed without interfering with our free will. . . .

THOMAS LYNCH

Faith and Fashion Blunders:
Shifting Metaphors of Mortality

———〜———

I want to thank the good for professor for that tasteful obituarial intro-
duction. To be spoken of in the present tense is very nice. When there
are flowers around and people are gathered, to be upright is no bad thing
either. I'm delighted with the invitation to be here. As all the poets, my
brothers and sisters in that trade, know, you cannot let an audience this
size pass without reading a poem or two. So I think today I'll begin with a
poem, and end with a poem which will relieve you of the obligation of
knowing when I am through.

But first, an explanation. Do you know those calendars that we get
every year with a new word on them? My wife gives me one every
Christmas. We're supposed to impress our friends with our expanding
use of the vocabulary. We say "imbroglio" a dozen times, and people
say, "My, he's enjoying the calendar this year." One March, I got the
word "grimalkin," a word I'd never heard before. It's a German-rooted
word for a fat, old, lazy, gray she-cat. Shakespeare used it, I think, in
Macbeth. At the time, I was inhabiting a home with a cat of just exactly
that description — a cat that I hated. As this poem takes pains to
point out. But the boy to whom the cat belonged, my son Michael,
loved the cat, and all of you who are parents, I suppose all of you who
are human, know how it is to love someone and hate something they
love. I should say in advance, for those of you who have cats and love

225

them, do so with my blessing. It's not the feline in general that I so much dislike — it's this cat in particular that I hated. And you'd have hated too.

Grimalkin

One of these days she will lie there and be dead.
I'll take her out back in a garbage bag
and bury her among my son's canaries,
the ill-fated turtles, a pair of angelfish:
the tragic and mannerly household pests
that had better sense to take their leaves
before their welcomes or my patience had worn thin.
For twelve long years I've suffered this damned cat
while Mike, my darling middle son, himself
twelve years this coming May has grown into
the tender if quick tempered manchild
his breeding blessed and cursed him to become.
And only his affection keeps the cat alive
though more than once I've threatened violence —
the brick and burlap in the river recompense
for mounds of furballs littering the house,
choking the vacuum cleaner, or what's worse:
shit in the closets, piss in the planters, mice
that winter indoors safely as she sleeps
curled about a table leg, vigilant
as any knickknack in a partial coma.
But Mike, of course, is blind to all of it —
the gray angora breed of arrogance,
the sluttish roar, the way she disappears for days
sex-desperate once or twice a year,
urgently ripping her way out the screen door
to have her way with anything that moves
while Mike sits up with tuna fish and worry,
crying into the darkness, "Here kitty kitty,"
mindless of her whorish treacheries
or of her crimes against upholsteries —

the sofas, love seats, wingbacks, easy chairs
she's puked and mauled into dilapidation.
I have this reoccurring dream of driving her
deep into the desert east of town
and dumping her out there with a few days feed
and water. In the dream, she's always found
by kindly tribespeople who eat her kind
on certain holy days as a form of penance.
God knows, I don't know what he sees in her.
Sometimes he holds her like a child in his arms
rubbing her underside until she sounds
like one of those battery powered vibrators
folks claim to use for the ache in their shoulders.
And under Mike's protection she will fix her
indolent green-eyed gaze on me as if
to say: "Whaddaya gonna do about it, Slick,
the child loves me and you love the child."
Truth told, I really ought to have her fixed
in the old way with an airtight alibi,
a bag of Redi-mix and no eyewitnesses.
But one of these days she will lie there and be dead.
And choking back loud hallelujahs, I'll pretend
a brief bereavement for my Michael's sake,
letting him think as he has often said
"Deep down inside you really love her don't you Dad?"
I'll even hold some cheerful obsequies
careful to observe God's never-failing care
for even these, the least of His creatures,
making some mention of a cat-heaven where
cat-ashes to ashes, cat-dust to dust
and the Lord gives and the Lord has taken away.
Thus claiming my innocence to the end,
I'll turn Mike homeward from that wicked little grave
and if he asks, we'll get another one because
all boys need practice in the arts of love
and all their aging fathers in the arts of rage.

I never say that poem without remarking that the boy and the cat featured in said narrative were both twelve when I wrote it. By the grace of God, the boy will be twenty-six next month. The cat lived to be twenty-one.

Actually, I remember very well the details of its demise. It was Ash Wednesday, 1999, when I was with several of my co-religionists getting that little tribal smudge on the forehead. You know, to remind us of our mortality (like I needed that). Remember, man, that you are dust? I was thinking maybe that would work with cats, too. I was casting about for something to put on her forehead, to remind her of her impending mortality, when I thought better of it, and I instead went home to email my son, Michael, away at a good state college.

"Michael," I wrote, "when you come home for Easter this year you are going to notice great changes in your pet cat. You'll notice that her toilet habits have become entirely unpredictable. You'll also notice that she seems vexed about coming in and going out: if you hold the door open when she roars to go out, she won't go out. If you hold it when she wants to come in, she won't come in. There are lumps all around her. (I knew this to be bad grooming, but I used the word "tumor.") When you come home for Easter you are going to have to be prepared to do the right thing."

And I think he knew what I was talking about. At the same time, I was making preliminary phone calls to Dr. Clark, our local veterinary surgeon — who I have to thank for the cat's longevity, I suppose. I remember we assembled in this windowless room in the doctor's emporium with earth-tone wall covering and some Enya music piped in from a source I couldn't make out. There were just the five of us, if you count the cat: Dr. Clark, Dr. Clark's rather comely assistant, my dear son Michael, his miserable cat Greta, and me.

The conversation was going exactly as I had planned. Dr. Clark was saying sensible things, like "Michael, you've been such a good friend to Greta, lo these many years. Now you're going to have to make the most difficult decisions about her and her end of life care."

Mike was nodding, and I was nodding. The cat was nodding. Everybody was pretty much in agreement on this — we were here to do the needful thing. Then, something happened that I never could have predicted. There was one drop of water coming out of my son's right eyeball, working its way down the edge of his cheek southwards. He wasn't shaking or sobbing; there was no seizing up about the thing, but it was unmistakable — you'd call it a tear, I suppose. I could see that the comely assistant saw it too because there was suddenly panicked eye contact between her and Dr. Clark.

The conversation took an unfortunate turn: "Michael, perhaps a shot of cortisone would give dear Greta some comfort in these her final months."

"Months?" I exclaimed. "I've come for a dead cat *today*." I was ready. I had gone to the trouble, as we mortuarial types do, of arranging a small box for the occasion. It was home in the garage, awaiting our sad return. And I'd had one of my factotums (another calendar word) at the office arrange for a very tastefully engraved Vermont granite stone, to wit:

Greta
1978-1999
Gone.

It was all there. Instead, they brought in a huge syringe, filled with a vile colored substance, and shot the beast in the hind quarters. I thought that would kill her for sure. She went very still, and after what you'd call a sensible pause, Dr. Clark said, "You may take her home now, Michael."

"Of course," I thought, "he wants her to have the good death, at home, in the company of people who know her." We took her home, and she didn't move for most of two hours. But two hours after that, she started to rattle. "That's the death rattle," I thought, "she'll be dead before the morning." Two days later she was up and moving; two weeks after that, there was a kind of bounce in her limp; and two months after that, she was looking at me as if to say "I showed you." And of course, she had.

I'm a member of one of those twelve-step groups that advise me to "Let go, let God." I did. I let go. I let God. I was doing pretty well until about Thanksgiving that same year, when I called Mike in for another audience about his cat.

"Michael," I said, "I can take a joke the same as the next guy, but I'm not the kind of guy to make a liar out of gravestones." Now, I admit I get them on the cheap. It wasn't the money. It was the pure existential vexation that Martin Luther King, Jr., Mahatma Gandhi, and Mother Teresa only occupied one millennium — and this cat was on the edge of living in two. It was more than I could take. So I told Michael if God or Mother Nature or whoever's in charge here didn't do the right thing, I would — New Year's Eve, 1999. It would not see another year, another century, another millennium.

He took me seriously. Towards dusk on the seventh of December, when he came home from school, he went into the back yard, where my delphinium used to prosper, and he dug a hole. He came back the next afternoon and gathered up the cat and disappeared. I should have known something was up because his brother, who is a fishing guide and rarely comes home, came home that day. His sister, who works at DePaul University in Chicago, came home that day, for no apparent reason. Friends of their youth gathered all around. My wife and youngest son had laid in a bunch of finger food. About forty-five minutes later, Michael came back with the cat wrapped up in a blanket, dead.

"Do you still have that box?"

"I do." I put it on the picnic table on the patio, and he wrapped it in the little blanket and placed the cat in the box. And do you know that people stood around for the better part of an hour, talking about Greta as if they really knew and liked her. Then, without warning, without a signal, Michael bent and kissed Greta, put the lid on the box, and started a slow walk out to the garden where a grave had been prepared.

I walked with him. On the way, he said something I will not soon forget: "In as much as my heaven would be incomplete without this cat, oughtn't we to pray?"

And as we walked, he did. When we were at the grave, he knelt down and placed the box in the hole. As he stood up, his shoulders began to shake, and he said, "I can't thank you enough for being here with me, but some things I have to do on my own."

As I walked back, I turned and watched while he covered the grave with dirt. How very proud of him I am — to know that this young man had learned, without any particular instruction, the value of what Dr. Thomas Long calls, "sacred community theater," these ways we process the dead. He had learned that it has nothing to do with how much we spend or how much we save. It has little to do with the boxes or doodads. It has mostly to do with what we do.

When October next came around, Michael had conspired with his sister and brothers to get me a kitten for my birthday. It was one of those little striped things, tiger cats, I think they call them. Michael thought it would repair my damaged ideas about the feline. I was calling her "Bruiser." I kept her in the garage, but I was getting in the habit of going out mornings, with an increasingly costly tin of designer cat food, and having those mindless conversations that you do, saying, "When I was your age, Bruiser . . ." or, "You should have known Greta. Now there was a cat." Things were really going good, and in fact, my youngest son, Sean, a rock star/funeral director, who has exactly the opposite daily schedule that I do, would go out, as part of his evening office, and feed the cat again. I think he was also having useful conversations.

Things continued really good for most of three weeks, until the older boy came home with, at the time, his only companion, a mad-eyed wolf-ish kind of cross-bred dog. After the long drive home, he pulled up and opened the garage door. I imagine the kitten, hearing the door slam and thinking it was its lord and master home, came out to see. Imagine the worst case scenario and then double it. Double it again for the way that nature is so speedy and tidy — the way, the dog by nature, snaps the neck. The way the blood spatters on the white door of the garage. Double it again because there I was out in the back yard in my boxer shorts at midnight with a dead cat, a hole in the geography, and my son saying things to me like, "Why wasn't God watching?"

And it occurred to me then — why wasn't God watching? Here was a cat I hated for twenty-one years and could not kill, and here was one I liked for twenty-one days and could not keep alive. Doesn't God, who-ever she is, like a practical joke from time to time?

But it also occurred to me that this is precisely why I like being a parent and precisely why I like being a funeral director: for those times in our lives when we belly up to those sad events or those remarkably wondrous events for which there is no bottom line, there is no particular Bible verse, there is no easy answer. There is just the power of our presence, our being there. Our willingness to go the distance with people —

231

whether that distance is to the grave, the tomb, the fire, whatever oblivion to which we consign them.

A man that I work with named Wesley Rice once spent all of one day and all of one night carefully piecing together the parts of a girl's cranium. She'd been murdered by a madman with a baseball bat. The morning of the day it happened, she'd left for school dressed for picture day: a school girl, dressed to the nines, waving at her mother, ready for the photographer. The picture was never taken. She was abducted from the bus stop. After he'd raped her and strangled her and stabbed her, he beat her head with a baseball bat, which was found beside the child's body. She was found a day later in a stand of trees, just off the road. The details were reported dispassionately in the local media, along with the speculation as to which of the wounds was the fatal one: the choking, the knife, or the baseball bat. No doubt these speculations were the focus of the double post-mortem the medical examiner performed on her body before signing the death certificate: multiple injuries.

Most embalmers faced with what Wesley Rice was faced with, after he'd opened the pouch from the morgue, would have simply said, "closed casket," treated the remains enough to control the odor, zipped the pouch, and gone home for cocktails. It would have been easier — the pay was the same. Instead, he started working. Eighteen hours later, the girl's mother who had pleaded to see her, saw her. She was dead, to be sure. And damaged. But her face was hers again, not the madman's version. The hair was hers, not his. The body was hers, not his. Wesley Rice had not raised her from the dead nor hidden the hard facts, but he had retrieved her death from the one who had killed her. He had closed her eyes and mouth, washed her wounds, sutured her lacerations, pieced her beaten skull together, stitched the incisions from the autopsy, cleaned the dirt from under her fingernails, scrubbed the fingerprint ink from her finger tips, washed her hair, dressed her in jeans and a blue turtleneck, and laid her in a casket — beside which her mother stood for two days and sobbed, as if something had been pulled from her by force. It was the same when her pastor stood with her and told her, "God weeps with you," and the same when they buried the body in the ground. It was then, and always will be, awful, horrible, unappeasably sad. But the outrage, the horror, the heartbreak belonged, not to the murderer or to the media or to the morgue, each of whom had staked their claims to it, but it belonged to the girl and to her mother. Wesley had given them the body back. "Barbaric" is what some people call this fussing over a dead body. I say the monster with the baseball bat was barbaric. What Wesley Rice did was a kindness — and to the extent that it is easier to grieve the loss that we see than the one we imagine or read about in the papers or hear of on the evening news, it was what we undertakers call "a good funeral." It served the living by caring for the dead.

A "good funeral," that oxymoronic trope, has dogged me all of my life, ever since my father said we should be in the business of "good funerals." I wanted to know how such a thing could happen.

The Center for the Ethnography of Everyday Life at the university invited me to present at their recent conference, "Doing Documentary Work: Life, Letters and the Field." Where I come from, upstream on the Huron from smart Ann Arbor, we rarely offload words like "ethnography" unless we are appearing before the zoning board of appeals or possibly trying to avoid jury duty. All the same, I thanked the organizers and marked the dates and times in my diary.

To be on the safe side, I looked it up — "ethnography" — and it says "the branch of anthropology that deals with the description of various racial and cultural groups of people." And "anthropology" — I looked that up too — which is "the study of the origin, the behavior, and the physical, social and cultural development of human beings." I looked up "human" and "human beings" too and got what you'd guess, but came across "humic" which sent me to "humus" which has to do with the "a layer of soil that comes from the decay of leaves and other vegetation and which contains valuable plant food." It is a twin of the Latin word for soil, earth.

Which put me in mind of a book I'd been reading by Robert Pogue Harrison, *The Dominion of the Dead,* in which he speaks about our "humic density," we human beings, shaped out of earth, fashioned out of dirt, because we are primally bound to the ground our shelters and buildings and monuments rise out of and our dead are buried in. We are "rooted" in the humus of the home place — to the stories and corpses that are buried there.

Isn't that just like people? Ethnographically speaking? Or anthropologically? To think of the place where their ancients lived and worked and are buried as sacred, central to their own identity.

Maybe you want to know what I said at the conference?

I said it looked like a "paradigm shift," from a sense of holy ground and grounding, to a kind of rootlessness — spiritually, ethnographically, anthropologically speaking, humanity-wise. At which point in the proceedings I removed from my bag and placed upon the table, a golf bag cremation urn. Molded, no doubt, out of some new age resin or high-grade polymer, it stands about fourteen inches high and looks like everyone's idea of the big nut-brown leather bag with plump pockets and a plush towel and precious memories that "Dad" or "Grandpa" or "Good Old (insert most recently deceased golf-buddy's nickname)" would have kept his good old golf clubs in. The bottom of the golf bag urn is fashioned to look like the greensward of a well maintained fairway. So the whole thing looks like a slice of golf heaven. There is even a golf ball resting beside the base of the bag, waiting for the erstwhile golfer to chip it up for an easy putt. The thing is hollow, the better to accommodate the two hundred some cubic centimeters, give or take, most cremated human beings will amount to.

I confess that the idea of the urn only came to me at the last moment because I wanted to see the looks on their faces. It's a character flaw. Still, I wanted to see the look on their faces when I presented, as an article of documentary consequence, as an anthropological artifact, as a post-modern relic of a species that had accomplished pyramids, the Taj Mahal, and Newgrange, the ethnographically denatured and, by the way, chemically inert, plastic golf bag shaped cremation urn. It's one of a kind. It came from a catalogue. And I wanted to tell them about the paradigm shift that it signified.

I came up burying Presbyterians and Catholics, devout and lapsed, born again and backslidden Baptists, Orthodox Christians, an occasional Zen Buddhist, and variously observant Jews. For each of these sets, there were infinite subsets. We had right old Calvinists who only drank single malts and were all good Masons and were mad for the bagpipes, just as we had former Methodists who worked their way up the Reformation ladder after they married into money or made a little killing in the market. We had Polish Catholics and Italian ones, Irish and Hispanic and Byzantine, and Jews who were Jews in the way some Lutherans are Lutheran — for births and deaths and first marriages.

My late father, himself a funeral director, schooled me in the local orthodoxies and their protocols as I have schooled my sons and daughter who work with me. There was a kind of comfort, I suppose, in knowing exactly what would be done with you, one's ethnic and religious identities having established long before the fashions and the fundamentals for one's leave-taking. While the fashions might change, the fundamental ingredients for a funeral were the same — someone who has quit breathing forever, some others to whom it apparently matters, and someone else who stands between the quick and dead and says something like "Behold, I show you a mystery."

"An act of sacred community theater," Dr. Thomas Long calls this "transporting" of the dead from this life to the next. "We move them to a further shore. Everyone has a part in this drama." The dead get to the grave or fire or tomb whilst the living get to the edge of a life they must learn to live without them. Ours is a species that deals with death (the idea of the thing) by dealing with our dead (the thing itself).

Late in the last century, there was some trending towards the more homegrown doxologies. Everyone was into the available "choices." We started doing more cremations — it made good sense. Folks seemed less "grounded" than their grandparents, more "portable," "divisible," more "scattered" somehow. We got into balloon releases and homing pigeons done up as doves to signify the flight of the dead fellow's soul towards heaven. "Bridge Over Troubled Water" replaced "How Great Thou Art." And if Paul's Letter to the Romans or the Book of Job was replaced by Omar Khayyam or Emily Dickinson, what harm? *After great pain, a formal feeling comes,* rings as true as any sacred text. A death in the family is, as Miss Emily describes it: *First — Chill — then Stupor — then the letting go.*

Amidst all the high fashions and fashion blunders, the ritual wheel that worked the space between the living and the dead still got us where we needed to go. It made room for the good laugh, the good cry, and the power of faith brought to bear on the mystery of mortality. The dead were "processed" to their final dispositions with a pause sufficient to say that their lives and their deaths truly mattered to us. The broken circle within the community of folks who shared blood or geography or belief with the dead, was closed again through this "acting out our parts" as Reverend Long calls it. Someone brought the casseroles, someone brought the prayers, someone brought a shovel or lit the fire, everyone was consoled by everyone else. The wheel that worked the space between the living and the dead ran smooth.

Lately I've been thinking the wheel is broken or gone a long way off the track or must be reinvented every day. The paradigm is shifting. Bereft of faith, the script has changed from the essentially sacred to the essentially silly. We mistake the ridiculous for the sublime.

Take Batesville Casket Company, for example. They make caskets and urns and wholesale to funeral homes all over the globe. Their latest catalogue is called "Accessories" and includes suggested "visitation vignettes" — the stage arranged around neither cross nor crescent nor Star of David, but around one of Batesville's "life-symbols" caskets featuring interchangeable corner hardware. One "life-symbol" looks like a rainbow trout jumping from the corners of the hardwood casket, and for dearly departed gardeners, there is one with little plastic potted mums. There is the "sports dad" vignette done up like a garage with beer logos, team pennants, hoops and hockey skates, and, of course, a casket that looks a little like a jock locker gone horizontal. There's one for motorcyclists and the much publicized "Big Mama's Kitchen" with its faux stove, kitchen table, and apple pie for the mourners to share with those who call. Instead of Methodists or Muslims, we are now golfers, gardeners, bikers, and dead bowlers. The bereaved are not so much family and friends or co-religionists as fellow hobbyists and enthusiasts. I have become less the funeral director and more the memorial caddy of sorts, getting the dead out of the way and the living assembled within a theater that is neither sacred nor secular but increasingly absurd — a triumph of accessories over essentials, of stuff over substance, gimmicks over the genuine. The dead are downsized or disappeared or turned into knickknacks in a kind of funereal karaoke.

Consider the case of Peter Payne, dead at forty-four of brain cancer. His wife arranged for his body to be cremated without witness or rubric, his ashes placed in the golf bag urn, the urn to be placed on a table in one of our parlors with his "real life" golf bag standing beside it for their son and daughter and circle of friends to come by for a look. And if nobody said "doesn't he look natural," several commented on how much he looked like, well, his golf bag. The following day the ensemble was taken to the church where the minister, apparently willing to play along, had some things to say about "life being like a par three hole with plenty of sand traps and water hazards," to wit, all too short and full of trouble. And heaven was something like a "19th hole" where, after "finishing the course," those who "played by the rules" and "kept an honest score" were given their "trophies." Then, those in attendance were invited to join the family at the clubhouse of Mystic Creek Golf Course for lunch and a little commemorative boozing. There is already talk of a Peter Payne Memorial Tournament next year. A scholarship fund has been established to send young golfers to PGA training camp. Some of his ashes will be scattered in the sand trap of the par five on the back nine with the kidney shaped green and the dogleg right. The rest will remain, forever and ever, perpetual filler for the golf bag urn.

Whether this is indeed a paradigm shift, the end of an era or, as Robert Pogue Harrison suggests, an "all too human failure to meet the challenges of modernity" is anyone's guess. But we are nonetheless required, as he insists, to choose "an allegiance — either to the posthuman, the virtual, and the synthetic, or to the earth, the real and the dead in their humic densities."

"So, which will it be," I posed rhetorically to the conference audience, (which seemed oddly fixed upon the *objet de mort*) "the golf bag urn" (read posthuman, virtual, and synthetic), "or some humus — the ground and graveyard, village, nation, place or faith — the nitty gritty real earth in which human roots link the present to the past and future?"

They looked a little blankly at me, as if I'd held up five fingers and asked them what the square root of Thursday was. There was some shifting in seats, some clearing of throats. I thought I might have numbed them with the genius of it or damaged them in some nonspecific way. I thought about wrapping up with a joke, but I thought the better of it and closed instead with an invitation to engage in a question and answer session.

A man in the second row whose eyes had widened when I produced the urn and who had not blinked or closed his mouth since the thing appeared raised his hand to ask, "Is there anyone in there?"

"Why, no, of course not," I assured.

There was a collective sigh, a sudden flash of not-quite-knowing smiles and then the roar of uneasy silence, like a rush of air returned to the room.

The Director of the Center for the Ethnography of Everyday Life hurriedly rose to thank me for "a thought-provoking presentation," led the assembled in polite applause, and announced that the buffet luncheon was ready and waiting in a room across the hall. Except for a man who wanted to discuss his yet to be patented "water reduction method" of body disposition, there was no further intercourse between me and the assembly.

It's only now, months later, the conference come and gone, that it occurs to me what I should have said. I should have said that ethnography seems so perilous just now, no less the everyday; that "life and letters and the field" seem littered more than ever with the wounded and the dead. That ethnicity, formerly a cause for celebration, now seems an occasion for increasing caution. That ethnic identity — those ties by which we are bound to others of our kind by tribe and race, language and belief, geography and history, costume and custom and a hundred other measures — seems lately less a treasure, more a scourge.

Such is the dilemma of the everyday. We rummage among books and newspapers, watch the fire go to ash, pace the room, walk in the woods, watch the snow give way to humus. The loons return. The first insuppressible flowers bloom. We find in our theatres and times, like Vladimir and Estragon, that life is waiting, killing time, holding to the momentary hope that whatever's supposed to happen next is scheduled to occur — wars end, the last thin shelf of ice melts and the lake is clear and blue, we get it right, we make it home — if not today, then possibly tomorrow.

And I should have read them a poem. For birthdays, I write myself a sonnet every year. Some people eat cake, some people do sonnets, some people do both. Actually, it turned out to be a 15-line poem because, as you know, the older you get, the harder it is to count. Thus the title, "Refusing at 52 to Write Sonnets."

It came to him that he could nearly count
how many late Aprils he had left to him

in increments of ten, or say, eleven.
Thus 63, 74, 85.

He couldn't see himself at 96.
Humanity's advances, notwithstanding, in health care, self-help
    and New Age regimens,
What with his habits and family history, the end is nearer
    than you think.
The future thus consigned to its contingences, the present
    moment opens
Like a gift
The brightening month, the green week, the blue morning,
The hour's routine, the minute's passing glance
All seem like godsends now.
And what to make of this? At the end,
the word that comes to us is
Thanks.

KATHERINE PATERSON

- -

Making Meaning

When I was here last time, I received a copy of Professor Dale Brown's book *Of Fiction and Faith* in which he interviews twelve writers who talk about how their faith informs, shapes, intersects, or otherwise affects the writers that they are. In his conversation with Walter Wangerin Jr., Dr. Brown engaged Wangerin with the question of meaningfulness by commenting that the novelist Michael Malone has characterized most modern literature as sophomoric because the cynicism is "too easy."

Wangerin agrees. "That's right," he says. "It is. It is the shattering sense of meaninglessness we get in adolescence. But eventually, we begin to use our wit to search for meaning. We get old. And writing is about that process, the seeking, the trying to name."

Last month, I went to see a production of *The Miracle Worker*. I know many of you have seen the play or the movie, and you remember that Annie Sullivan is determined to give the gift of language to a child who, from the age of eighteen months, has been blind, deaf, and consequently, mute. Over and over again, Annie makes Helen feel objects and then spells the name of the object into her palm.

"Doll," Annie says, "it has a name. D-O-L-L."

But Helen can't make the connection between the object and the marks Annie is making in her hand.

"Cake," says Annie, stuffing a piece of cake into Helen's mouth. "It has a name. Cake. C-A-K-E."

This painful process is repeated on and on through tantrums, sullen rebellions, and more tantrums — until that astounding awakening at the water pump when the exasperated Annie shouts into Helen's unhearing ears as she writes in her palm, "Water, it has a name. W-A-T-E-R." Suddenly, Helen stops struggling to get away. The whole audience holds its breath as they watch the child's frozen mouth begin to move until finally it makes the sound, "Wa." I let out a sob, a sob so loud that the people in the row in front of me turned around and stared. But I couldn't help it — it *was* a miracle.

Martin Smith, a very wise Anglican priest that I know, says that God in Genesis creates by speech, and it is by language that we humans create meaning. We give voice to the images and the metaphors, Smith argues, and the chaos that surrounds us gives way to narrative, to story.

Perhaps few modern poets do this better for me than Mary Oliver. One Sunday in early Lent, our co-pastor brought one of Oliver's poems to share with our adult class. The poem is entitled, "White Owl Flies Into and Out of the Field."

> Coming down out of the freezing sky
> with its depths of light,
> like an angel, or a Buddha with wings,
> it was beautiful, and accurate,
> striking the snow and whatever was there
> with a force that left the imprint
> of the tips of its wings — five feet apart —
> and the grabbing thrust of its feet,
> and the indentation of what had been running
> through the white valleys of the snow —
> and then it rose, gracefully,
> and flew back to the frozen marshes
> to lurk there, like a little lighthouse,
> in the blue shadows —
> so I thought:
> maybe death isn't darkness, after all,
> but so much light wrapping itself around us —

as soft as feathers —
that we are instantly weary of looking, and looking,
and shut our eyes, not without amazement,
and let ourselves be carried,
as through the translucence of mica,
to the river that is without the least dapple or shadow,
that is nothing but light — scalding, aortal light —
in which we are washed and washed
out of our bones.

I don't think, once having read this poem, I could ever think of death the same way again. "What a wonderful, wonderful image," I said to Carl.

"Yes," he replied, "that was what I thought."

But Gina, his wife and our co-pastor, countered, "That's all very well, unless you're that little mouse running across the field."

But isn't that exactly the point? We are that mouse. We human beings scrabble through life, unseeing, unhearing, and suddenly the owl is swooping down upon us. That, friends, is not the time to say to the mouse, "Never mind, sweetie, it's all part of a grand and beautiful design." It is probably not the moment for a sermon at all. In the midst of suffering, in the midst of death, we are not often supported by argument or consoled by discourse. But we may — indeed, we often are — comforted by art. I know on September 11th, a day of fear and terror, I finally had sense enough to turn off the television and put on a CD of Brahms's *German Requiem.*

But I'm guessing that most of us gathered here tonight don't rate ourselves as a Mary Oliver, much less a Johannes Brahms. I'm a writer for children. What is my role as meaning-maker in a world gone mad?

It was a week after September the 11th. We were finally having to give up the last faint hope that Peter, our son John's brother-in-law and close friend, would be found somewhere unconscious in a hospital, or wandering, senseless in a distant locale. I looked at my calendar and was distressed to see that I was slated to speak to middle school students in Hinesburg, Vermont, the next day. What was I going to say to twelve- and thirteen-year-olds in the midst of this grief and terror that had not only our extended family, but our entire nation in its death grip? Finally, I decided to start by reading them a passage from *Bridge to Terabithia,* which I had written out of another time of family grief and tumult.

> That night as he started to get into bed, leaving the light off so as not to wake the little girls, he was surprised by May Belle's shrill little "Jess."
>
> "How come you're still awake?"
>
> "Jess. I know where you and Leslie go to hide."
>
> "What do you mean?"
>
> "I followed ya."
>
> He was at her bedside in one leap. "You ain't supposed to follow me!"
>
> "How come?" Her voice was sassy.
>
> He grabbed her shoulders and made her look him in the face. She blinked in the dim light like a startled chicken.
>
> "You listen here, May Belle Aarons," he whispered fiercely, "I catch you following me again, your life ain't worth nothing."
>
> "OK, OK." — she slid back into the bed — "Boy, you're mean. I oughta tell Momma on you."
>
> "Look, May Belle, you can't do that. You can't tell Momma 'bout where me and Leslie go."
>
> She answered with a little sniffing sound.
>
> He grabbed her shoulders again. He was desperate. "I mean it, May Belle. You can't tell nobody nothing!" He let her go. "Now, I don't want to hear about you following me or squealing to Momma ever again, you hear?"
>
> "Why not?"
>
> "'Cause if you do — I'm gonna tell Billy Jean Edwards you still wet the bed sometimes."
>
> "You wouldn't!"
>
> "Boy, girl, you just better not try me."
>
> He made her swear on the Bible never to tell and never to follow, but still he lay awake a long time. How could he trust everything that mattered to him to a sassy six-year-old? Sometimes it seemed to him that his life was delicate as a dandelion. One little puff from any direction, and it was blown to bits.

"I don't know about you," I said to those children, "but I'm feeling a lot like a dandelion today." I could see them visibly relax. Here was an adult, willing to tell the truth. We can't make meaning for anyone, much less for the young, unless we are willing to first tell them the truth. Otherwise, we are like Pangloss, Candide's false mentor, who, in the face of earthquake, inquisition, war, and pestilence, merrily insists that "all is well, all is for the best in the best of all possible worlds." A glib and foolish optimism strikes us as almost obscene. The world our children live in, the one we cannot protect them from, is a world where evil and suffering and injustice is rampant. It is useless to pretend to children that all is well in our world. But cynicism, as Malone says, is the easy way out for writers confronted with the world as it is. There are writers for the young as well as for the old who choose this route. But we who are people of faith must seek against all odds to wring meaning out of what would be easier, and in the world's eyes more realistic, to dismiss as meaningless. Indeed, Freud says we are, at best, infantile, to even try. But it's not Freud we're arguing with. If the God of Abraham, Isaac, and Jacob does not exist, there's no contest. It is precisely because we have faith, because we believe in a God of justice and steadfast love, that we find ourselves in a painful, sweating, wrestling match in which the adversary is God. Six years ago at the Festival, Elie Wiesel said, "Mine is a religion that believes we must argue with God." Then he paused and took a long look at those of us in front of him as if to ask, "How about yours?"

I've told this story many times. It is a story that I went on to tell that morning in Hinesburg. I feel the need to tell it again in the context of this talk because I think it says what we as writers often do, often must do, and that is use art to somehow make sense for ourselves. Something that makes no sense otherwise. It is our way of demanding our blessing from the divine adversary with whom we are, in times of crisis, locked in mortal combat.

The story begins a little more than thirty years ago. A small school that our children attend is closed, and all the students are moved to a much larger elementary school across town. David, our second grader, is miserable. In the rural school, he was both the class artist and the class clown. In the new school, he is simply weird. Every day, he comes home and declares that he "is never, never going back to school and you can't make me!" And I, his mother — who had been in fifteen different schools by the time I was eighteen and had been initially despised at nearly every one of them — am over-identifying with my seven-year-old, probably exacerbating his misery, but nevertheless, getting him up every morning and grimly pushing him out the door, fearing that his unhappiness will never end. And then one afternoon, without any warning, the bright, funny little boy we thought we had lost walks into the house: "Me and Lisa Hill are making a diorama of *Little House in the Big Woods*," he announces cheerily. I'd never heard the name before, but from then on, I'm to hear hardly any other name.

Now I'd like to promise you girls that I was thrilled that my son's best friend was a girl but unfortunately, all I could think was, "They thought he was weird before. If his best friend is a girl, he'll never fit in." But then, I meet Lisa and my worries evaporate. Anyone would be fortunate to have her for a best friend. She is bright, imaginative, and funny. She laughs at his jokes and he at hers. She's the only girl daring enough to invade the second grade boys t-ball team. She and David play together after school in the woods behind her house and talk to each other in the evenings on the phone. "It's your girlfriend, David," his older brother says. But David takes the phone unperturbed: girlfriends are people who chase you down on the playground and grab you and kiss you. Lisa is no more a girlfriend than Rose Kennedy is a Playboy bunny.

The first seismic shock of the year comes in April. I go to the hospital for a suspicious lump that turns out to be cancerous. We are all deeply shaken. Aside from the occasional gerbil, our family has had few close brushes with mortality.

Then on an August day, the phone rings. It is a call from the Hills' next door neighbor. "I thought you ought to know," Mrs. Robinson says, "that Lisa was killed this morning."

While her family was on vacation at Bethany Beach, on a day when the lifeguards sensed no danger from thunder far off in the distance, a joyful little girl, dancing on a rock above the beach, was felled by a bolt of lightning from the sky.

How am I to make sense of this to my eight-year-old son? I can't make sense of it for myself. David tries. One night after his prayers, he tells me that he knows why Lisa has died. "It's not because Lisa was bad," he says, "Lisa wasn't bad. It's because I'm bad and now God is going to kill Mary (his little sister) and you and Daddy and Lin and John," going down the list of his family and loved ones, all of whom God will kill in punishment for his real and imagined sin. This is not the God I know, not the God we thought we had taught our children about. But this was one child's earnest struggle to find meaning.

Which is why finally I began to write a story — I was trying to make sense of a tragedy that didn't make sense to any of us. As a writer, I know that a story needs to make sense. It has to have a beginning, a middle, and an end, and when you come to the end you look back and even if it is unexplainable intellectually, emotionally you know you have made the journey from chaos to order, from senselessness to meaning. Often you are at a total loss when someone asks you what your book is about. You can't put it into a neat verbal summary because if you've done your job, the whole story is the meaning.

As I began to write the story that was to become *Bridge to Terabithia*, I wrote in pencil in a used spiral notebook, so that if it came to nothing, I could pretend that I'd never been very serious about it. Eventually, I transferred those first smudged pages to a typewriter. It was going along fairly well for a first draft — until the day came when I realized that, when I went to work the next morning, Leslie Burke would die. I solved that problem: I just didn't go to work. I answered my back correspondence, I rearranged my bookshelves, I cleaned the house, I scrubbed my kitchen floor — anything to keep Leslie alive.

In the midst of this, I went to a friend's house for lunch.

"How's your new book coming?" she asked.

No one is ever supposed to ask me about my current project; even the members of my family don't do that. But Estelle and I'd been in school together, and she has no respect. So I blurted out that I was writing the story of a friendship between a boy and a girl in which the girl dies, but I couldn't do it. I just couldn't let her die.

"I guess," I said, thinking I was being very wise, "I just can't go through Lisa's death again."

Estelle looked me straight in the eye, "I don't think it's Lisa's death you can't face, Katherine."

I knew she was right. Surely part of the task of finding the meaning of our own lives is the obligation to confront the end of them.

When, thanks to Estelle, I realized that it was my own death that had to be faced, I returned to the typewriter, and with sweat pouring down from under my arms, wrote the dreaded chapter, and went on to finish the draft. Then, because it was simply too painful to keep around the house, I mailed the manuscript to my editor, before the sweat had evaporated. As soon as I'd mailed it, I realized I'd made a hideous mistake. Even the rankest of amateurs knows better than to mail off early drafts. My editor Virginia would think I'd lost my mind — or at least my ability to write. I waited in agony for the envelope returning my manuscript with a polite farewell from the wonderful editor who had lavished such care on my first three books.

Instead, I got a phone call. "I want to talk about your new manuscript," she said. "I laughed through the first two thirds and cried through the last." Somehow, even though she knew nothing of the traumas of the previous year, she'd understood what it was I was trying to do. "Now," she said gently, "let's turn it into a story."

Then, she asked me the right question: What is this story about? Is this a story about death, or is this a story about friendship? Until that moment, I had thought that it was a story about death. It had been a year about death, we were consumed with death. But as soon as she asked the question, I knew I had been wrong.

"Oh," I replied, as though I'd known it all along, "it's a story about friendship."

"That's what I thought," she said, "now you have to go back and write it that way."

If writing the early drafts had been a march through hell, revising the book became an exercise in joy. As the prophet Hosea has said, the valley of trouble had been turned into the gate of hope. Writing as well as reading fiction can provide us with, in the words of Barry Lopez, healing and illumination.

Besides Brahms's *Requiem*, another source of great comfort to me in the dark days after September 11th was a taped series of talks by Father Martin Smith entitled, "Co-Creators with God." It was very healing, in the midst of terror, death, and chaos, to set my mind on creation. In his talks,

Smith states that for two thousand years, Christians have tended to go to one extreme or another in explaining our task as people of God. At one end of the spectrum are those who feel that God has a plan for every individual life, what we typically call "God's will for my life." In this model, "It is our duty by prayer and study to get a peek into our personal file and then act out what we find there." That was the sort of religious atmosphere in which I, and I dare say many of you, were raised. Find out God's perfect plan for your life — and stray from it to your peril.

At the other end of the spectrum are those that leave a person's life work totally up to each individual. That's what the gift of free will is all about, they maintain. God doesn't really have all that much to say about who we are and what we become. God has given us intelligence and freedom, and it's up to us as free, intelligent beings, created in the image of God, to find the meaning of our lives.

What we fail to do, Smith argues, is to examine all of those scriptural passages that call us co-workers with God, that say we're partners with God as meaning-makers. Jesus sets us a wonderful model in the parables by telling stories that challenge human nature and often human notions of justice — and leaving it to the listener to make sense of the story. This is what writers do: they tell the story and invite the reader to help create the meaning, a meaning which will be different for each reader because every reader brings to the writer's story a unique life story of his or her own. God, as Smith eloquently reminds us, calls us not to blind obedience nor to a lonely, stumbling through the dark, but into a creative partnership. I love to think of the work I do everyday as a creative partnership with God. In turn, we as writers do the same thing when we give our creations to readers and invite them to make the meaning of our story, for their own particular lives.

I know my gift is limited. I know I cannot stand toe to toe with philosophers or theologians nor solve for myself or anyone else the problem of evil, either natural or moral. But we who are writers can tell a story, or write a poem. Where rational argument will always fail, somehow, miraculously in metaphor and simile and image and simple narrative, there is both healing and illumination. We write stories not because we have answers, but because we have questions. The writing of a story *is* the wrestling with the angel. Rabbi Abraham Joshua Heschel has said that art is boring unless we are surprised by it. The writer may have some notion of the ending of the plot, but she is seeking much more than plot. She writes to struggle for a meaning which we do not already know. The first reader, who is of course the writer herself, will inevitably be surprised by the blessing wrestled from the angel.

The amazing thing I've learned, time after time, is this: when I am willing to give the deepest part of myself, whether admirable or not, when I am willing to share my own struggle, my own wrestling, readers are able to respond to what I have written in their own deepest core.

About sixteen years ago, I was invited to speak to a book club that was discussing *The Great Gilly Hopkins*. The reading group was comprised of prisoners, incarcerated in the Chittenden Correctional Center in Burlington, Vermont. Though my brave husband had spent time in the Selma jail during the civil rights era, it was my first trip to prison. Now that airline security has become so much tighter, my entrance into prison wouldn't seem quite so strange, but then it was quite frightening. I registered at the window and divested myself of purse and briefcase, which were very closely examined; took off my coat and sent it through the x-ray; put my belt, my necklace, and my earrings in the basket. Even so, when I walked through the metal detector, the alarm rang.

"I have no more metal on me," I protested.

"You have buckles on your shoes, the guard said, accusingly.

Having passed security, I went through a series of heavy doors, the first shutting behind me before the next opened. Finally, I was in the room where the prisoners were waiting. Twenty men and four women were seated around a long table with their instructor. After an initial awkwardness, we began to talk in earnest about the book they had read and what it had meant to them. One of the young men shared that when he was a teenager, he had been briefly in a foster home with a foster mother who had been truly kind to him. She had wanted him to read *Gilly Hopkins* at that time, "But I was a kid who didn't want anybody telling me what to do. I guess that's why I ended up in here. Now that I've read the book, I know what she was trying to say to me."

"Just out of curiosity," the instructor asked, "how many of you were ever in foster care?"

Every single person raised a hand.

As part of the program, each participant was given a paperback copy of the book, and at the end of the session, the inmates lined up to have their books autographed.

"What's your name?" I asked a young man handing me his book.

"Oh, it's not for me," he answered. "It's for my daughter. Her name is Angel."

It had been an emotional afternoon, but that one sentence was the one that haunted me for nearly thirteen years.

Finally, I began to write my fourteenth novel about a child whose father was in prison. My editor wanted me to change both the title of the book and the name of my eleven-year-old heroine. In fact, every single person hated my title. So I let them change the title of the book, but I was adamant about the name of the central character: Angel.

But one idea does not a novel make. If you try to write a book based on a single idea, you're not likely to get beyond the third chapter. It takes more than one strand to weave the fabric of a story.

At least a dozen years after that day in the Vermont prison, I was in California and a friend gave me a copy of a small magazine that her husband was editing. On the back of the magazine was a dramatic photo of super nova remnant Cassiopeia A, and under the picture, this quotation, "When the Chandra telescope took its first image in August of this year, it caught not just another star in the heavens but a foundry, distributing its wares to the rest of the galaxy. Silicon, sulphur, argon, calcium and iron were among the elements identified from Chandra's image. 'These are the materials we are made of,' said the project scientist." The thrill that every writer recognizes went through my body. I knew I had an idea for a book in that quotation. What would it mean to a child to learn that she is made of the same stuff as the stars? In my novel, *The Same Stuff as Stars,* I examined that question this way:

"It's scary," Angel said.

"What's scary?"

"How big everything is, how far away. I'd be just like an ant to that star."

"Nah, not nearly that big. The whole world isn't that big!"

"You mean, we're like nothing? The whole world is like nothing?" It frightened her to think of herself, her whole world like less than a speck in the gigantic sky, like nothing at all.

"Yeah, we're small. But we aren't nothing," he said. "Wanna know a secret?"

"What?"

He reached over and pinched her arm.

"Ow," she said. It didn't hurt so much as surprise her.

"See this," he said, lifting her arm up where he'd pinched it. "See this stuff here?

"This is the stuff of stars."

"What do you mean?"

"The same elements, the same materials that make those stars up there is what make you. You're made from star stuff."

It didn't make sense.

"They're burning in the sky, and I'm just standing here not shining at all!"

"Well, yes, but that doesn't mean you're made from different stuff, just that something different is happening to those same elements. You're still close kin to the stars."

She was trembling out there in the August night in nothing but her pajamas, but it wasn't because of the cold.

One of my great frustrations as a writer of stories for children is the adults who are afraid to entrust meaning making to the young. This results in book banning. But even those eager to share a book may feel the need to dictate meaning. I have a friend whose young son had never been much of a reader until one day she gave him a copy of Natalie Babbitt's masterpiece, *Tuck Everlasting*. For those of you who have never read the book, the question being wrestled with on its pages is that of everlasting life. Not eternal life, in the biblical sense, but living on forever on earth. Would it be a blessing, as some believe, or a curse? Somehow, this ten-year-old, who had been struggling with the fact that his birth mother had given him up for adoption, found in *Tuck Everlasting* a healing and comfort no one could have imagined would be provided by a book, especially when to the ordinary reader the story had nothing whatsoever to do with rejection or adoption. While he couldn't articulate why the book made sense to him in this strange way, he declared that he loved it and read it over and over again, loving it more with every reading. Chris found in its pages meaning for his life.

As it happened, it was the very book that his fifth grade teacher chose for the class to study that year. At first, he was thrilled: the whole class would be reading his book, the first book he had ever read that truly belonged to his heart. Then the discussions began, and worst of all, the tests. And they were not about his book at all. They were about a book chock-full of esoteric symbolism and philosophical messages that meant nothing at all to his life. On the final exam, he made a C-. He had no idea what the Ferris wheel stood for in chapter one, or why the villain's suit was yellow. He only knew that it was a book that had changed his life. Now it was as though he and the teacher had read two different books, and her book was the right one. He never opened his again.

In her book, *When God Is Silent,* Barbara Brown Taylor speaks of the narrative style of Jesus and points out how courteous and respectful of the listener it is. "Story and image," she goes on to say, "both have great pockets of silence in them. They do not come at the ear in the same way advice and exhortation do. Although they are, I believe, even more persuasive, perhaps this is because they create a quiet space where one may lay down one's defenses for a while. A story," she continues, "does not ask for decision; instead, it asks for identification, which is how transformation begins."

Despite the genealogies, the laws, the exhortations, the Bible comes to us chiefly as story. The story of God and humankind. And what is the climax of the story? Incarnation. God with us. God identifying with us. Which is how transformation begins.

In *Candide,* the wandering hero tries desperately to cling to the teaching of his mentor and believe, against all the evidence, that all is well, that everything happens for the best here in the best of all possible worlds. Finally, he is forced to face reality. To anyone with his eyes open, it is a tragic and devastating world. What can a human do in the face of overwhelming evil, both natural and moral? Candide concludes all one can do is tend his garden. Thus work, even though there is no guarantee that it will endure or bear fruit, is the only way to confront the chaos that life is.

Contrast *Candide* with another story — that of the prophet Jeremiah. Jeremiah is in jail — and rightly so, for he has been saying a lot of very unpatriotic things. He has insisted on publicly declaring that his country is bringing destruction down upon itself by its evil-doing. Just when his prophecy is coming true and the Babylonians are advancing on the gates of the city, pretty much guaranteeing that Jerusalem's inhabitants will end up either dead or captive, Jeremiah does a very peculiar thing: he sends out his friend, Baruch, to buy a piece of Judean real estate.

The difference between Candide and Jeremiah, it seems to me, is that Jeremiah knows he's in partnership with God. Against all odds, he believes the word of the Lord that someday that field will be tended and the fruits of that field will flourish. Jeremiah's truth is not simply the reality of evil, but the reality of God's faithfulness in the midst of evil. Jeremiah stakes his life as well his money that God will continue to call God's children to be co-creators in this world.

There's not much temptation for a children's writers to write meaningless fiction, where no one changes and the story goes nowhere. Children won't put up with it. But even if they did, I wouldn't write it. As co-creators with God, we are, by definition, meaning-makers.

As I was preparing this talk, I was enjoying thinking of myself, the writer, as meaning-maker and co-creator with God, when in the midst of my delight, I remembered my usual audience is not fellow writers, but teachers. All too often, I have one of these over-worked, under-valued, heroic saints say to me wistfully, "I wish I could write a book," somehow valuing my life's work above their own. It makes me deeply ashamed. What about all those people in whatever field of endeavor who are serving their neighbors and their neighbors' children? All those people who think of themselves as ordinary and envy writers for being creative. Is there anything more creatively demanding than nurturing a child's growth and development, than helping a child learn how to become a full human being? I don't think so.

On Easter Sunday, our pastor told a story about a visiting teacher who was sent to the hospital to tutor a child confined there. The lesson she was told that the child must have in order to catch up with his class was on nouns and verbs. The teacher wondered why on earth a sick child should be burdened with learning parts of speech, and she was even more perplexed when she was taken to the ICU to meet her horribly burned student. She was in shock, and hardly knowing what to do, and so she talked to this almost comatose child about nouns and verbs for the required length of time and fled the hospital.

When she returned somewhat trepidatiously the next day, a nurse met her on the way in.

"What did you do yesterday?" she demanded.

The teacher began to apologize, saying that, inappropriate as it seemed, she'd been told to teach the child about the parts of speech. She was very sorry — her supervisor was probably unaware of the child's condition.

"No, no, no," the nurse explained. "We thought he was going to die. He'd given up trying. But after you left, he rallied. We think he might live after all."

Later the child himself was able to explain just what had happened:

"It was terrible. I was sure I was going to die. But then, this teacher came in and started talking about nouns and verbs. I knew they wouldn't send someone to teach me about nouns and verbs if they thought I was going to die!"

It was the first time I'd ever thought of English grammar lessons as words of hope. But certainly not the first time I've known a teacher to provide hope to a child in what seemed to be a hopeless situation. Many teachers I know do this on a regular basis, every day of the week. And they call *us* creators.

Not long ago, I was asked to speak to a group of public school teachers who would be taking their classes to see a production of the play *Bridge to Terabithia*. I spent more than hour describing how the book came to be written and how Stephanie Tolan and I had adapted it into the play that their classes would be seeing. At the end of the usual question time, a young male teacher thanked me for what I had told them that morning.

"But I want to take something special back to my class," he said. "Could you give me some word to take back to them?"

I was momentarily silenced. After all, I'd been talking continuously for almost an hour and a half. Surely, he could pick out, from that outpouring, a word or two to take home to his students. Fortunately, I kept my mouth shut long enough to realize what I ought to say.

"I'm very biblically oriented," I responded, "and so for me, the most important thing is for the word to become flesh. I can write stories for children and young people, and in that sense, I can offer them words. But you are the word become flesh in your classroom. Society teaches our children that they are nobodies unless their faces appear on television. But by your caring, by your showing them how important each one of them is, you become the word that I want to share with these children."

If you ask me what message a book of mine contains, I'll get testy, but that doesn't mean that I think I have nothing to say to my readers. What I want my story to say to isolated, angry, fearful youth — to all of the children who feel their lives are worthless in the eyes of the world — is you are seen. You are not alone. You are not despised. You are unique and of infinite value in the human family.

As a writer I can try to make meaning for these lost children through the words of a story, but I can't stop there, thinking that my task as meaning-maker is done. Nor, I dare say, can you. It is up to each of us not simply to write the words, but to *be* the word of hope, of faith, of love. To be the word made flesh.

Acknowledgments

Copyright has been retained by the author of each piece. The editor gratefully acknowledges the kind permission to reprint the following:

"Whispering Hope" by Doris Betts. Festival 1994. First published in *Image*, Issue #7, Fall 1994. Reprinted by permission of Doris Betts.

"The Eyes of the Heart" by Frederick Buechner. From *Secrets in the Dark*. © 2006 by Frederick Buechner. Reprinted by permission of HarperCollins Publishers.

"Writing as Subversion" by Will Campbell. Festival 1990 (Contemporary Christian Writers in Community). Printed by permission of Will Campbell.

"Tired of Victory, Bored by Defeat: Restoring Proper Sadness to Christian Art" by Betty Smartt Carter. Festival 2000. Printed by permission of Betty Smartt Carter.

"The Collision of Faith and Fiction: Cleaning up the Wreckage" by David James Duncan. Festival 1998. Printed by permission of David James Duncan.

"Writing as an Act of Worship" by Elizabeth Dewberry. Festival 2004. Printed by permission of Elizabeth Dewberry.

"Faith and Fiction" by Ron Hansen. Festival 2002. First published in *A Stay Against Confusion: Essays on Faith and Fiction* (Harper Collins). Reprinted by permission of Ron Hansen.

Acknowledgments

"No Bible-Beating Allowed" by Silas House. Festival 2004. Printed by permission of Silas House.

"The Miracle and the Myth" by Jan Karon. Festival 2002. Printed by permission of Jan Karon.

"An Interview with Joy Kogawa." Conducted by Henry Baron. Festival 1998. Printed by permission of Joy Kogawa and Henry Baron.

"An Interview with Anne Lamott." Conducted by Linda Buturian. Festival 2000. An earlier version appeared in the *Oregon Extension Journal*. Reprinted by permission of *Oregon Extension Journal* and Linda Buturian.

"The Cosmic Questions" by Madeleine L'Engle. Originally titled "An Evening with Madeleine L'Engle." Festival 1996. Printed by permission of Lescher & Lescher, Ltd.

"Why Have We Given Up the Ghost? Notes on Reclaiming Literary Fiction" by Bret Lott. Festival 2004. First published in *Image*, Issue #43, Fall 2004. Reprinted by permission of Bret Lott.

"Faith and Fashion Blunders: Shifting Metaphors of Mortality" by Thomas Lynch. Festival 2004. Printed by permission of Thomas Lynch.

"An Interview with Kathleen Norris." Conducted by Linda Buturian. Festival 2002. Printed by permission of Kathleen Norris and Linda Buturian.

"Image and Imagination" by Katherine Paterson. Festival 1998. Printed by permission of Katherine Paterson.

"Making Meaning" by Katherine Paterson. Festival 2004. Printed by permission of Katherine Paterson.

"Writing and Knowing" by James Calvin Schaap. Festival 1998. First published in *Fifty-Five and Counting: Essays and Stories* (Dordt College Press). Reprinted by permission of James Calvin Schaap.

"An Interview with Paul Schrader." Conducted by Garry Wills. Festival 2000. First published in *Perspectives*, August/September 2001. Reprinted by permission of Paul Schrader, Garry Wills, and the editors of *Perspectives*.

"Reversing Entropy" by Luci Shaw. Festival 2004. First published in *Image*, Issue #41, Winter 2003-4. Reprinted by permission of Luci Shaw.

"Way Beyond Belief: The Call to Behold" by Barbara Brown Taylor. Festival 2004. Printed by permission of Barbara Brown Taylor.

"Glory into Glory" by Walter Wangerin Jr. Festival 2000. Printed by permission of Walter Wangerin Jr.

Made in the USA
Middletown, DE
17 November 2022

15360678R00161